Microsoft

Comprehensive

Strategies

HIPAA COMPLIANCE
>> Solutions >>

from Microsoft

and

Washington Publishing

Company

Steve Bass
Lisa Miller
Bryan Nylin

PUBLISHED BY
Microsoft Press
A Division of Microsoft Corporation
One Microsoft Way
Redmond, Washington 98052-6399

Copyright © 2002 by Steve Bass, Lisa Miller, Bryan Nylin

All rights reserved. No part of the contents of this book may be reproduced or transmitted in any form or by any means without the written permission of the publisher.

Library of Congress Cataloging-in-Publication Data
Bass, Steve, 1952-
    HIPPA Compliance Solutions / Steve Bass, Lisa Miller, Bryan Nylin.
       p. cm.
    Includes bibliographical references and index.
    ISBN 0-7356-1496-2
    1. Insurance, Health--Continuation coverage--Law and legislation--United States. 2. Insurance, Health--Continuation coverage--United States--Automation.   I. Miller, Lisa, 1961-   II. Nylin, Bryan, 1961-   III. Title.

KF1183 .B37 2001
368.38'2'00973--dc21   2001044964

Printed and bound in the United States of America.

1 2 3 4 5 6 7 8 9   QWT   6 5 4 3 2

Distributed in Canada by Penguin Books Canada Limited.

A CIP catalogue record for this book is available from the British Library.

Microsoft Press books are available through booksellers and distributors worldwide. For further information about international editions, contact your local Microsoft Corporation office or contact Microsoft Press International directly at fax (425) 936-7329. Visit our Web site at www.microsoft.com/mspress. Send comments to *mspinput@microsoft.com*.

BizTalk, Microsoft, Microsoft Press, and Windows are either registered trademarks or trademarks of Microsoft Corporation in the United States and/or other countries. Other product and company names mentioned herein may be the trademarks of their respective owners.

The example companies, organizations, products, domain names, e-mail addresses, logos, people, places, and events depicted herein are fictitious. No association with any real company, organization, product, domain name, e-mail address, logo, person, place, or event is intended or should be inferred.

Acquisitions Editor: Alex Blanton
Project Editor: Jean Cockburn

Body Part No. X08-41930

Dedicated to Earl J. Bass

His work still sets the standard.

Contents

Preface—Preparation for Change: HIPAA and the Remaking of Health Care Administration

Introduction

The Solution	x
OnlyConnect Framework	xi
BizTalk Server 2000	xi
Microsoft BizTalk Accelerator for HIPAA	xii
WPC and Microsoft Consulting Services	xii
Microsoft Solution Offering (MSO) Support	xii
Independent Software Vendors and Systems Integrators	xiii
A Fiscally Responsible Solution	xiii

Chapter 1
HIPAA

Minding the Business of Health Care	1
K2 Trek: A Look at the Regulation	2
EDI	4

Chapter 2
To Implement HIPAA, or Not to Implement?

Who Must Comply?	21
Publication in the *Federal Register*	22
The Business Value of EDI	25
The X12 Approach	27
HIPAA-Phobia	29
Pessimistic Voices	31
The Cost of Implementation	31
Beyond Expediency: The Value of Implementing HIPAA for the Entities That Must	33

Chapter 3
The HIPAA Solution Offered by Microsoft and Washington Publishing Company

Core Technologies	36
Specialized Technology and Consulting	36
Partners	37
The OnlyConnect Framework	38
The Solution in Action	44

Chapter 4
Technical Deployment Overview

Working in Tandem	56
BizTalk Server 2000	56
BizTalk Mapper	57
The OnlyConnect Gap Analysis Tool	68
OnlyConnect FirstPass	71

Chapter 5
The New Health Care Economy: A Vision of Fundamental Change

Technology Empowering Consumers	73
The Health Care Landscape	74
Provider Organizations and Physicians	75
Payers	77
Device Manufacturers	78
Private Sector Employers, Public Sector Agencies: Funding Health Care	78
Vision for a New Health Care Economy	79
The New Healthscape	81

Appendix A
What Is the Federal Register?

The Final HIPAA Rule for Transaction and Code Set Standards	84

Timeline   106

HIPAA Supplemental Information

Part I
A HIPAA Glossary & Acronymary   114

Part II
Consolidated HIPAA Administrative Simplification Final Rule Definitions

    45 CFR 160.103 Definitions   140

    45 CFR 160.202 Definitions   145

    45 CFR 162.103 Definitions   146

    45 CFR 164.501 Definitions   147

    45 CFR 164.504 Uses and Disclosures: Organizational Requirements   153

Part III
Purpose & Maintenance

    Purpose   154

    Maintenance   154

Index   155

Preface

Preparation for Change: HIPAA and the Remaking of Health Care Administration

The methods used in the practice of medicine in the United States are not accidental or improvised. They are the mutually agreed upon results of decades of scientific enquiry. The body of knowledge grows and is applied to help patients because, through their professional organizations, health care providers practice self-scrutiny and share their results. Health care providers follow medical conventions because they respect the process that establishes them. Within that process, those most qualified by their education and experience assess the results of experimentation and practice. Disagreements are aired and efforts are made to resolve conflicting judgments before old methods are adapted or new ones adopted. Procedures rooted in convention are changed by consensus because those who perform them put the good of the patient—and of all potential patients—above other concerns.

Bringing providers together in allegiance to the primacy of the empirical method, the umbrella groups of health care—such as the American Medical Association and American Hospital Association—are forums for the examination and exchange of their members' experience. Health care progresses because those who provide it tacitly agree to adopt methods that bring success, as measured in relief provided, health maintained or restored, and lives preserved and improved.

While medical science and treatment have been progressing, the administrative functions necessary to the system have been expanding, becoming more elaborate and costly. The processes by which treatment is obtained and paid for has become more difficult without improving, as is exemplified by the referral paperchase. Health care providing organizations are overburdened by administrative needs. Clerical procedure normally does not follow the medical model of peer review and empirical assessment. As treatment and diagnostic procedures that employ advanced technologies proliferate, accounting for them lags behind on methods of the past.

The soon-to-be implemented Health Insurance Portability and Accountability Act of 1996 will bring about a single, unified, electronic system of health care administration throughout the United States. Microsoft and Washington Publishing Company offer the means for all elements of the provider-payer continuum to make this mandated transition.

Introduction

Microsoft has long been the source of technology products—including operating systems, back-end servers, word processors, spreadsheets, and hardware. The versatility of their platform allows their use across the whole range of industries and disciplines. But now, in response to new Federal law, Microsoft and Washington Publishing Company are delivering a technology suite to solve the specific problems of the business end of the health care industry.

Among these problems is the familiar experience of having to wait while a practitioner's office staff laboriously prepares a paper referral—the ticket to seek an appointment with a specialist. That referral will also be a vital component of the health care insurance claim that will follow the visit with the specialist.

The Health Insurance Portability and Accountability Act of 1996 (HIPAA) set an electronic format for, and standardized the content of, most of the transactions surrounding health care insurance claims. Washington Publishing Company (WPC) is the publisher of nearly all of these formats (and most of their content) and is specified as such in the HIPAA regulation. Health care providers—doctors, dentists, hospitals, and dozens of others—that choose to transact electronically must adhere to standardized formats and content when, for example, submitting a claim to an insurance company for payment.

HIPAA was enacted primarily to make individual and group health insurance coverage in the United States less prone to interruption by such events as an insured person changing jobs. It will make insurers' responses to claims more uniform and their actions more transparent.

The goal of HIPAA is to reduce costs without adversely affecting health care providers and receivers. Today, 400 different transmission formats for health care claims exist, each with different content. After HIPAA takes effect (currently slated for October 16, 2002), all payers must accept one content set in one format.

It isn't just for submitting claims: enrollment in a health plan, premium payment, eligibility, referrals, claim status, claim review, and claim payments are also mandated by HIPAA. Health care providers will still be able to use paper claim forms that don't employ the electronic standard, but a provider clinging to paper-dependant methods will be opting out of the benefits of automated business processes—such as quicker payment and reduced clerical hours.

The American National Standards Institute (ANSI) is a private non-profit organization that administers and coordinates the U.S. voluntary standardization and conformity assessment system. The HIPAA data format and content published by WPC were devised by a subcommittee of the ANSI Accredited Standards Committee for Electronic Data Interchange (EDI), ASC X12. The insurance subcommittee, X12N, is, like all X12 subcommittees, a consensus-building organization of volunteers. X12N's members represent health care providers, payers, insurance claim clearinghouses, software vendors, consultants, and other interested parties. The members collaborate from their various locations on a continual basis and meet face-to-face three times a year. The degree to which X12N sponsoring organizations put the volunteer committee's work to use has been at each organization's discretion; with HIPAA in effect, using the standard becomes mandatory for all covered entities.

X12 volunteers are drawn from the ranks of business professionals and information technology (IT) professionals. The X12 standards were designed to

- be a structured method for business professionals to harmonize business process information across multiple competing enterprises without revealing exact details of those processes; and
- subsequently convey that information to the IT professionals charged with automating those processes.

The X12 meetings, a mix of business politics and technology discussions, have been taking place in various forms since 1968. The resultant standards are not perfect; they reflect a consensus that is often a compromise.

The Solution

In the summer of 2000, WPC was a participant of Microsoft's BizTalk Server 2000 early adopter program. BizTalk Server ships with some X12 templates for generic supply chain management, such as purchase orders, ship notices, and invoices. But WPC wanted to use BizTalk for health care insurance information.

Because the HIPAA X12N implementation guides named in the regulation are generated from a database, a logical extension of WPC's book generation application was to create not simply templates but fully functional document specifications, or *schemas*. The schema generation module pulls meta-data—data about data—directly from the same database that is used to build the implementation guides.

Microsoft and WPC saw that the enterprise integration features of BizTalk Server 2000 could be applied to the content-rich schemas to create a combined software, consulting, and best practices Solution for the health care insurance industry.

The Microsoft BizTalk Accelerator for HIPAA helps bridge the gap between an organization's business analysts and its IT staff. Business analysts describe the information their organization uses in a business context; the IT department supports and automates the manipulation, storage, and transmission of that information for users inside and outside the organization.

This Microsoft Solution Offering (MSO) is made up of several components:

- OnlyConnect Framework, a blueprint for HIPAA compliance
- The Microsoft BizTalk Accelerator for HIPAA
- Microsoft BizTalk Server 2000
- Microsoft SQL Server 2000
- Microsoft Windows 2000 Advanced Server
- WPC and Microsoft Consulting Services (MCS), consulting and training
- Microsoft Solution Offering (MSO) support packages
- Independent software vendors and systems integration partners

OnlyConnect Framework

The OnlyConnect Framework combines WPC's OnlyConnect Methodology—a way to become HIPAA-compliant—with the Microsoft Solutions Framework.

Early in the planning phase of the BizTalk Accelerator for HIPAA, WPC shared with Microsoft its staff's experience of HIPAA-compliance assessments for large payer organizations. The OnlyConnect Methodology was the product of those assessments, which WPC had conducted over the course of several years. The methodology was loosely based on the concepts of the Microsoft Solutions Framework. What has emerged—the OnlyConnect Framework—is the best practices path to solving the very complex (indeed, at times, seemingly overwhelming) problems of achieving HIPAA compliance.

The OnlyConnect Methodology reduces the cost of implementing HIPAA transaction standards by using existing, or *legacy*, systems. By keeping legacy systems in place, employees will not need new training on new software, so day-to-day business processes will continue without interruption.

The methodology's initial step, the OnlyConnect Gap Analysis Tool, identifies those fields in a legacy system's database structure that will no longer be populated. It also identifies new fields to be added to the legacy system. Updates to the tool will be issued as the implementation guides change, assuring a solid path to continued compliance.

The second step includes analyses of the past one to five years of data from the legacy system. That body of data is fed into a HIPAA-compliant database structure to provide custom analytical reports generated from SQL Server 2000 databases. Orphaned data components are identified and their instances of use are counted. The Analyses verify the Gap Analysis results by checking years of data and identifying any fields in the HIPAA-compliant database that are not populated. This process guarantees data integrity and double-checks for gaps.

Next, a subject matter expert analyzes all applications fed from the database structure, identifying, with the help of IT staff, areas to be modified. Once identified, recommendations are made on how to implement these modifications.

The design-and-build step integrates dynamic, distributed business processes with legacy systems, bonding them in a common design environment. This environment allows new technology, existing business processes, and legacy systems to interoperate seamlessly, yielding a transparent solution for the end users. This design-and-build step uses the OnlyConnect architecture, which

- acts as a receiving and sending gateway for legacy systems,
- extends the functionality of legacy systems to new, often smaller, business partners, and
- maintains transactions with all current business partners.

BizTalk Server 2000

A member of the Microsoft .NET Enterprise Server family of products, Microsoft BizTalk Server 2000 unites, in a single product, enterprise application integration (EAI) and business-to-business (B2B) integration. BizTalk Server 2000 enables developers, IT professionals, and business analysts to easily build—over the Internet—dynamic business processes that span applications, platforms, and businesses.

In addition to BizTalk Server 2000, Microsoft, with industry partners, has led innovation of enabling technologies necessary for Internet-based business solutions. These initiatives include BizTalk Framework 2.0, which is platform-independent, and Extensible Markup Language (XML) framework for application integration and electronic commerce. BizTalk Framework 2.0 is not a standard, but it builds upon such existing standards as the Simple Object Access Protocol (SOAP). SOAP is also a key technology in other members of the .NET product line, namely Microsoft Visual Studio 7.0. BizTalk Framework 2.0 provides the basis for interoperable, reliable messaging for BizTalk Server 2000.

For more information about BizTalk Framework 2.0 and BizTalk Server 2000 (product resources for community services, a large library of schemas, and white papers), go to the Microsoft BizTalk Server 2000 Web site (*http://www.microsoft.com/biztalk*).

Microsoft BizTalk Accelerator for HIPAA

Health care organizations affected by HIPAA can use the integration capabilities of BizTalk Server 2000, along with HIPAA resources provided by WPC, to automate business processes and quickly build integration solutions. This helps them to comply with Federal law while leveraging existing IT investments. The interoperability of BizTalk Server 2000 with health care organizations' legacy systems, combined with BizTalk HIPAA schemas, provide the health care industry with the tools to meet the HIPAA mandate.

Early adopters of the Accelerator have stated that its value is easily discernable. The WPC schemas and the Microsoft parser create a solid foundation on which an IT staff can easily create a cutting edge HIPAA Solution, without fiscal bleeding and with limitless possibilities.

WPC and Microsoft Consulting Services

The Solution concept is a new model for Microsoft. Rather than a product being the primary focus, the Solution to a set of problems is the focus. At the core of this Solution is Microsoft Consulting Services health care practice, led by the team of Bill Reid, Rob Oikawa, David Ferro, and Pushkar Sule. They have created something not just for serving customers, but for serving partners. The goal of the Health Care Core Solution Team is one of empowerment and knowledge transfer to partners and clients to assist and enable their path toward compliancy.

Microsoft Solution Offering (MSO) Support

The Microsoft Solution Offering (MSO) support services program provides a set of service offering packages that are customized specifically for the HIPAA Solution. These support packages go beyond the traditional product support approach by covering all aspects of the Solution with one contract.

The most basic package includes such services as solution workshops and advisory services for setup, configuration, and operations. More advanced packages can include rapid onsite support, onsite advisory services, architecture review, and access to scalability and benchmark test labs.

Independent Software Vendors and Systems Integrators

Partners, partners, partners! The partnership model is the key to the Microsoft HIPAA Solution. The partners themselves are its strength. Sharing knowledge through robust client relationships is the path to the successful implementation of the Solution. Integration with legacy systems, and an informed staff, will yield the best HIPAA Solution for both the implementers' existing clients and many new ones they stand to gain. HIPAA provides ISV's and SI's with new business models, new services and new opportunities to benefit their clients. That kind of atmosphere is the intent of HIPAA.

A Fiscally Responsible Solution

To reiterate, the Solution builds atop legacy systems. Health care claim adjudication systems that have been developed over the past 20 years need not be dismantled and rewritten. They do their job and will continue to operate. Inflowing data is transformed from a HIPAA X12N transmission into extensible markup language (XML) and then into the input format the legacy system requires. Data flowing out takes the opposite route: from legacy data structures (such as National Standard Format [NSF]), it is transformed into XML, then into HIPAA X12N transmissions and sent to trading partners.

The Solution is flexible. It enables the direct use of the XML representations of the data, allowing access to very powerful XML data manipulation tools. A substantial XML research and development effort is underway as that language moves toward replacing the current language of the Internet, hypertext markup language (HTML). The Solution can provide a clear migration strategy for replacing legacy systems, if desired, with XML data and tools.

Many—if not most—enterprises employing the Solution will experience a measurable return on their investment. For example, a large hospital system that has grown through acquisitions might have a hundred separate systems, and none able to directly share and exchange information. They communicate outside the enterprise, perhaps through a clearinghouse, to payer organizations. But aggregate data is not available to the enterprise's Chief Information Officer (CIO). Installing the Solution in those hundred systems will put those formerly discrete, unconnected systems in communication with each other, as well as with trading partners outside of the enterprise. Using On-Line Analytical Processing (OLAP) tools, the CIO will be able to assemble aggregate views of data across the enterprise and therefore measure the effectiveness of business processes and associated clinical outcomes.

Acknowledgments

We are indebted to the following persons for their help in writing this book:
   David Lubinski, whose vision is expressed in Chapter 5;
   John Wall of Healthaxis, an Early Adopter whose case study enlivens Chapter 3;
   Bruss Bowman of QCSI, another influential member of the Early Adopters Program;
   Zon Owen, for his definitive contribution, the Glossary.

We are also grateful to these uniquely qualified reviewers of various portions and versions of this book:
   Jean Narcisi of the American Medical Association
   George Arges of the American Hospital Association
   Robert Lapp and Frank Pokorny of the American Dental Association
   Lee Anne Stember and Lynne Gilbertson of the National Council for Prescription Drug Programs
   Kendra Martin of the American Petroleum Institute
   Margaret Weiker of EDS
   Whitney Gilliam of Springs, Inc.

For their invaluable editorial expertise we thank Jean Cockburn of Microsoft Press and Margaret Burke of Washington Publishing Company.

   Steve Bass
   Lisa Miller
   Bryan Nylin

Chapter 1

HIPAA

Minding the Business of Health Care

The business landscape of health care is an overgrown maze of systems—some interactive and others autonomous—in which patients, providers, and payers often find confusion and delay. More than four hundred electronic health care claim file formats are currently in use. Relationships among trading partners; requirements that differ by region, by state, and by local circumstance; and the secondary status that administrative concerns rightly occupy in the practice of medicine, contribute to the intricacy of this landscape. Proliferation of paper forms, content standards and guides in use has resulted in many options for the transfer of administrative data—an essential part of the day-to-day business of health care. But as avenues for this information have multiplied, their variety and the complexity of choosing among them have increased the administrative burden.

For over twenty years, EDI (Electronic Data Interchange) has functioned smoothly and economically as the business-to-business link for essential exchanges within a wide range of industries. At last, HIPAA establishes for the health care sector a single, unifying form of electronic interchange based on proven standards, adapted to meet the unique needs of health care administrators, and capable of changing as those needs change.

The one unified data content set that HIPAA mandates will ultimately simplify health care administration and clerical methods, but the prospect of the many changes to come as HIPAA is implemented has engendered trepidation, and even alarm, in many whose work is directly affected. In the offices of care providers and payers, staffers are asking: How are these administrative transaction standards to be implemented? What will it cost, and what good will implementation do? A lack of hard information has inspired widespread skepticism and gloomy conjecture with some in the industry questioning the efficacy of the selected standard. Doubt about whether the deadline for implementation imposed by the law can be met is common; the fear that it will cost too much is general.

The intention behind this book is not to deny that difficulties will be encountered during the implementation task, but to explain what that task entails so decision makers can make the best choices for their organizations. As the date by which the new systems must be in place approaches, many conflicting claims are being made by newly minted experts purporting to know how to bring a health care organization's office up to electronic speed. It can be difficult to distinguish between bombast and what might prove useful. This book aims to convey an understanding of HIPAA processes that will enable the careful reader to ask the right questions of anyone offering a plan to make an organization HIPAA compliant. As changes wrought by the regulation are discussed, the business value of HIPAA will be demonstrated. If this should serve to dispel some of the trepidation and fear that accompany the anticipation of change on such a scale, the authors join in the sighs of relief.

William R. Braithwaite, senior policy advisor of the U.S. Department of Health and Human Services, said during a recent presentation, "HIPAA is not meant to do harm; rather, to do no harm." HIPAA can add value to any organization that chooses to implement the transaction standards. Making an organization HIPAA compliant, even in consultation with outside help, is very difficult unless members of that organization have the ability to ask informed questions. Anyone who grasps the facts presented in this book will gain that ability and, with it, a far greater chance of being able to recognize the peddlers of HIPAA-bunk.

Administrators who have already chosen a path to HIPAA compliance might find in these pages assurance that they have made the correct choice. They stand to gain ways to more effectively guide their staffs as that solution is implemented. And if their chosen path should be revealed as a poorly delineated one, the value of this assembly of information will be even greater.

K2 Trek: A Look at the Regulation

The countdown to HIPAA implementation began with the August 17, 2000 issue of the Federal Register, the official daily publication for Rules, Proposed Rules, and Notices of Federal agencies and organizations. The Register's Volume 65, number 160, contains the "Final Rule on Standards for Electronic Health Care Transactions," a portion of the Health Insurance Portability and Accountability Act of 1996. Known during the legislative process as the Kennedy-Kassebaum bill ("K2" to abbreviators), the enacted legislation is referred to by its acronym HIPAA (pronounced HIP-uh). The Health Insurance Portability and Accountability Act directly affects all health care organizations in the United States and, indirectly, everyone who obtains American health care.

The countdown's "...3, 2, 1," is scheduled to occur on October 16, 2002 (as of this printing); its equivalent of "liftoff" is the requirement that a plan for HIPAA's implementation be in place on that date by the following: all health care providers, from the largest hospital systems to one-doctor medical practices; most health plans; many employers; insurance companies; billing organizations; the government's Medicare and Medicaid agencies; health insurance clearinghouses; and most systems vendors in the market. The smallest health plans—those with annual receipts of less than $5 million—have an additional year to complete their implementation plans. To find the most current information about the status of HIPAA implementation, see the U.S. Department of Health and Human Services' *Administration Simplification* Web site at *http://aspe.dhhs.gov/admnsimp/*.

Providers will still be able to conduct health insurance–related activities using the longstanding paper-based system, but in doing so they will not gain the benefits of electronic claim submissions, the first of which is time. Complying with HIPAA ends insurance-related paper-shuffling by care providers' office staffs; ignoring it in favor of old modes of operation will prove costly in clerical hours.

To realize the advantages of electronic claim submissions, health care providers will adopt the newly prescribed format and content. Most of the other organizations listed above have no choice—HIPAA requires their participation. Non-compliance with the transaction and code set standard is discouraged by, in the language of the Act, "a penalty of not more than $100 for each such violation, except that the total amount imposed on the person for all violations of an identical requirement or prohibition during a calendar year may not exceed $25,000."[1]

---

1. From Title XI, Section 1176 of the Social Security Act.

The consequences of particular violations of the Act's privacy provision are more severe: "If the offense is committed with intent to sell, transfer, or use individually identifiable health information for commercial advantage, personal gain, or malicious harm, [the offender may] be fined not more than $250,000, imprisoned not more than 10 years, or both."[2]

The effects of HIPAA will be many and far reaching. Enacted August 21, 1996 as Public Law 104-191, HIPAA altered several titles within the United States Code. Title II, subtitle F added a new part to Title XI of the Social Security Act of 1935: "C, Administrative Simplification." This regulation makes a set of electronic transaction provisions (for claims, referrals, payments, and related information) the congressionally mandated means of conducting health care administration (the place of transaction provisions relative to the whole of HIPAA is shown in Figure 1-1). Those transaction provisions—where they came from, what they do, and how their use will transform health care administration—are the primary subject of this book.

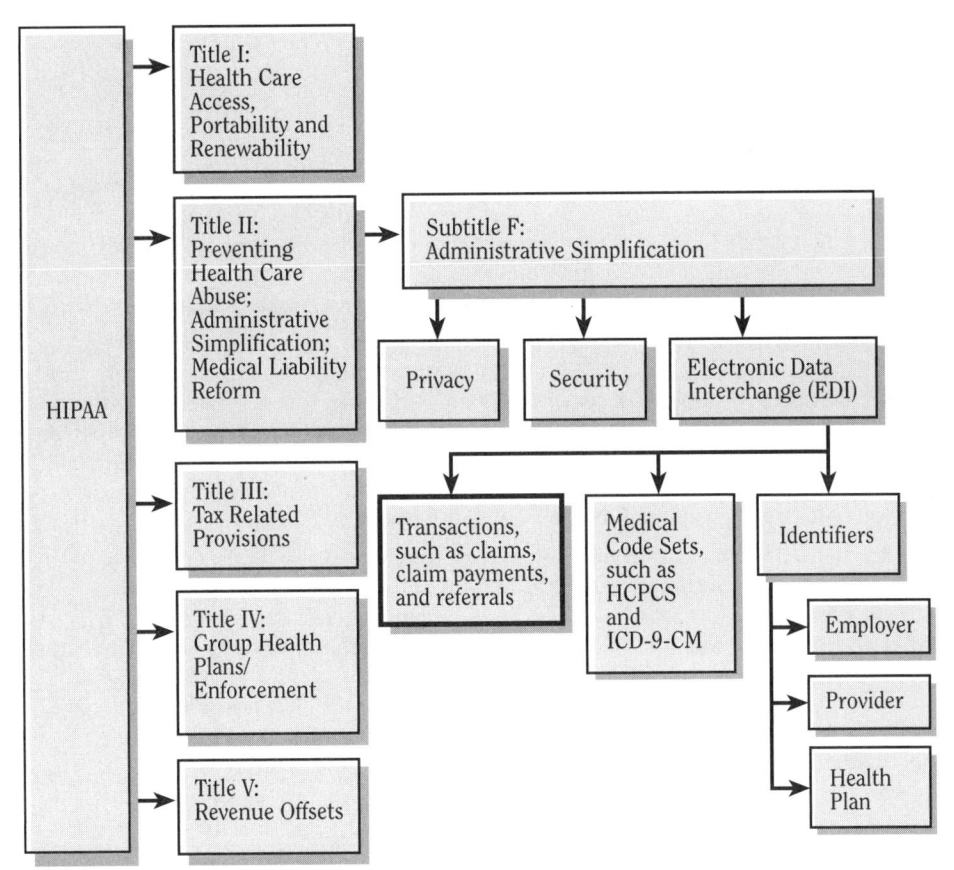

Figure 1-1. *The place of the transaction provisions relative to the whole of HIPAA*

---

2. From Title XI, Section 1177 of the Social Security Act.

Of the many provisions of subtitle F, the transaction rule was the first to be published. Because it engenders change in a complex set of administrative procedures, the process of implementing the transaction rule will require many segments of the industry to apply funds, as well as staff members' attention, to achieve it. But despite this initial financial outlay, the preamble to the regulation states that the transaction rule is expected to save the health care industry $29 billion in the first ten years of its implementation.[3]

The final privacy rule was published in December 2000 and took effect on April 14, 2001. A two-year period for implementation follows its effective date; that period is scheduled to end April 14, 2003. The privacy rule is expected to cost the industry $17.6 billion over 10 years according to the preamble of the regulation. The final security rule has not yet been published.[4]

To understand how the transaction rule can be expected to result in $29 billion in savings, it is useful to know about the series of efforts to build standards for electronic communication that led to this standard. All these precursors have proven to significantly reduce costs; the first one also made history.

EDI

The Berlin Airlift and TDCC

In June of 1948, military forces of the Soviet Union halted all land and water traffic into the western-controlled sector of the German capital city, Berlin. Western powers had to choose between two alternatives: abandon the city, or supply its people with the necessities of life by air. For the next eleven months, the sector's 2.5 million residents would be fed by way of one of the greatest feats in aviation history: the Berlin Airlift.

United States Air Force Colonel Ed Guilbert was the Airlift's traffic manager, responsible for all aspects of supply movement: unloading, loading, accounting, and delivery to the right locations in the city. Guilbert was an innovator. Shortly after the supply flights began, he instituted the use of straps made of strongly webbed material to bundle cargo in large portions. This enabled unloading in sections of far greater bulk and cut the time it took to empty a typical cargo plane from half an hour to five minutes.

This rapid unloading of cargo led to planes landing in West Berlin at the rate of one every three minutes. In that pit stop atmosphere, the documentation accompanying each planeload of supplies had to arrive before the plane. The situation required a way to communicate each plane's manifest—the list of what it carried—independently. Accounting for what the Airlift brought in had to be separate from the flights themselves. Guilbert ordered that all manifests be in English and transmitted by telex before landing. The efficiency this brought to that massive and unprecedented undertaking made possible the continuous flow of cargo, from aircraft to ground transportation to its final destination without warehousing. Guilbert's electronic

---

3. From the Preamble to the Final Rule, Part VI, Final Impact Analysis, Section H. Updated Cost & Benefit Assumptions, Subhead – Impact of Change.
4. From the Preamble to the Final Privacy Rule, Part IV, Final Regulatory Impact Analysis, Section B. Summary of Costs & Benefits.

manifest was the beginning of Electronic Data Interchange (EDI) and made Ed Guilbert "the father of EDI."

After his air force service, Guilbert further developed his innovative ideas. In 1968, Guilbert convened the first meeting of the Transportation Data Coordinating Committee (TDCC). TDCC played a unique role in making the electronic interchange of business data a reality by publishing in 1975 the first set of EDI standards. These first standards—specifically for air, ocean, motor, and rail transportation—drew on what Guilbert had accomplished 20 years earlier in the Airlift. Joseph Carley, who served as Program Director for TDCC while the EDI standards were being developed, conceived the overall strategy that guided the organization. Ralph Notto was a systems engineering consultant to TDCC. His ground-breaking work has changed very little since 1975. He designed the standard format to be unambiguous yet highly versatile.

Also serving as a systems consultant to TDCC during the initial days of EDI development was Earl J. "Buddy" Bass. He designed the structure of the documentation and coined many of the terms EDI still uses. Bass strove for precision in his naming conventions. He avoided using then-current words and phrases that he saw as having preconceptions attached to them. What others were calling an *electronic document*, Buddy Bass termed a *Transaction Set*. That which might have been deemed a *record*, he named a *Data Segment*, and what seemed to others to be a *field*, he called a *Data Element*. Playing a minor role was Bass's son, Steve, who drew the flowcharts in that original multi-volume set of EDI documentation.

The Uniform Code Council

A series of meetings between members of the Grocery Manufacturers of America (GMA) and the distributors of those manufactured goods, the National Association of Food Chains (NAFC), brought forth a consensus decision in September 1969 to seek a standard *Interindustry Product Code*. Four years of research culminated in the establishment of the Universal Product Code (U.P.C.). On June 26, 1974, a 10-pack of Wrigley's chewing gum became the first item scanned at a grocery store—a Marsh Supermarket in Troy, Ohio. The world of retail distribution would never be the same. The logical next step was to combine the efficiency gained through U.P.C. with an electronic means to transmit those product identifiers among the systems of the manufacturer, the warehouse, the transporter, and the retailer.

In January of 1972, the first Board of Governors of the Uniform Grocery Product Code Council (UGPCC) met in Chicago. The primary mission of the UGPCC was to administer the nascent U.P.C. UGPCC became the Uniform Product Code Council (UPCC) in 1974. In 1977, the UPCC commissioned the A.D. Little Corporation to research the feasibility of using EDI in the food and grocery industry. The results of the study indicated that substantial savings could be attained.

As an outgrowth of the A.D. Little study, Touche Ross was retained to help prepare the Uniform Communication Standards (UCS) printed in May 1981. TDCC agreed to supply project management for the UCS pilot. Following very successful pilots, in May of 1983, UPCC agreed to administer the UCS. In 1984 it dropped the word "Product" from its name, becoming the Uniform Code Council (UCC) (*http://www.uc-council.org*), a bit of streamlining meant to reflect changes in the organization's functions.

Generic EDI

In 1977, TDCC embarked on another initiative: BUSAP (a contraction of *Business Applications*, pronounced BYOO-sap). The BUSAP standard was composed of traditional buying and selling transactions, such as a request for a price quote, a response to that request, purchase orders, and invoices. While the original 1975 standards contained, for example, a unique invoice for each of the four modes of transportation, BUSAP contained a single invoice. In 1979, ANSI chartered a committee, dubbing it "X12," to develop standards for Electronic Data Interchange. The present X12 standard began as BUSAP with Credit Research Foundation as secretariat and the TDCC staff serving as paid technical advisors. These new transaction sets were generic and versatile in nature. They would be adopted by various industries, applied according to an industry's needs, and documented with industry-specific implementation guides.

Implementation Guides

The Voluntary Interindustry Commerce Standard (VICS) (*http://www.vics.org*) EDI Retail Users Group was initially formed in the latter part of 1986 when 18 companies began development of a common interpretation of the X12 Purchase Order. By October 1987, 46 companies, including retailers and their suppliers, were involved in this development effort.

The *VICS Purchase Order Implementation* was published in April 1987; by the end of that year the *Conventions and Implementation Guidelines for VICS EDI* had been expanded by several transaction sets.

Washington Publishing Company

Steve Bass had been a contractor to TDCC since the initial standards were published in 1975. In his position as Art Director of Upper Valley Press in Bradford, Vermont, Bass participated in a 1978 beta project of the Varityper division of Addressograph-Multigraph. This beta project connected mainframe computers to typesetting machines with a 300 baud modem. The melding of the two technologies was successful, as Bass demonstrated when he prepared the TDCC books for publication: more than four thousand pages were typeset in a mere two months! The craft of typesetting was undergoing fundamental changes by being linked to the computer.

Since the 1970s, six generations of standards publishing systems have been developed. That ancestral data dump from a mainframe directly into a phototypesetting machine required hand manipulations of the final camera-ready pages, as previous systems did. The personal computer applications that followed generated Standard Generalized Markup Language (SGML) for the same Varityper machine. Desktop publishing solutions emerged from this progression. That which had taken several people months of work is now handled by one person in hours.

In 1987, the VICS EDI Retail Users Group asked TDCC to publish the portion of the X12 standard used by the retail industry, augmented as necessary with information needed to use it, in the form of an industry implementation guide. TDCC declined the request. Steve Bass formally incorporated Washington Publishing Company (WPC) that year to meet the challenge and publish that retail industry-specific subset of the X12 standard. WPC has published VICS EDI ever since. WPC is also the publisher of the Uniform Communication Standard and other EDI-based standards for the UCC. In addition, WPC has published EDI implementation guides for several other industries:

- Transportation
    - The Association of American Railroads (AAR)
    - The American Trucking Association (ATA)

- Information System Agreement, a consortium of ocean carriers (ISA)
- Telecommunications
  - The Telecommunications Information Forum, a committee of the Exchange Carrier's Association (TCIF)
- Petroleum
  - Petroleum Industry Data Exchange, a committee of the American Petroleum Institute (PIDX)
- Publishing
  - Book Industry Systems Advisory Committee (BISAC)
  - Serials Industry Systems Advisory Committee (SISAC)
- Manufacturing
  - Automotive Industry Action Group (AIAG)
  - National Association of Purchasing Managers (NAPM)
  - American Iron and Steel Institute (AISI)
  - The Aluminum Association

X12 standards continue to be developed by volunteers, while industry action groups usually develop implementation guides for their constituents. The Credit Research Foundation was replaced by TDCC as the X12 secretariat, and TDCC was replaced by the Data Interchange Standards Association (DISA), the present X12 secretariat. For many years, WPC published and distributed the X12 standard for DISA. WPC continues to publish implementation guides for UCC, AAR, and PIDX.

DISA sponsors the Ed Guilbert Professional Award, given each year to a leader of the standards community. Among the recipients of the award in its early years have been founding shapers of EDI Joseph Carley, Ralph Notto, and Buddy Bass. A former chairman of the X12 committee as well, Buddy Bass, as he accepted the Guilbert Award, expressed an essential tenet of the standards setting process: "…leave your corporate hat at home and wear your industry hat; come to negotiate and compromise and don't push your own company's systems and procedures—that way we'll end up with the best standards."

Health Care EDI

Below, listed in the chronological order of their founding, are descriptions of the many diverse organizations that are involved in health care EDI. EDI has two main components: format and content. For the most part, the X12 family of standards supplies the format and various other organizations supply the content. Committees that established standardized health care claim forms contribute much of the content. EDI removes data entry forms as they are no longer needed, but the functions of their content remain the same.

The National Committee on Vital and Health Statistics

The National Committee on Vital and Health Statistics (NCVHS) was founded in 1949 in response to a very successful international conference held in Paris the previous year. The 1948 gathering, the Conference for the Sixth Decennial Revision of the International Lists of Illnesses and Causes of Death, was sponsored by the United Nations'

World Health Organization (WHO). The NCVHS was started to address issues that had been raised in Paris. Service on the NCVHS has always been voluntary; its members are selected, as the 1949 NCVHS Report states, "to represent a point of view, an area of interest, or a field of knowledge essential to the carrying out of the Committee's responsibilities."[5]

In her history of the first fifty years of the National Committee on Vital and Health Statistics, Susan Baird Kanaan writes, "It was viewed from the outset as a technical committee—a cooperative, non-governmental effort without particular authority."[6] Its early years were focused on improving the collection and use of health data on a national basis. NCVHS worked closely with the National Center for Health Statistics (NCHS) of the Federal Department of Health, Education and Welfare (HEW, now CMS, Centers for Medicare and Medicaid Services).

In 1964, the NCVHS created a subcommittee on the epidemiological use of hospital data, beginning an effort to standardize such data in order to broaden its usefulness. These seminal efforts came to fruition more than thirty years later, when the Committee was named in HIPAA as an advisor to standards setting and maintenance organizations.

The NVCHS, over its long history, has undertaken a variety of missions both national and international in scope. From the 1960s onward it has focused on improving the quality and amount of health data on specific populations at risk of being poorly served by health care systems, such as people with low incomes, racial and ethnic minorities, the elderly, those with disabilities, and the uninsured, among others.

Recognizing the Need for Health Data Uniformity
In the 19th century, Florence Nightingale, the great modernizer of patient care, expressed the idea that public health would be better served if all hospitals required patients to furnish the same information upon admittance. But it took another international conference, this time in Virginia in 1969, before concerted efforts toward this goal began. That conference generated a specific request for the NCVHS to develop a minimum data set for hospital discharges. In 1972, the Committee published its criteria for a data item's inclusion in or exclusion from the minimum data set for hospitals. The resulting Uniform Hospital Abstract Minimum Data Set was published in 1973. It was adopted by several key private sector national organizations and, in 1980, became official HEW policy. This was the first uniform data set for hospital discharges, and it became the de facto standard.

The NCVHS has continually emphasized that privacy safeguards are imperative to any developing electronic standard.

Another NCVHS accomplishment that prepared it for its later HIPAA role was in the area of external cause of injury codes (E-codes). The Committee's work applying hospital data to categorize causes of injury led the National Uniform Billing Committee to add a space for E-codes to its Uniform Bill for Hospitals (UB-92).

---

5. *The National Committee on Vital Health Statistics, 1949-1999 – A History,* by Susan Baird Kanaan. *http://ncvhs.hhs.gov/50history.htm*
6. *ibid*

The NCVHS is named in HIPAA as an advisory body to the department of HHS on data standards concerned with these functions:
- Transaction standards for
  - Health claims or equivalent encounter information
  - Health claims attachments
  - Enrollment and disenrollment in a health plan
  - Eligibility for a health plan
  - Health care payment and remittance advice
  - Health plan premium payments
  - First report of injury
  - Health claim status
  - Referral certification and authorization
- Identifier codes for payers, providers, employers, and individuals
- Medical code sets and classification systems
- Security safeguards
- Electronic signatures
- Privacy
- The electronic medical record

These areas have long been of concern to the NCVHS, but HIPAA intensified the committee's focus on electronic transactions, shifting its attention away from its original pursuit of health data content.

American Hospital Association and the National Uniform Billing Committee

Since the latter half of the 1960s, the American Hospital Association (AHA), with the federal government's Health Care Financing Administration (HCFA, pronounced HICK-fa but now known as the Centers for Medicare and Medicaid Services, CMS) and a panel of volunteers from private and public entities allied to health care, had worked toward a common goal: to create a single billing form that all hospitals in the United States would use to submit claims to institutional payers, such as insurance companies. By 1972, thirteen different form designs had been developed in succession, but none had been used, even on a trial basis. In 1973, the fourteenth version of the claim form was field tested in Georgia, modified again, and introduced for a second trial, this time in Wyoming.

Brought together by the AHA, the volunteer advisory panel that had been involved in the effort all along became formally organized as the National Uniform Billing Committee (NUBC) in 1975. Its membership, then as now, included representatives of all the major health care payer and provider organizations.

Following additional pilot tests with HCFA and discussions at NUBC meetings, the billing form was further modified. Finally, at the NUBC meeting in May of 1982, the form and a manual for its use were approved. It was named UB-82 for Uniform Billing and the year it was finalized.

Entrusted with the continuing task of determining the content of the Uniform Billing data set, the NUBC tries to balance demonstrated need for particular data against the difficulty of providing it. Usually essential data—once it has been identified as necessary for claims processing—is assigned a position on the form. Each position on the form is assigned a unique number; these are referred to as Form Locators.

Data that is used only in some transactions is positioned in general fields bearing assigned codes that convey such information as dates and amounts. This use of qualifying codes replaces attachments that used to be added to the billing form. The UB manual contains code definitions and notes detailing situational usage of the data set. In addition, the UB manual identifies the requirements for preparing Medicare, Medicaid, Tricare (formerly CHAMPUS, the Civilian Health & Medical Program of the Uniformed Services), Blue Cross/Blue Shield (BCBS), and other insurance claims.

The NUBC has a counterpart in each of the states—the State Uniform Billing Committees (SUBCs)—which handles state implementation and disseminates state UB manuals containing notes pertinent to the particular state's requirements.

The NUBC imposed an eight-year moratorium on changes to the original data set. After the moratorium ended, the National Committee used SUBC surveys to evaluate how well UB-82's data set met the needs of providers and payers. Survey results contributed to the creation of UB-92, which incorporated the most useful aspects of UB-82 along with other changes to further reduce the need for attachments.

In addition to the paper form, HCFA/CMS maintains an electronic form of the UB, called Electronic Media Claims (EMC). More than 98% of hospital claims submitted for Medicare payment are sent as EMC formatted data. Including private payers, more than 80% of institutional claims are submitted electronically.

The NUBC's primary role is to maintain the integrity of the UB-92 data set. It serves as the forum for discussions that might lead to consensus agreement on data elements for claims, as well as the preliminary forum for data elements to affect claim-related transactions. The NUBC played a key role in the development of the X12N Health Care Claim: Institutional, adopted under HIPAA.

The NUBC is meticulous in its maintenance process. Confidence in the UB data set can be gauged by its selection by the public health sector—among others—as the medium of research projects to monitor health care delivery and to set new health policy directions. Recognizing this important usage, the NUBC in 1998 expanded its membership to include representatives from public health and health research. It also recognized the importance of developments in the design of electronic transactions by adding representatives from X12N.

The NUBC is recognized in the HIPAA Administrative Simplification provisions as one of four organizations that the National Committee on Vital and Health Statistics (NCVHS) must consult in the development of the HIPAA administrative standards.

National Council for Prescription Drug Programs

In July 1996, after a two-year effort, the National Council for Prescription Drug Programs (NCPDP) became an ANSI-accredited Standards Development Organization (SDO). NCPDP members, through consensus-building processes, define standards for transmitting prescription information from pharmacies to payers and for receiving approval and payment information. NCPDP standards are used billions of times each year to enable electronic transmission of retail pharmacy information.

"NCPDP is excited that the HIPAA final standards for electronic health care transactions were released," said Lee Ann C. Stember, NCPDP President, who was recently asked to comment. "The pharmacy services sector has been eagerly anticipating the rulings in order to move forward with the implementation of Telecommunication Standard Version 5.1. The pharmacy services sector has always led the way among health care with respect to electronic claims, and we anticipate this to continue. It is through the diligent work of NCPDP members, who created Version 5.1, that our standards are able to keep up with the ever-evolving marketplace."

The HIPAA regulation adopted the NCPDP Telecommunications Standard Format Version 5.1 and the NCPDP Batch Standard Version 1, Release 0 for retail pharmacy claims, health care eligibility benefit inquiry and response, health care services review, referral certification and authorization, and coordination of benefits. The Batch Standard uses the Telecommunication Standard as part of the implementation guidelines. The regulation is expected to be edited to name the NCPDP Batch Standard Version 1.1 with the Telecommunication Standard Version 5.1 as the Detail Data Record.

The final rule incorrectly states that NCPDP Telecommunication Standard Version 5.1 cannot support the billing of professional pharmacy services because it does not support HCPCS J-codes to identify the pharmacy procedure or service. But Version 5.1 does clearly support HCPCS J-codes as qualifiers. The rule named the *ASC X12N 837 Health Care Claim: Professional*, Version 4010, to perform this function. A correction has been requested. NCPDP members are working to have Telecommunication Standard Version 5.1 and Batch 1.1 added for retail pharmacy professional services.

In the final rule, NCPDP Telecommunications Standard Version 5.1 was named for pharmacy remittance advice transactions. The Telecommunications Standard does not support remittance advice information such as check number and amount. CMS/HCFA will correct the final rule in the preamble and the section on remittance advice.

In the final rule, the Eligibility section and page 50364 mention prior authorization transactions using ASC X12N 278. In Technical Corrections, DHHS published a revision to the final rule that named the NCPDP Standards for Referral Certification and Authorization.

Health Level Seven

Founded in 1987, Health Level Seven (HL7) became an ANSI-accredited Standards Developing Organization (SDO) in June of 1994. HL7's mission statement (published in their Web site, *http://www.hl7.org*) is: "To provide standards for the exchange, management, delivery, and evaluation of health care services. Specifically, to create flexible, cost effective approaches, standards, guidelines, methodologies, and related services for interoperability between health care information systems." HL7 standards are widely used to interface the independent systems in health care institutions concerned with clinical information.

HL7's involvement with HIPAA began in 1996 with the formation of a Special Interest Group (SIG) for claims attachments. The Attachment SIG was formed to standardize the content and format of supplemental information needed to support health care insurance and other electronic commerce transactions. The Secretary of HHS was to name applicable standards not later than 18 months after the date of the law's enactment, August of 1996. Standards relating to claims attachments were excepted from that deadline and given until not later than 30 months after that date to be formally adopted. The initial step following the enactment is the publication of a Notice of Proposed Rule Making (NPRM) in the Federal Register.

The NPRM for health care transaction standards and code sets was published on May 7, 1998; a public comment period began that day and ended on July 6, 1998. The final rule was not published until August 17, 2000. The NPRM for attachments is expected to be published in 2001. It will name two X12N implementation guides:

- Health Care Claim, Request for Additional Information (277)
- Additional Information to Support a Health Care Claim (275)

and six HL7 booklets, each covering one of the following:

- Ambulance
- Clinical Reports
- Emergency Department
- Laboratory Results
- Medications
- Rehabilitation Services

The implementation guides and booklets are available on the WPC Web site (*http://wpc-edi.com*). Between the date when the transaction standard and code sets NPRM were published and the publication of the final rule more than two years had passed. The attachments mandate might also take that much time to become official.

The Workgroup for Electronic Data Interchange

In 1989, President George H. W. Bush appointed Dr. Louis W. Sullivan Secretary of Health and Human Services (HHS)–a position Dr. Sullivan held through 1992, the end of that administration. As HHS secretary, Dr. Sullivan convened a forum of health care and insurance industry leaders to determine how health care administrative costs could be reduced. The group concluded that converting the administrative processes of health care to EDI—already in widespread use in the grocery, warehousing, supply chain management, and transportation industries—would yield substantial savings.

As a result of the Federal forum, the Workgroup for Electronic Data Interchange (WEDI, pronounced WEE-dee) was established in the latter part of 1991 to address administrative costs in the nation's health care system. WEDI is a voluntary, public/private task force created to streamline health care administration by standardizing electronic communications across the industry.

Initially co-chaired by Bernard R. Tresnowski, President of the Blue Cross and Blue Shield Associations, and Joseph T. Brophy, former President of The Travelers Insurance Company, WEDI fostered the vision of a health care industry that would conduct all business electronically, using one set of standards and interconnecting networks. An early recommendation was to use the ANSI ASC X12 family of EDI standards.

In 1992, WEDI formed a steering committee of health care leaders representing private payers (insurance companies), government payers (Medicare, Medicaid administrators), providers (doctors, nurses, hospitals), and allied businesses. This steering committee was asked to outline steps toward two goals: to make EDI a routine means of conducting business between payers and providers by 1994, and to extend the full benefits of administrative automation across the health care industry by 1996. Fifty technical experts known as the WEDI Technical Advisory Group (TAG) supported the Steering Committee. Lee Barrett, who was at that time Chair of the X12 insurance subcommittee, X12N, was one of the original Steering Committee members. Asked recently about HIPAA, Barrett said, "There were many people in the industry that shared the vision back in '92 and the subsequent years that a set of standardized transactions was critical for the industry. We needed to address the need to evolve from 450 different electronic claim formats to a singular format. The momentum and commitment from the industry through the efforts of WEDI, ASC X12N, and other industry coalitions was tremendous and, therefore, the focus was achieved to implement the transactions through HIPAA."

By July 1992, WEDI had presented a report to Dr. Sullivan that outlined aggressive goals to propel the health care industry toward the use of EDI. WEDI was committed to realizing these goals through a public/private partnership and industry initiative. The report outlined the necessary steps to make EDI routine for the health care industry by 1996.

William J. Clinton defeated President George H. W. Bush in the election of November 1992. As a candidate, Bill Clinton had run on a platform that included health care reform. After his election, the executive branch's Health Care Reform Task Force began to develop health care reform legislation. WEDI's 1992 report played a critical role in educating the administration and members of congress about the savings possible with complete EDI implementation. Many of the new Clinton administration's proposals were built on WEDI's work and recommendations.

WEDI recommendations that were carried out in 1992 and 1993 include:

- X12N approved standardized health care claim and eligibility transactions
- X12N established new workgroups to develop other standards required by the health care industry
- HCFA initiated the use of claim and claim payment transactions for Medicare consistent with the X12 standards
- The private sector began developing EDI implementation guides, including several for the Health Industry Business Communications Council that were published by WPC
- Efforts toward standardizing data content increased
- EDI awareness and participation were heightened

WEDI participation increased 500% from 1992 to 1993. Over 5,000 copies of the 1992 WEDI Report were distributed to various parties including the Federal government, health care providers, trade associations, consumer groups, employers, vendors, state governments, and payers. All members of the United States Senate and House of Representatives received a copy of the report. WEDI representatives met with members of President Clinton's Health Care Reform Task Force to discuss WEDI's plan for achieving the aggressive goals outlined in the 1992 WEDI Report. WEDI representatives met with key Congressional staff working on health care reform issues to educate them on the WEDI work plan and industry EDI initiatives. As a result of all of this activity, the membership of X12N increased 50% between 1992 and 1993.

WEDI met in 1993 in an effort to overcome obstacles and achieve the goal of complete implementation by 1996. The Workgroup was divided into 11 Technical Advisory Groups (TAGs):

1. Standards Implementation and Uniform Data Content
2. Network Architecture and Accreditation
3. Confidentiality and Legal Issues
4. Unique Identifiers for the Health Care Industry
5. Education and Publicity
6. Health Identification Cards
7. Short-Term Strategies
8. State/Federal Role
9. Financial Implications
10. Coordination of Benefits
11. Health Care Fraud Prevention and Detection

The members of TAG 1 were successful in building implementation guides based on the generic X12 standards. But rather than having to go to both WEDI meetings and X12 meetings, they sought to do their X12 generic standards work and their implementation guide work at the same time.

X12N – The Insurance Subcommittee

The insurance subcommittee of X12, known as X12N, is comprised of several task groups with several work groups under each task group. Three separate areas, or lines, of the insurance business are associated with the subcommittee:

- Property & Casualty
- Life & Annuity
- Health Care

In an effort that began in 1994 and was completed in 1995, all X12N task groups finalized plans to have subcommittee X12N publish insurance industry–specific implementation guides for the generic X12 transaction standard. For the first time, the generic standards developing body, X12N, sought to develop its own implementation guides. Prior to this all EDI implementation guides were developed by industry action groups outside of X12 itself.

WPC was selected as publisher and copyright holder for X12N in 1995. The first X12N implementation guide, published for the Property & Casualty task group in 1995, was concerned with automobile liability insurance reporting. The second was for health care–covered claim payments and had been begun as a WEDI guide. Since then over 100 industry-specific implementation guides have either been published or are under development. The nine HIPAA guides are just a part of what this very active X12 subcommittee is accomplishing.

X12N has a diverse membership: Insurance companies such as State Farm, The Hartford, American Family Insurance, and the Blue Cross/Blue Shield Association and fifteen of its franchisees; many government agencies, such as the National Association for Public Health Statistics & Information Systems and the National Association of State Medicaid Directors; clearinghouses; systems vendors; and consultants.

American Medical Association and the National Uniform Claim Committee

In 1980, CMS/HCFA developed the first version of the HCFA-1500, an adaptation of a claim form recommended by the American Medical Association (AMA). In 1981, a Uniform Claim Form Task Force was convened to design a form that could be easily used by all physicians and insurers. The task force was co-chaired by the AMA and CMS/HCFA, with input from insurance organizations such as the Blue Cross/Blue Shield Association and the Health Insurance Association of America.

The task force was reconvened in 1984 and again in 1986 to revise the form. The 1984 version was approved by the Office of Management and Budget and CMS/HCFA mandated its use for all Medicare claims. It allowed providers to choose between two ways of recording diagnoses and procedures: by using codes or through narrative entries, or both. At the time, not all insurers required the use of the CMS/HCFA Common Procedure Coding System (HCPCS, pronounced HIX pix) or of the International Classification of Diseases, 9th Revision, Clinical Modification (ICD-9-CM). HCPCS and ICD-9-CM were specified in HIPAA as mandated medical code sets.

The 1986 version of the claim form was mandated for use by July 1992. A significant change was the elimination of diagnostic and procedure narratives. Improvements to HCPCS and ICD-9-CM had increased their specificity, removing the need for narrative accounts.

The National Uniform Claim Committee, modeled after the NUBC, replaced the Uniform Claim Form Task Force in May of 1995. Chaired by the AMA and CMS/HCFA, it has a broad base of provider, payer, standards developer, and government membership. NUBC is also a voting member.

NUCC took over the responsibility for the HCFA 1500 claim form and conducted considerable research into whether and how to revise it in response to HIPAA. A prototype replacement was developed by HCFA and WPC in 1998. The NUCC then conducted focus group sessions in several cities across the U.S. NUCC concluded at that time that although the new form could be ready for HIPAA and eliminate ambiguity, the cost to implement it far exceeded any projected gains. Many software/hardware systems depend on the existing HCFA 1500 in its current image. The NUCC is currently exploring the development of national instructions for completing the form while considering the possibility of very minor revisions to HCFA 1500 to make it compatible with a HIPAA 837 transaction.

The NUCC also developed a uniform data set for non-institutional claims and played a key role in the construction of the X12N Health Care Claim: Professional Implementation Guide, adopted under HIPAA. With development completed, the NUCC approved its standardized data set in July of 1997. Published by WPC, the data set was designed to be technologically and architecturally independent, and intended to apply to the claims and equivalent encounters and Coordination of Benefits (COB) transactions specified in the HIPAA. The data set was constructed based on the combined universe of fields included in the HCFA 1500 paper claim form, the Medicare National Standard Format (NSF), the NCVHS core data set, and the X12N *Health Care Claim: Professional Implementation Guide* that was subsequently adopted for HIPAA.

The American Dental Association and the Dental Electronic Content Committee

The American Dental Association has served members of the profession and others within the dental community through the development and promotion of standards for recording and conveying information on services provided to a patient. Such efforts began in the mid-1960s and, as the decade ended, first results included the national standard for tooth numbering; for paper claim form submission; and for dental procedure coding, named the *Code on Dental Procedures and Nomenclature (the Code)*. Both the paper claim form standard and the dental procedure codes have evolved with revisions on approximately a five-year cycle. The most recent versions of the ADA Dental Claim Form and of the *Code* were published in the latter half of 1999 with a January 1, 2001 effective date. Both items are published by the American Dental Association in a manual titled "cdt-3 / version 2000."

Long-term American Dental Association achievements in the standards arena have been recognized under the HIPAA legislation as well as its final rule on standard transactions and codes and the Federal Register notice that named the Designated Standards Maintenance Organizations. The final rule on transactions and code sets also established the *Code on Dental Procedures and Nomenclature* as the national standard medical code set for reporting dental procedures.

Code maintenance has been the historic responsibility of the Association's Council on Dental Benefit Programs. This body has also undertaken review and revision of the ADA Dental Claim Form. Evolution of the *Code* has followed a path that incorporates changes arising from members of the profession and the third-party payer community. Revision to the paper claim form has followed a similar path, recognizing that the needs of dentistry at times vary from the claim reporting needs of the medical profession. This is why the ADA Dental Claim Form has some similarities to, as well as differences from, the HCFA 1500 form used for other professional claim submissions. Such differences are also reflected in the HIPAA standard claim transaction implementation guides, where there is one each for dental claims, professional claims (physician, for example), and institutional claims.

To fulfill its role as a consultant to the HHS Secretary under the HIPAA legislation, the Association established the Dental Content Committee (DeCC). The DeCC was established by the American Dental Association Board of Trustees and is a voting body with balanced membership from the payer, general interest (such as other content committees and WEDI), and provider sectors of the dental community. As a DSMO, the Dental Content Committee is concerned with the data elements that comprise all standard transactions, bringing the dental perspective to consideration of all requested changes. The DeCC is not, however, involved in changes to the *Code on Dental Procedures and Nomenclature*, which has been identified as an external code set that is conveyed by a data element in a standard transaction.

Designated Standards Maintenance Organization

HIPAA required the Secretary of HHS to adopt standards for health care transactions after consulting with the following Data Content Committees (DCCs):

- National Uniform Billing Committee (NUBC)
- National Uniform Claim Committee (NUCC)
- Workgroup for Electronic Data Interchange (WEDI)
- American Dental Association (ADA)

The final HIPAA transaction rule established a new category of organization, the *Designated Standards Maintenance Organization (DSMO)*. In the same August 17, 2000 issue of the Federal Register that contained the final rule, the Secretary of HHS named six organizations that had agreed to maintain the standards using criteria specified in the rule. The Secretary designated the following organizations as DSMOs:

1. Accredited Standards Committee X12
2. Dental Content Committee of the American Dental Association
3. Health Level Seven
4. National Council for Prescription Drug Programs
5. National Uniform Billing Committee
6. National Uniform Claim Committee

The DSMOs contracted with WPC to build a Web site (*http://www.hipaa-dsmo.org*; see Figure 1-2) to implement the process specified in the rule and embodied in a Memorandum of Understanding (MOU) among the DSMOs.

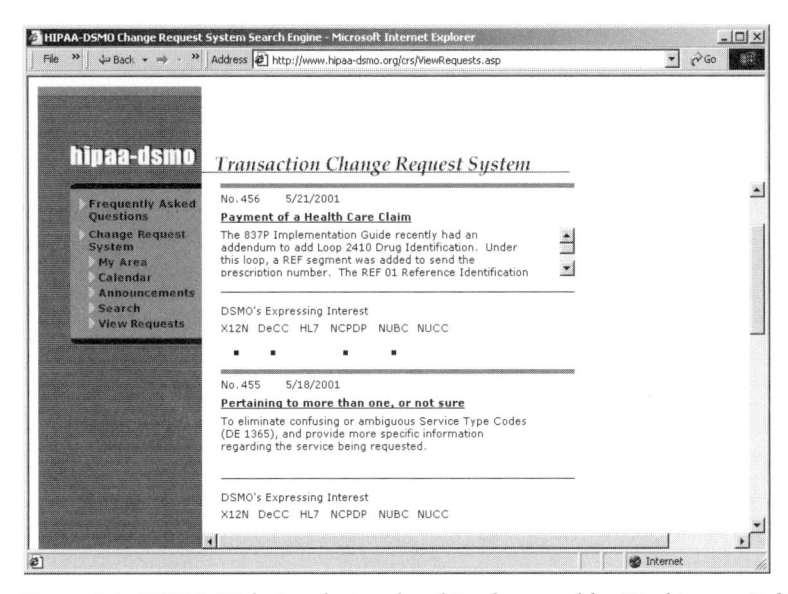

Figure 1-2. *DSMO Web site, designed and implemented by Washington Publishing Company*

The X12 standards are protean and unfinished. As business processes evolve, the transaction standards undergo continual change. HIPAA transaction standards can be changed once a year. It is expected that they will change every year in small, subtle ways, and sometimes dramatically.

Changes to the implementation guides occur through the DSMO process. The following guiding principles described in the MOU are adhered to by the DSMOs:

- Public Access – Single Point of Entry

    Any person or organization will have the opportunity to submit a HIPAA Change Request through a single, consistent point of entry and a coherent process.

- Timely Review of Change Requests

    The DSMOs agree to establish or maintain a methodology or process that ensures timely reviews and responses to all HIPAA Change Requests. Since the Secretary can promulgate new or revised HIPAA rules no more frequently than once a year, each organization's process should be designed to work within that time frame.

- Cooperation and Communication

    The organizations agree to cooperate and communicate with one another as each organization looks at new transactions, changes in technology, or other changes in the health care industry.

- Consider all Viewpoints

    The process allows for input and consideration of the various viewpoints of health plans, providers, and other entities involved in or affected by the HIPAA transaction rules.

- Evaluate Impact of Change Requests

    The organizations agree to consider the overall impact of any HIPAA Change Request on all the HIPAA transactions. While a request might seek a change to one transaction, that change might affect other transactions, and such eventualities must be anticipated.

- Maintain a National Perspective

    The organizations agree to maintain a national perspective in satisfying the business needs of the health care industry while fostering administrative simplification.

- Conform to Legislation

    All changes recommended shall be consistent with HIPAA statutory and regulatory provisions.

The DSMO Steering Committee will annually provide NCVHS with a change summary and with recommendations for changes. NCVHS reviews these and makes its recommendations to HHS. In turn, HHS initiates HIPAA rule modifications. A Federal Rule making process might be invoked. If so, an NPRM is published, to be followed by a 60 day public comment period, which is followed by a period during which responses to the comments are formulated. Finally, a new final rule is published that includes a compliance date. That date cannot be less than 180 days after publication.

The process calls for a five business day period monthly during which each DSMO has the opportunity to express interest in change requests entered into the Web site in the previous month. Each DSMO representative then has 90 days to enter the consensus opinion of his or her organization. Within 15 days following the 90-day period, the DSMO representatives meet to formulate a harmonized response to each change request. If more time is required, any DSMO representative can ask for a single 45-day extension.

After the harmonized response is posted to the Web site, the original submitter or any DSMO representative can appeal the decision. After the appeal process concludes, the decision becomes final. The appropriate standards setting organization's process of implementing each approved change request begins. The SSO can begin its implementation process before the change request is decided, but it cannot implement any proposed change until the end of the DSMO process.

The DSMO Web site was launched in October of 2000. In an effort to identify and repair major impediments to implementation, NCVHS asked the DSMOs to alter their procedures and institute a fast track process for the first six months of operation, October 2000 through March of 2001. Two hundred thirty-one change requests went through the DSMO process with a final resolution of each request posted to the Web site in June of 2001. For change requests entered as of April 2001 and after, a rolling schedule of DSMO resolutions every month has been achieved, dating back to July 2001.

Chapter 2

To Implement HIPAA, or Not to Implement?

Who Must Comply?

Determining which parties must comply with HIPAA is not always simple and straightforward. In some instances, it is obvious exactly to whom the regulation applies (health plans, health care clearinghouses); in other instances, it seems open to interpretation. If doubt exists as to whether an organization is required to comply, the organization should comply, because in doing so, it will be adopting the best practices available for health care administration in the United States.

The *best practice* concept is familiar to health care professionals. Clinical care procedures are determined by what has been proven to bring about the best results in patients. These best practices achieve a level of care far higher than the one that would be attained by doing merely what is necessary for patient survival.

In applying that logic to the administrative side of health care, *business matters* are what must be best served. Far from removing patient interest from consideration, establishing the best administrative practices available decreases patient frustration by reducing what is generally known as *red tape*. As EDI transforms the business of health care, office staffs and the people receiving care will find they spend less time on administrative tasks, whether doing them or waiting for them to be done.

HIPAA compliance is mandatory for health plans. See the Regulation in Appendix A, § 160.102 for a statement about who must comply and § 160.103 for a definition of those mentioned in § 160.102. Table 2-1, on the following page, lists the organizations included in the mandatory compliance.

Table 2-1. Organizations Included in Mandatory Compliance

Health Plans	For Example:
	• Group health plans
	• Health insurance issuers
	• HMOs
	• Issuers of Medicare supplemental policies
	• Issuers of long-term care policies
	• Employee welfare benefit plans
	• Any other arrangement offering or providing health benefits to the employees of two or more employers
	• Government health plans
	   • Active military personnel and veterans
	   • CHAMPUS (the Civilian Health and Medical Program of the Uniformed Services)
	   • Indian Health Service
	   • Federal Employees Health Benefit Program
	   • Approved state child health plans
	   • Medicaid + Choice

Health Care Clearinghouses	For Example: • Billing services • Repricing companies • Community health management information systems • Value-added networks • Switches
Health Care Providers (who choose to conduct business electronically)	For Example: • Doctors • Dentists • Hospitals • Clinics

Publication in the *Federal Register*

On August 17, 2000, the Office of the Secretary, Department of Health and Human Services, published the final rule titled *Health Insurance Reform: Standards for Electronic Transactions* in the *Federal Register, Volume 65, Number 160*. The regulation defines *health plan* as, "an individual or group plan that provides, or pays the cost of, medical care . . ." (§ 160.103) It specifies group health plans, health insurance issuers, HMOs, issuers of Medicare supplemental policies, issuers of long-term care policies (except "nursing home fixed-indemnity" policies), and employee welfare benefit plans "or any other arrangement . . . offering or providing health benefits to the employees of two or more employers." (§ 160.103) All of these entities must implement HIPAA.

The regulation further states that the Health Plan category also includes, "when applied to government funded programs, the components of the government agency administering the program." (§ 160.103) It specifies as health plans the health care programs for the following:

- Active military personnel and veterans
- CHAMPUS (the Civilian Health and Medical Program of the Uniformed Services)
- Indian Health Service
- Federal Employees Health Benefit Program
- Approved state child health plans
- Medicaid + Choice

All of these entities must implement HIPAA. HIPAA compliance is also mandatory for the following:

- Health care clearinghouses

   The term *health care clearinghouse* is defined in the regulation as any public or private entity that

   "(1) Processes or facilitates the processing of information received from another entity in a nonstandard format or containing nonstandard data content into standard data elements or a standard transaction."

   Or

   "(2) Receives a standard transaction from another entity and processes or facilitates the processing of information into nonstandard format or nonstandard data content for a receiving entity." (§ 160.103)

   The regulation states that clearinghouses include but are "not limited to, billing services, repricing companies, community health management information systems or community health information systems, and [if they perform functions (1) and (2), above] value-added networks and switches." (§ 160.103)

- Health care providers that electronically transmit any information related to:
  - Health care claims or equivalent encounters
  - Payment and remittance advice
  - Coordination of benefits
  - Health care claim status
  - Enrollment or disenrollment in a health plan
  - Health plan eligibility
  - Health plan premium payments
  - Certification and authorization of referrals
  - First reports of injuries
  - Health claims attachments

All of these are *transactions*. The regulation defines *transaction* as "the exchange of information between two parties to carry out financial or administrative activities related to health care." (§ 160.103) These Regulated Transactions (RTs) describe business processes that are encoded in the X12N Implementation Guides. The Implementation Guides specify the parts of the generic EDI standard that perform a particular business function. Initial capitals are used here when referring to HIPAA's Regulated Transactions, a set of business functions, to differentiate them from the X12 Standard's transaction sets. Singly and in combination, EDI transaction sets carry out the RTs electronically. Table 2-2 shows the RTs and the implementation guide or guides whose transaction sets carry out that business process.

Table 2-2. Standard Implementation Guides That Correspond to the Regulated Transactions

The Regulated Transactions (RTs)	X12 Transaction Set Identifier Implementation Guide Name (X12N Identifier)
Health Care Claims or Equivalent Encounters	837 Health Care Claim • Institutional (004010X096) • Dental (004010X097) • Professional (004010X098) Pharmacy Claim • NCPDP standard mentioned in Chapter 1, National Council for Prescription Drug Programs
Payment and Remittance Advice	835 • Health Care Claim Payment/Advice (004010X091)
Coordination of Benefits	837 Health Care Claim • Institutional (004010X096) • Dental (004010X097) • Professional (004010X098) 835 • Health Care Claim Payment/Advice (004010X091)
Health Care Claim Status	276 & 277 • Health Care Claim Status Request and Response (004010X093)
Enrollment or Disenrollment in a Health Plan	834 • Benefit Enrollment and Maintenance
Health Plan Eligibility	270 & 271 • Health Care Eligibility/Benefit Inquiry and Information Response
Health Plan Premium Payments	820 • Payroll Deducted and Other Group Premium Payment for Insurance Products (004010X061)

Table 2-2. Standard Implementation Guides That Correspond to the Regulated Transactions

Certification and Authorization of Referrals	278 • Health Care Services Review – Request for Review and Response (004010X094)
First Reports of Injuries	The standard for this transaction has not been established. Consult the Department of Health and Human Services Web site for updated information: *http://aspe.dhhs.gov/admnsimp*
Health Claims Attachments	Although not yet established, in conjunction with the HL7 booklets mentioned in Chapter 1, Health Level Seven, the X12 Transaction Sets 277 & 275 will become the mandated standard for attachments. 277 • Health Care Claim Request for Additional Information (004010X104) 275 • Health Care Claim Response to Request for Additional Information

After HIPAA formally goes into effect, all U.S. health care providers who send and receive administrative data electronically to and from a trading partner will accomplish those RTs using one, HIPAA-specified, set of data elements. See § 160.102 of the Regulation in Appendix A under the title *Applicability*. The regulations do not force health care providers to use EDI; they merely require those who do employ it to use the same electronic standard. In the post-compliance era, the economic and procedural advantages of using the transaction standards will be realized by payers and by those providers who choose to participate. Business procedures will become more efficient as the standards are employed, and EDI-shy providers will adopt them too.

Additional information about who must implement the HIPAA transaction standards is available at these Web sites:

http://aspe.dhhs.gov/admnsimp

http://www.wedi.org

The Business Value of EDI

EDI is the *lingua franca* of ocean shipping and motor and rail transport; and of the grocery, energy, and retail industries, among others. Unlike the discipline of health care, these industries adopted EDI voluntarily, without the legislated imperative of Federal regulation. Decision makers within many, disparate areas of commerce—from the automotive industry to fresh produce—set aside the fractiousness that is common in groups of competitors and agreed to change the form of their participation in the marketplace. Why? Because EDI made that marketplace more profitable and efficient for whole industries, from appliances to toys. The new speed and accuracy of electronic transactions enabled retailers and wholesalers to adopt the Just-In-Time approach to inventory. They eliminated costly warehousing because, with EDI, production could closely track demand.

The people who are now expected to change the way they conduct the business of health care might not have used EDI before, but they are familiar with its effects whether they are aware of it or not. Wal-Mart, the largest retail chain in the world, issued its own, non-governmental mandate when it advised its trading partners that, to continue to supply the giant of retail, they must use EDI. A walk through Wal-Mart's endless aisles of consumer goods is all it takes to understand the broad range of producers and suppliers, in the U.S. and around the world, who started implementing EDI as a result of the retailer's decision.

Another conspicuously successful corporation that utilizes EDI is the United Parcel Service (UPS). Those ubiquitous brown trucks and the packages they carry reach their destinations through a unique application of EDI embodied in UPS's EDI Implementation Guide.

Chris Miller, Washington Publishing Company's (WPC's) Chief Technical Officer (CTO), previously worked for Current Components, Inc., an importing and exporting distributor of small printers and printer-related hardware and supplies. Chris explains Current Components' business model:

> Goods are purchased overseas or through large U.S. distribution centers and are distributed nationally by UPS and other carriers. Essentially, product arrives on big trucks and leaves on little trucks.
>
> UPS has a number of ways to accept manifest entries. The manifest contains data detailing destination address, size, weight, content, and so on, for each parcel shipped. Often, UPS installs a computer at a shipper's location. The shipper is then required to input each customer's name and address; as a box is prepared, the shipper inputs its size, weight, etc., and a label is created. At the end of each business day, data is uploaded by modem to the UPS processing center. A disadvantage of this approach is that the customer is required to maintain two database systems: one for internal processes, such as accounting, and one to support UPS. Another drawback is that tracking data, namely the barcode created by the UPS system, is not available to the host accounting system.
>
> Current Components did not want to maintain two systems. It required that tracking data be available to customer service personnel. The company chose to implement EDI, enabling it to link up with the UPS system, in which EDI data is uploaded each night by HTTPS over the public Internet. UPS provided Current Components with an implementation guide that detailed the required EDI file structure as well as the various checksums and methods for creating barcodes. Once the initial design was completed, Current Components was able to maintain one database. Tracking information was available to everyone in the company in real time. And Current Components' Web site, which accesses the central database, allowed customers to track shipments in real time, even before the parcels are picked up by UPS. UPS's EDI implementation also provided for richer data content to be transmitted. Thus, package details, including content descriptions, are available during tracking. Data entry errors were eliminated because there was no second database requiring maintenance. Billing errors were greatly reduced because UPS personnel were no longer required to hand-key barcode or ZIP code information.

Implementation design was accomplished quickly. The system has been running flawlessly for a number of years without modification. EDI provided a cost effective, simple, and elegant solution for exchanging data between Current Components and UPS.

Implementation Guides for the HIPAA transaction standards, published by WPC as stated in the regulation, are available to all areas of the health care industry (see Table 2-2). Payers and providers employ these Guides to attain HIPAA compliance.

Because of HIPAA, the coupling of EDI and health care administration is imminent. It is ironic that health care, encompassing a huge range of services and products essential to people's well-being—and some upon which lives literally depend—is converting to an advanced, more reliable method of administration only after it has been proven in less vital fields. When the mandated means of interchanging health insurance data is routinely and uniformly employed, the clerical staff of medical practices will drastically reduce the time they spend repeatedly inputting the same information in various forms and formats. Costly inputting errors that would inevitably have occurred will be avoided. Money saved and mistakes avoided by eliminating duplication of effort are the positive effects of converting to EDI that other industries have experienced. The system for securing health care ought to function at least as well as those through which we buy household goods and send packages. The importance of the health care "product" demands it.

The X12 Approach

X12 EDI, the format for health care content, streamlines administrative methods. In the world of objects, something *streamlined* has no part that protrudes or projects to interrupt the flow around it of whatever medium (usually air or water) the object moves through. A thing with parts extending into the currents that surround it encounters *turbulence* as those extensions resist the streaming flow. The pre-HIPAA financial and administrative systems used in health care are bulky with attachments and paper forms. They cause such turbulence as the shaken feeling that comes over a patient on discovering his or her referral is no longer valid when a long-awaited office visit is set to occur.

A system with HIPAA implemented is less prone to turbulence. Its sleek profile was achieved by eliminating duplication of efforts. A single piece of information—patient's last name, for instance—is retained in this system, its meaning reflected by its position and available as needed, without the requirement of retyping it at each stop along the way from doctor visit to claim payment. Another aspect of the sleek nature of EDI comes from its connectedness: computer-to-computer communication drastically reduces the tedious, error-prone task of data entry.

Other categories of EDI have reshaped how the retail, warehouse, and automotive industries, as well as rail, motor, and sea transport, conduct business. This health care data set provides a content framework on which better business applications will be built. Because changing the data set requires industry consensus, EDI will be a unifying factor within health care administration. When the regulation takes effect, all entities doing any electronic care-related administrating must employ the HIPAA standard, the single replacement for the Babel of 400 modes of transmission. The new frugality of form of expression will yield coherence and economy, without disparate business data content sets to reconcile.

Kendra Martin, CIO of the American Petroleum Institute and former chair of ASC X12, has reflected on the energy industry's continuing use of EDI. Her observations and recollections follow:

> The emphasis of early EDI was primarily on data entry: getting duplication of efforts in data entry out of the way, and reducing the number of entry mistakes. The crucial focus, simply put, was on getting better information more quickly. We weren't even talking about Just-In-Time inventory and quick response. We were basically talking about trying to automate the volumes and volumes of data to improve day-to-day operations.
>
> Companies such as 3M—a very diversified, large corporation with interests in more than 200 different industries—began looking around and saying, in effect, "OK, we really like this EDI. But. We do business in all these industries—transportation, grocery, retail, warehousing, and many others. Do we have to use a separate set of EDI standards for each of them?" Thus evolved the very apparent need to move to a trans-industry, inter-functional, generic set of EDI standards. It seemed logical to pursue that goal, and the Accredited Standards Committee (ASC) X12 became the vehicle for that pursuit.
>
> A significant shift in the mindset of standards developers occurred in the mid-1980s when two things happened. First, we started looking at the needs of smaller companies and working with some to develop solutions that would fit. EDI was not just for the *Fortune 500* companies. In fact, it wouldn't be of benefit if the majority of your trading partners weren't EDI-enabled. Second, there was the explosion of the personal computer market. For so many in the business world, personal computers just changed everything. The advent of personal computers allowed small businesses to participate in an activity that was traditionally reserved for mainframe shops.
>
> To expand EDI to where it would make a significant economic impact, it became clear that we needed to get to the smaller trading partners. A lot of progress could be measured in the number and types of X12 transaction sets that came into being around that time. But the challenge that companies really struggled with was getting one hundred percent of their trading partners signed up and ready to go. The GMs and Fords could get maybe ten to fifteen percent of their large suppliers doing EDI with them, but beyond that, it became a battle. So we experienced a lot of frustration in those first years.

This is the same frustration that many health care CIOs and CTOs are feeling today. Kendra Martin continues:

> We had to spend several years trying to overcome that reluctance to implement EDI. But once more, advances in technology intervened. Now it seems almost everyone has an Internet connection for their home personal computer. And we talk not about EDI but about electronic commerce. People now understand that EDI is a tool for doing electronic commerce.

Diverse industries and most of the *Fortune 500* companies have implemented EDI and found good business value in it. (In 1994, 483 of that year's *Fortune 500* companies purchased EDI documentation from WPC.) Now, health care stands to reap some of the same business value that more commercial fields have realized for years.

HIPAA-Phobia

An informal survey of HIPAA-related articles in health care industry media suggests that administrators are responding to the challenge of implementing HIPAA by trying to delay meeting it. On March 30, 2001, the Blue Cross Blue Shield Association (BCBSA), the American Medical Association (AMA), and the American Public Human Services Association (APHSA) sent a letter to Congress requesting a delay in the implementation of HIPAA, citing several key factors in support of an extension:

- The staggered release and implementations of HIPAA administrative simplification regulations will require multiple systems upgrades, undermining efficient planning and budgeting.
- Compliance costs of implementing the transactions and code sets regulations are much higher than anticipated.
- More time is needed for the development and testing of compliance software.
- The elimination of local procedure codes must be accompanied by a significant investment of time and resources to avoid disruption of administrative services during the transition to national standard codes.

Scott P. Serota, President and Chief Executive Officer of BCBSA, believes that an extension would benefit consumers, physicians, and hospitals:

> Under the current timeframe, wholesale change to the claims and billing platform for the entire health care industry must be done by October 2002[1]. That's a challenge even more complicated than Y2K, and time is running out. Thousands of electronic codes used in physician offices, hospitals, clinics, and pharmacies—including codes designed to address local reimbursement issues—will disappear and be replaced by federally mandated codes.
>
> A rushed implementation risks a disruption of services and payments. Physicians, hospitals, and health plans need time to test new systems. Given the stakes and the importance of a smooth transition, an extension to get it right is critical.

Congress responded with proposed legislation in the House and the Senate:

- Sen. Larry Craig (R-Idaho) introduced S.836 on May 7, 2001, titled: A Bill to Amend Part C of Title XI of the Social Security Act to Provide for Coordination of Implementation of Administrative Simplification Standards for Health Care Information. S.836 was referred to Senate committee the same day. The legislation calls for setting back the date upon which entities must be compliant with

---

1. Editor's Note: At the time of this printing, delays in HIPAA implementation were being debated by Congress. To find the most current information about the status of HIPAA implementation, see the U.S. Department of Health and Human Services *Administrative Simplification* Web site *http://aspe.dhhs.gov/admnsimp*.

the administrative simplification standards until two years after all rules have been promulgated, and the national provider and health plan identifiers are ready and available. The legislation does not affect the privacy regulation.

- Rep. John Shadegg (R-Arizona) introduced H.R.1975 on May 23, 2001. Its title is: To Modify the Deadline for Initial Compliance with the Standards and Implementation Specifications Promulgated Under Section 1173 of the Social Security Act, and for Other Purposes. H.R.1975 was referred to House subcommittee on June 4, 2001.

On June 25, 2001, the Medical Group Management Association (MGMA) responded to the proposed legislation with a letter from William F. Jessee, MD, CMPE, MGMA's President and Chief Executive Officer, to Senator Max Baucus, Chair of the United States Senate Committee on Finance.

In the letter, the MGMA acknowledged that a delay in the implementation of transactions and code sets was reasonable, but it opposed legislation that would delay the implementation of administrative simplification provisions of HIPAA. The MGMA gave several reasons for its opposition, including the likelihood that the legislation would result in an indefinite delay in the adoption of HIPAA provisions and that the lack of an explicit compliance date for HIPAA would result in uncertainty and confusion in the medical community, which would lead to the stagnation of HIPAA implementation.

In organizations directly affected by the regulation, the people who direct the flow of information, the use of technology, and the management of finances will fail in their jobs if they continue to merely wish the new strictures would go away. Such an attitude might be fostered by the tenor of industry commentary that gave rise to the previously mentioned two legislative attempts to eviscerate HIPAA.

Industry buzz that exaggerates the inherent difficulties of implementation or the perils of non-compliance is potentially damaging in other ways, too. This buzz might instill in decision-makers susceptibility to purveyors of software touted as "HIPAA-compliant." Some vendors even offer to "certify" that those who buy their wares are thereby in compliance with HIPAA.

In and of itself, a software package cannot be "HIPAA-compliant," nor can it confer that status. To truly attain implementation, an organization must change internal conditions in ways that go beyond the function of software. Assistance is available on the path to HIPAA compliance that accounts for all the necessities: assuring network security, deciding how to deploy the data set, and meeting privacy commitments. Decision-makers for implementing organizations must determine whether or not vendors' offerings encompass such a solution. Any approach to implementing HIPAA that addresses a single organization's needs will not have efficacy because it is one-sided. Vital to health care EDI is the primacy of the trading partner–to–trading partner relationship, just as it has been in EDI practiced for years by other industries.

Any organization can obtain the elements to build HIPAA compliance. Converting to the prescribed data set might be the easiest part, with HIPAA implementation guides furnishing the means. Again, further reliable information is available at the DHHS Web site and the WEDI Web site:

http://aspe.dhhs.gov/admnsimp

http://www.wedi.org

Pessimistic Voices

Respected organizations within health care have reported that their constituents are unable to comply with the dictates of the regulation. Yet many of these organizations were deeply involved in the process that determined the very standards they denounce. This stated inability to comply by the deadline, despite having been involved in the process from the beginning, requires examination.

Political efforts to extend the deadline or remove rules should not be perceived by any covered entity as a signal to wait. Rather, entities that are required to implement should be moving toward fulfilling the terms of the regulation in a prudent and fiscally responsible manner.

The implementation guides are maintained by volunteers who represent, and are answerable to, all sectors of the health care community. The guides reflect a consensus of industry opinion with the force of the HIPAA regulation behind it. To ensure relevancy and current status, all implementation guides are subject to redrafting, as industry representatives work toward the next expected annual version release. New business issues, errors, and conflicts of opinion are addressed, and (presumably) resolved, in the course of this normal standards maintenance process.

The Designated Standards Maintenance Organization (DSMO) and Standards Development Organization (SDO) processes are in place to address issues of concern to organizations affected by the regulation. With the coming of implementation, all the various elements dealing with health care administration will become more fluent in their use of these processes. Confidence in their efficacy, and the efficacy of the standards they result in, will spread as people gain actual experience with them. Protestations from within the health support professions claiming that the HIPAA standards or their implementation guides won't work will subside as the standards and guides begin working.

The Cost of Implementation

One might as well ask, "Who knows the cost of implementation?" Anyone who replies, "I do," is invited to weigh in with an answer. Determining how to implement, where and how to even begin, and what dollar amount to allocate for the task at hand requires informed analysis of factors pertaining to the complying entity as well as those that pertain to its trading partners. Along with the HIPAA regulation, the Department of Health and Human Services (DHHS) published figures expressing an idea of the cost of implementation. The department also projected the cost *benefits* that an organization implementing the HIPAA transaction standard might expect as a result. The cost/benefit tables, and a complete explanation of how the department calculated these ratios, can be found in the preamble to the regulation (*Federal Register*, p. 50366) and are also available in HTML form on the Internet: *http://aspe.dhhs.gov/admnsimp/final/txfin00.htm*

According to studies by several organizations, the Gartner Group and the Nolan Company among them, the original DHHS estimates of implementation costs were unrealistically low.

The projected cost of implementation has been compared to that of Y2K readiness efforts, an analogy that—if it asserts similarity between the two—illuminates nothing about HIPAA, whose processes are continuous and open-ended. Making systems ready for the changeover to 2000 called for effecting a single, consistent change per system, tied to a specific date, that corrected a sin of omission. The disaster of summary systems crashes was averted but, beyond that, Y2K readiness efforts are not seen as having generated a positive return on the time and money invested in them. If a pre-millennial parallel exists, it is one of mood: the dread of HIPAA implementation among those most affected echoes the fear that chaos would descend with the calendar change.

To focus on the real return on this investment, taking into account the parts of HIPAA that will require spending not soon recoverable—namely, the cost of meeting the regulation's privacy and not-yet-established security provisions—requires a leap into the future, ten years after health plans, clearinghouses, and participating providers have initiated implementation.

Many people are troubled by large health care expenditures that are not directly related to improving medical or patient services. The HIPAA regulation's provisions that are collectively termed *Administrative Simplification* might seem to fall under this category, but the electronic infrastructure they comprise will serve patients far better than previous administrative methods.

Even if the cost of fulfilling the regulation's privacy and security requirements is viewed as a drain upon resources, in time the savings will be appreciable.

Implementation dollars are best spent on improving an organization's current, or *legacy*, environment. This entails retraining current staff, augmenting legacy systems, and effecting a general upgrade guided by the HIPAA template. It might mean replacing existing implementation plans with a more comprehensive solution.

First, a well-informed staff will be enabled to evaluate an organization's situation regarding Administrative Simplification. While many consulting services offer their expertise, few can empower an entity's staff to contribute toward their own solution. For years, care-giving organizations have promoted patient education, which increases patients' participation and sense of control regarding their own treatment. It is time for health care administrators to embrace the same concept for their IT infrastructure. If current staff members are encouraged and empowered to help decide upon a solution, they will assert their ownership of it in practice. These are the people who know where the problems of legacy systems lie. Consulting companies that offer a "HIPAA assessment" are apt to approach the task from the top, producing expensive charts for highest echelon personnel. Unless this work is based on data and procedures employed in the day-to-day administrative process *as practiced* by staff at the core of the organization, it will be of dubious value.

The next step in developing a solution—and controlling its cost—is examining the legacy data content set. Knowing whether it shares any elements with the HIPAA-sanctioned data set is the beginning of understanding how business processes must change. If a process is still predominantly paper-based, will the solution be more costly than that of an electronic legacy environment? Not necessarily. The paper-based legacy system might even provide a better starting point: A new electronic system, freshly installed, will significantly undercut the former costs of preparing paper claims and other paper transactions. The health care industry estimate of $8.00 to prepare a paper-based claim is an extravagance compared to the cost of an electronic claim, which is likely to be as low as between $2.00 and $3.00.

The benefits of the functional improvements—eligibility, referrals, electronic claims status, and electronic payments—far outweigh their costs. Ultimately, more health care dollars will be available for patient care and services and for the improved employee benefits that enable institutions to hire and keep personnel of the highest quality.

The benefits provided by implementing the Administrative Simplification portion of HIPAA are greater than the costs, but the accompanying privacy and (not yet final) security requirements will delay the realization of some of that savings.

Beyond Expediency: The Value of Implementing HIPAA for the Entities That Must

The benefits that come with implementation vary according to the nature of the implementing entity. What the regulation requires also necessarily depends on which role the entity plays: that of payer for, or provider of, health care.

Payer

The payer community is the sector most affected by HIPAA, which is, more than anything else, a vehicle for insurance reform and regulation. In the past, payer entities have defined their own business processes and content, in effect imposing them on providers and consumers. This regulation stops and remakes what had been payer organizations' normal business processes. Managers of these businesses have expressed the fear that provider organizations currently dealing with them electronically through standards other than the HIPAA-mandated one will revert to paper-based systems for these business transactions, rather than implement the mandated X12N EDI transaction standards. Unlike payers, a provider entity can choose to conduct its administrative functions via non-electronic means; that is, through the physical movement of paper on which the required data is recorded. Payer organizations must accommodate such systems, even as they increasingly seem to be holdovers from a receding past. But is HIPAA implementation likely to produce, as payers fear, the opposite of its intended effect, providers switching from electronic dealings to paper? This eventuality is unlikely because those providers, having already experienced improvement in how their offices function when some tasks are performed electronically, are expected to recognize that switching from an unsanctioned standard to the X12N EDI transaction standards will yield further improvement, widening the breadth of what can be achieved electronically.

Payers will benefit from HIPAA, starting with the simplifying effect of the regulation's essential attribute, the EDI standard. One data content set for virtually all business associates, and any provider that communicates electronically—meaning most providers—will foster improvements within payer organizations. Streamlining internal business processes will cut payers' costs. The smooth flow of information between payer entities and providers will drastically reduce errors such as those that come in the course of entering and reentering data.

The payer community will gain the capability of instantaneously delivering information—to all parties who depend on it—about eligibility, referrals, and payment. Subscribers rarely initiate contact with their payer entities unless facing a life-changing event such as catastrophic illness. Once they are able to access benefit information electronically, using systems which HIPAA compliance allows payers to set up with relative ease, subscribers will find it easier to get information. They need not wait for a crisis to inform themselves of the terms of their insurance policies. Payers will find they can disseminate more information, all of it of unquestionable accuracy, while reducing the hours their personnel spend fielding questions.

With new fluidity, information will be channeled between payer and provider, provider and consumer, and consumer and payer. More efficient communication will serve the interests of all parties.

The payer community, required to invest in implementation, will offset the cost of that investment by developing innovative applications of the standard that increase efficiency while reducing the cost of doing business.

Provider

The provider community will implement to realize the advantages of electronic transactions. Providers will have the greatest potential return on their investment when they implement HIPAA. A provider communicates with many payer entities. The changeover from the turbulent system wherein payers use their choice of 400 data content sets that the provider must accommodate, to a streamlined system in which all parties use one uniform data content set, will relieve the administrative burden on providers more than that of any other segment of the care continuum. Pre-HIPAA, each payer could have different requirements, a source of immense confusion and an enormous clerical workload for providers. The electronic standard cuts through the confusion and reduces the workload. Providers will no longer be burdened with checking eligibility, obtaining referrals for patients, checking claim status, and reconciling accounts receivable. These functions will be automated and staff participation in them will be minimal; the information will be readily available at their fingertips.

One physician has said that the rapid and easy determination of a patient's eligibility for care during an office visit would relieve staffers of having to generate a bill; a fee of just $10, collected from each non-eligible patient receiving care, would put his practice in the black.

HIPAA brings to the provider community relief from the exorbitant cost of doing business. Another physician remarked that he had received a check from an insurance company for services that had been performed more than seven years previously. That check had seemed a bonus until he thought more about the situation. Why did his accounting staff not know that this payment had been due his practice? How many other checks should he have gotten? The benefits for providers of implementing HIPAA include relief from such nagging questions as these.

Chapter 3

The HIPAA Solution Offered by Microsoft and Washington Publishing Company

Microsoft believes that HIPAA offers health care organizations a rare opportunity for strategic action—to meet the requirements head on and use it as a catalyst for positive change. Recognizing the importance of this initiative to the health care industry, Microsoft research and development resources were focused to directly address the industry's unique needs.

Solving industry-specific needs required a new approach within Microsoft. An approach was taken that extends beyond traditional product development, including an increased investment in providing prescriptive guidance, training, consulting, and partner services into the overall solution offering. The partnership with Washington Publishing Company combined the best of product development with the industry-specific expertise needed to directly address the requirements of HIPAA.

The HIPAA Solution is composed of several components that, together, determine the form an organization's HIPAA compliance will take. The Solution might be viewed as a house built with an infrastructure of core technologies, appointed with specialized technology and consulting, and finished with the participation of partners (see Figure 3-1).

```
                    Client
┌─────────────────────────────────────────────────┐
│ Independent Software Vendors                    │
│ System Integration Partners                     │
├─────────────────────────────────────────────────┤
│ Microsoft BizTalk Accelerator for HIPAA         │
│ Specialized Training and Consulting Services    │
│ from Microsoft and WPC                          │
├─────────────────────────────────────────────────┤
│ Microsoft Windows 2000 Server                   │
│ Microsoft SQL Server 2000                       │
│ Microsoft BizTalk Server 2000                   │
└─────────────────────────────────────────────────┘
```

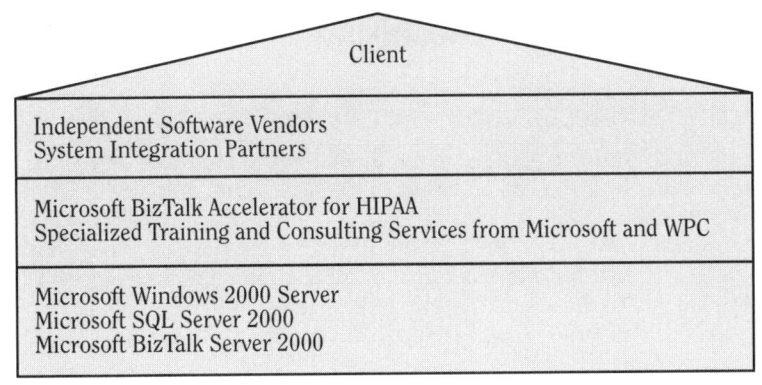

Figure 3-1. *The HIPAA Solution House—built on a foundation of core technologies and capped by the client*

Core Technologies

Microsoft Windows 2000 Server

The Windows 2000 Server operating system is designed to increase the value of existing hardware and software investments while lowering overall computing costs. This operating system is easier to deploy, configure, and use than other operating systems because of the centralized, customizable management services it provides. These services are flexible enough to work with existing management solutions and mixed-platform distributed networks. The result is maximum value from current IT infrastructure.

Microsoft SQL Server 2000

Microsoft SQL Server 2000 consists of a set of components that work together to store and analyze data. It is capable of meeting the data storage and analysis needs of the largest Web sites and enterprise data processing systems. The SQL Server 2000 relational database engine meets the requirements of sophisticated data processing environments. It protects data integrity while managing the actions of thousands of users, even as they modify the database concurrently, with minimal overhead costs.

Microsoft BizTalk Server 2000

A member of the Microsoft .NET Enterprise Server family of products, Microsoft BizTalk Server 2000 is a single product that performs two functions: enterprise application integration (EAI) and business-to-business (B2B) integration. BizTalk Server 2000 enables developers, IT professionals, and business analysts to easily build—over the Internet—dynamic business processes that span applications, platforms, and businesses.

Specialized Technology and Consulting

The Microsoft BizTalk Accelerator for HIPAA

The Microsoft BizTalk Accelerator for HIPAA is the first supported product developed by Microsoft to meet specific business requirements of the health care industry. It is designed to simplify and accelerate the process of meeting HIPAA standards for the electronic transfer of information among health care and insurance entities covered by the regulation. The HIPAA standards for administrative simplification apply to elements of the industry that perform any of these three functions: provide health care, pay for health care, or act as a claims clearinghouse.

The Accelerator contains the following features that allow Microsoft BizTalk Server 2000 to process and validate health care EDI transactions as defined by HIPAA:

- All 12 X12N HIPAA transaction sets as BizTalk Server schemas from Washington Publishing Company (WPC)
- The HIPAA implementation guides for the transaction sets as Microsoft HTML Help documents from WPC

- A HIPAA-specific parser
- Specialized support for splitting large health care claims, claim payments, and enrollment transactions into smaller, more manageable transactions

WPC and Microsoft Consulting Services: Consulting, Training

The concept underlying the HIPAA Solution differs from those on which other Solutions from Microsoft are based. At the core of the HIPAA Solution is Microsoft Consulting Services (MCS) for health care practices. The goal of MCS Health Care Core Solution Team is the empowerment of clients and their trading partners by transferring knowledge to assist and enable them to achieve HIPAA compliancy.

A properly trained staff is critical to implementation. The right preparation reduces the risks of deployment while speeding it up. Prior to beginning the process, an organization's implementation staff should complete a three-part training program that will acquaint them with what constitutes a state of institutional readiness for implementation. Training should be done in a development lab setting, with didactic content presented before hands-on lab work. Forming teams of learners that compete to accomplish specific assignments helps increase the effectiveness of the training experience.

Training to implement this Solution should include preparation in the following areas:

- HIPAA EDI
- BizTalk Server
- BizTalk Accelerator for HIPAA

Partners

Independent Software Vendors and Systems Integration Partners

The partnership model is key to the Solution; the partners themselves are its strength. Sharing knowledge through robust client relationships is both the path to, and a function of, successful implementation of the Solution. An informed staff performing actions that reflect the integration of legacy systems yields the best results, for both an implementer's existing clients and the many new ones that implementation positions it to gain. HIPAA provides Independent Software Vendors (ISV) and System Integrators (SI) with new business models, new services, and new opportunities to benefit their clients. Such an atmosphere of innovation and greater efficiency is intended by the authors of HIPAA.

The Client

The last component in the Solution is the customer or client, the organization required to meet the mandates of the HIPAA legislation. The client implementing it is the most important, capping element of the Solution.

The OnlyConnect Framework

The OnlyConnect Framework (OC Framework)—the OnlyConnect Methodology from WPC combined with the Solution Framework from Microsoft—is the basis for HIPAA compliance. The components of the Framework, working together, make up a software, consulting, and best practices Solution for health care–providing entities and the health care insurance industry.

The OC Framework is based on the Microsoft Enterprise Solutions Framework and WPC's OnlyConnect Methodology, a combination of Microsoft and WPC best practices. The OC Framework delineates a HIPAA-tailored approach to implementation planning, assessment, remediation, and deployment. It incorporates the following:

- WPC's OnlyConnect Methodology, for performing HIPAA Transaction Compliance analysis;
- Microsoft Solutions Framework, for remediation, planning, and deployment; and
- Microsoft Operations Framework, for ongoing operations.

The OC Framework, a set of best practices, is based on three core models:

- Team model

  This model is designed to improve internal cooperation by providing a flexible structure for organizing groups of staff by project. Discrete roles and responsibilities within a team make this model scaleable to a project's scope, a team's size, and team members' skills.

- Risk Management model

  This model helps teams identify priorities, make well-informed strategic decisions, and prepare for contingencies. It constitutes a structured process to create an environment fostering decisions and actions to continuously assess, prioritize, and deal with project risks.

- Process model

  This model is designed to improve control of the implementation project, minimize the risks it raises, improve its quality, and shorten the time it will take. It provides structure and guidance throughout the project's life cycle. The process model specifically describes the phases, milestones, activities, and deliverables of a project, and explains their relationship to the Team model.

Most implementation projects will pass through four phases. In the core Process model, these phases occur as follows:

- The Envisioning phase accomplishes the crystallization of the project's purposes and objectives, showing leadership agreement on its scope.
- The Planning phase turns the vision of phase 1 into specifications, courses of action and detailed schedules.

- The Development phase entails building the solution in accordance with the plans established in phase 2, and testing it.
- The Deployment phase releases the solution to the operating environment. It is the final phase, the point at which the Operations Framework begins functioning.

Envisioning

During the envisioning phase a team of consultants works closely with the customer to identify the vision and scope for the project. A primary goal is to fully understand the environment, with its particular challenges and opportunities, and to illustrate how the technology can meet, and even exceed, the requirements identified by an extensive business process review. Business goals and costs are key factors in developing the implementation plan. During this phase of engagement, the consulting team will help the customer define its resources and determine the project's budget and scope.

The key deliverables for this phase are three documents:

1. The Vision/Scope document, which includes these components:
- Business problem/opportunity statement
- Vision statement
- Solution concept statement
- Project success factors, which include the following:
  - Operational concept: sample scenarios for where and how the system will be implemented and how users will employ the new technology
  - Complete list of project deliverables that make the new product or service operational
  - Acceptance criteria: a checklist of requirements that must be satisfied as a precondition of production release
- User profile: identifies the users of the eventual solution so the team can assess expectations, risks, goals, and constraints; includes a full description of the users and how this solution concept will affect them
2. The Risk Assessment document, which describes the risks that have been identified and what their impact is expected to be.
3. The Project Structure document, which describes how the team will manage and support the project and details the administrative structure of the project team into the planning phase. It also encompasses change control and configuration management functions, and defines such project standards as templates, naming conventions, and status reporting guidelines.

Planning

The length of the planning phase depends largely on the level of staff and scope of the project as identified in phase one. Team assignments are finalized. A Risk Model is implemented, for risk identification and contingency planning. Key deliverables include a draft functional specification, architecture diagrams, draft master project plan and schedule, and a development environment. The master project plan itself contains several plans: addressing its pilot, deployment strategy, testing, training, security, facilities, purchasing, and security.

Key deliverables of the planning phase include:
- Functional specification document, containing these elements:
  - Vision/scope summary
  - Background information, to place the solution in a business context
  - Design goals, usability goals, deployment goals, constraints, and expectations
- Solution design document, containing these elements:
  - Usage scenarios
  - Features and services
  - Enterprise architecture documents
- Component specification
- Top 10 Risk List, identifying major risks and specifying complete remediation and contingency plans
- Project standards
- Project plan—a detailed description of the major activities to be completed to fulfill the project's vision/scope, including plans for the following:
  - Communication
  - Testing
  - Training
  - Deployment
  - Procurement
  - Pilot
  - Budget
  - Capacity
  - Security
  - Contingencies
- Project schedule—a time line for performing project plan tasks
- Team model with all major roles filled

Development

The development phase is centered on building and testing the Solution. The amount of time necessary to complete this phase depends on the implementer's vision and the implementation's scope. Tasks to be completed in the development phase include installation of hardware and software, configuration of applications and databases, and building forms. Progress through a fully validated pilot must reach the point where the solution is ready to deploy. During this time, instructional materials are produced and staff is trained. The final objective of this phase is to reach a decision to release the solution into production.

There are several interim milestones during this phase, including:

- Technology validation
- Proof of concept
- Pre-production testing
- Pilot test

Key deliverables from this stage include:

- Training material
- Communications
- Deployment processes
- Operational procedures
- Documentation
- Updated master project plan and schedule

Deployment

During the deployment phase the core solution and components are deployed and stabilized. The first few days of operation are closely monitored. The team works with customer staff to address any issues that arise and to accomplish a full transfer of knowledge. A project and customer satisfaction review is conducted. Once the customer's operations staff is ready to take over, the project will be closed and the consultants will sign off.

Deployment is marked by several interim milestones:

- The deployment of core technology
- The completion of site deployments
- The completion of stabilization

The key deliverables of this phase are the following:

- Operations and support information systems
- Documentation repository
- Project close-out report

Methodology

The OnlyConnect Methodology is a WPC Tool Suite/Partner-based Consulting Service composed of seven steps that result in an assessment of an organization's readiness for HIPAA compliance. The methodology is the result of WPC's experience assisting organizations to become HIPAA-compliant, and the gradual development within health care administration of the current best practices. When an organization follows all seven steps, the OnlyConnect Methodology can guide that organization's IT staff to find out what will be necessary to attain and maintain HIPAA compliance, including system modification and remediation. The OnlyConnect methodology assists not only in the identification of changes necessary for compliance (HIPAA remediation), but also in enabling IT staff to identify ways to improve legacy environments unrelated to the requirements of HIPAA.

The enhancements that go beyond the goal of compliance reflect the best administrative practices in health care. Through them, the OnlyConnect methodology can reduce the cost of implementing HIPAA transaction standards by leveraging the functionality of existing legacy systems. Because it calls for keeping legacy systems in place and as intact as possible, the methodology enables employees to continue working without new training on new software. Such minimal impact to the IT landscape means that IT staff can continue daily business processes, for a smooth transition to compliance.

Properly implemented, OnlyConnect's seven steps achieve HIPAA compliance through actions that begin with the smallest units of information. By starting with small units of information and proceeding upward through larger information structures, the implementation process increases in complexity as it progresses. This is why OnlyConnect is said to use a "bottom up" approach.

Step 1: Gap Analysis

The Gap Analysis of the legacy system's database structure identifies the following:
- Fields that will no longer be populated
- Fields that require some form of remediation
- New fields that need to be added to the legacy system

The OnlyConnect Gap Analysis Tool (GAT) is a graphical, Web-based application that reports any differences between what the HIPAA Implementation Guides require and what legacy environments provide. The GAT graphical interface allows non-IT staff to view the condition of the legacy system in relation to the HIPAA requirements.

Adopters of the Microsoft/Washington Publishing Company Solution can use the OnlyConnect GAT for another purpose. It functions as a Web-based, multi-user mapping tool, producing a BizTalk-compatible XML schema for the legacy data structure, as well as a map between the transaction and the legacy system. Updates to the OnlyConnect GAT will be provided by WPC as the implementation guides change, assuring that compliance will be continuous. The original investment in gap analysis is leveraged by XML utility. Organizations that improvise their own gap analysis are hampered by a lack of familiarity with HIPAA specifications. When the implementation guides change, this handicap will be compounded.

Step 2: Historical Analyses

In the historical analyses phase of the methodology, software collects the data of the previous one-to-five years from the legacy system and formulates analyses of it. These historical analyses are converted to XML and fed into the WPC HIPAA-compliant database structure. Custom analytical reports, generated from SQL Server 2000 databases, are then viewable—either with an intranet or over the Internet—at the user's location. The reports identify orphaned data components and list where these data components are utilized, so IT staff will know which data requires intervention. This approach narrows the focus of staff to the changes that are needed, saving valuable time and effort that might otherwise be spent on unnecessary changes. The Historical Analyses also verify Gap Analysis results with the perspective provided by several years of data. Any fields in the WPC HIPAA-compliant database that are not populated in the user's application will be identified. This process guarantees data integrity and verifies that any gaps in data will be eliminated.

Step 3: Application Analyses

OnlyConnect Partner subject matter experts analyze all applications fed from the database structure, and identify for the client-user's staff the areas that require modification. The subject matter expert then makes recommendations on how to implement these modifications. This analysis integrates with the overall architecture, again narrowing the scope of the client organization's efforts.

Step 4: Orchestration

An OnlyConnect Partner designs and builds a dynamic, distributed business solution, bonding legacy systems to new technology in a common design environment. This behind-the-scenes integration provides a transparent solution for the end users: staff might be unaware that any change has taken place, since they can continue using the same procedures. Utilizing the BizTalk Orchestration designer, the requirements of the HIPAA solutions architecture can be graphically rendered to replicate the structures the client had been using before compliance. The appearance of computer screens and the terms in use can remain the same, so existing staff does not need retraining. Orchestration adds the new functionality, scaled to legacy systems, required to complete the design of a HIPAA-enabled architecture.

Step 5: Implementation Architecture

OnlyConnect Implementation Architecture, once deployed, acts as a receiving and sending gateway for legacy systems. It allows older systems to accept transactions from all current business partners and extends that function to new business partners. The sending of transactions is also provided for by the Architecture. Smaller business partners who might not have been capable of communication with the legacy environment without manual data entry will now be able to interact with clients' systems on the same terms as the most technically sophisticated business partners. The investment required to implement the BizTalk HIPAA Solution will enable the client's legacy environment to be in contact instantaneously with more business partners and associates that a health care or insurance organization must communicate with on a daily basis.

Step 6. Transaction Testing

WPC's OnlyConnect FirstPass is a transaction format compliance application that runs in the Windows environment. It is a simple drag-and-drop application to test incoming transmissions, verifying format compliance before attempting actual transactions (going live) with a trading partner. This tool reduces the time it takes to bring on new trading partners.

Step 7: HIPAA Compliance

OnlyConnect Partners assist clients on their path to HIPAA compliance by implementing the regulation's requirements in phases. This approach ensures implementation that is expandable, reliable, and scaled to the client's needs.

Step 7 achieves the final goal of being compliant with the HIPAA regulation: putting its transaction and code set standards to work.

The amount of time it will take to implement each step is directly dependent upon the number of legacy systems involved. Steps 1 and 2, Gap Analysis and Historical Analyses, can be implemented separately from the rest of the tool suite, enabling IT staff to help their organization get a jump on the HIPAA timeline.

The Solution in Action

Healthaxis, a technology innovator in Irving, Texas, was an early adopter of the Solution. The following case study, by John Wall, Healthaxis CTO, provides a unique glimpse of a Solution user solving a real problem for its client.

Case Study

Having the opportunity to be an early adopter of the BizTalk Accelerator for HIPAA and the first OnlyConnect implementation was an excellent opportunity to test both a new product and process. The results were beyond our expectations and a great story to tell. This is an attempt to tell that story.

Healthaxis began working with the Accelerator for HIPAA and OnlyConnect even before the product had made it to Release Candidate status. With a lot of moving parts to consider deploying as an early adopter, having a process (OnlyConnect) to follow, plus a great client (a payer organization) and technology partners (Microsoft and WPC) made a recipe for success.

Our task was to deploy a HIPAA EDI solution for an independent insurance company. As part of the deliverables, we were to deploy a solution that got them up and running and, in the course of this transition, to impart the skills the client would need to continue supporting their EDI needs. This project ran for a total of 10 weeks (70 days), from concept to client acceptance; we had taken that long just to develop the maps for another in-house EDI product. Figure 3-2 shows a high-level diagram of how the 10 weeks went, with more specific details of the project to follow.

Week One	EAP Kick Off	Envisioning
Week Two	Client Kick Off	Planning
Week Three	Analysis	
Week Four	Mapping & Workflow	Development
Week Five	Mapping & Workflow	
Week Six	Mapping & Workflow	
Week Seven	Changes/Rework	
Week Eight	Testing & Tuning	
Week Nine	Production Installs & Testing	Deployment
Week Ten	Sign Off	

Figure 3-2. *Project timeline*

The Envisioning Phase

The envisioning phase started in early May 2001, when a large group—from Healthaxis, Microsoft Consulting, the BizTalk Accelerator Team, and WPC—met for an entire day and evening. During this meeting, to get the project rolling, we were able to define a major portion of the project, including:

- Business problem/opportunity statement
- Vision statement
- Solutions concept
- Operational concept
- Complete list of deliverables
- Risk Assessment
- Project Structure Document

Business Problem and Opportunity Statement

With this project, we were working to create business opportunities for everyone involved. This really helped in both motivation and commitment to the project. Below are some of the opportunities defined for this project:

- Provide infrastructure to have one HIPAA EDI solution for all of our client's systems
- Provide a rapid and accurate deployment model for HIPAA
- Provide a best-of-breed EDI solution to the client
- Solve a host of data transmission and HIPAA compliance issues, with minimum impact to the client
- Position Healthaxis as a leader with an end-to-end solution
- Establish BizTalk Accelerator for HIPAA as a superior EDI Platform

Vision Statement

The vision statement was the most critical part of this project. We wanted to deliver significant value for our client as well as position the client for future EDI work. In addition, we wanted to have a solution in place by the time BizTalk Accelerator for HIPAA went into production, giving the client the jump on its competitors for a winning business opportunity. After much discussion, the decision was made to tackle three of the hardest EDI transactions: the ones pertaining to Claims. We decided to tackle the transaction sets designated 837—Institutional, Professional, and Dental. Below is the statement from our Envisioning Document:

Deploy BizTalk Accelerator for HIPAA as key integration component, allowing for the client's internal claim system to accept and process X12N 837 Institutional, Professional, and Dental transaction sets. This Solution would then be utilized to deploy the remaining nine transaction sets into and out of the appropriate legacy systems.

Solutions Concept/Operational Concept

Being the first to build a solution is always a gamble. Performance is not known; details about how each part of the solution will work are just in the concept phase. Facing such unknowns is a risky part of being first. We had some good technology experience with BizTalk and an accurate idea of what we needed to do. Our solution concept for this effort ended up working out very well.

Our plan was simple: deploy a HIPAA EDI solution for our client that would have minimal impact to its existing legacy environments. A very simplified diagram of how we envisioned our solution working is shown in Figure 3-3.

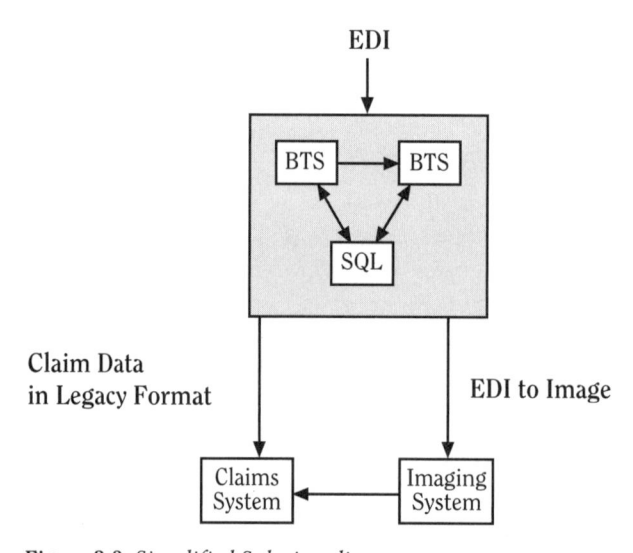

Figure 3-3. *Simplified Solution diagram*

Inbound Claim Data would enter BizTalk Accelerator for HIPAA where it would be saved, enhanced, mapped, and fed to two separate legacy systems in formats they already used. This would allow a "Bolt-on" Approach to be taken with their system.

Complete List of Deliverables

Building the deliverables list was very important in this phase of the project. It gave everyone an accurate idea of the project's scope as well as a set of building blocks for both the Risk Assessment and Project Documents. The major deliverables are identified below:

- 12 HIPAA-Compliant and Certified Transaction Maps
- End-to-End implementation of the 837 transactions (Institutional, Professional, and Dental)
- HIPAA Implementation Guides
- De-identification Tool to Ensure Privacy of Sensitive Data
- Transaction Warehouse

- WPC OnlyConnect
- Gap Analysis Tool (Schema Validation Tool)
- Instant Validation Tool (Syntax Checker)
- Automatic 997 (Functional Acknowledgment)
- Parsers (X12N, HIPAA)
- Business Workflows – Orchestration
- Transaction Re-association
- Cooperative Development Approach to Support Client Learning (Expert Knowledge Skills Transfer)
- Formal Tools & Process Training
- Enterprise Connectivity Platform

Risk Assessment

Risks were identified and tracked in this project with an adaptation of an FMEA (Failure Mode Effects and Analysis) tool. All risks were identified and scored based on three criteria: Severity of Failure, Ability to Detect and Prevent, and Probability of Occurrence. Scores were multiplied together and managed by priority. This allowed continuous monitoring of the project risks, with the relative scores showing how each risk compared to all other project risks.

Project Structure Document

The initial coordination on the project structure was challenging. With at least one month to go before BizTalk would be ready for production code release, some items would change during our planning and development stages. (This was a big item on our Risk Assessment.) After establishing some reliable timelines for when BizTalk code would be available, the task at hand was to define the major milestones for this project. The following is a list of milestones:

- 12 Transaction Set Maps
- Legacy Data Analysis
- Mapping and Crosswalk of Data
- Builds/Install/Testing of BizTalk Accelerator for HIPAA
- Business Workflow Defined
- Legacy Interfaces Defined
- Trading Partners Identified
- Training
- Testing
- Performance Tuning

The Planning Phase

Taking the work from the Envisioning documents and turning them into defined deliverables is where a lot of the technical and business work really begins to take hold. During the planning phase the following items were developed:

- Functional Specification
- Design Goals with constraints/expectations
- Solution design document
- Usage Scenarios
- Features and Services
- Enterprise Architecture Documents
- Component Specifications
- Risk Management: Failure Mode Effects and Analysis (FMEA)
- Project Standards
- Project Plan Constructed

Functional Specifications

The functional specifications were completely developed, with the project's deliverables defined by the work of three separate teams: the HIPAA team from Healthaxis, a technology team from the client, and the business experts from the client's Claims/EDI department. By including all of the key participants in both delivering and accepting this solution, a set of functional specifications were developed in a relatively short period of time.

Work started with a review of the Vision/Scope documents that had been composed earlier. Their content was expanded and put in the context of our client's business and technology needs.

Omitting details that might distract, a high-level picture of the system is shown in Figure 3-4.

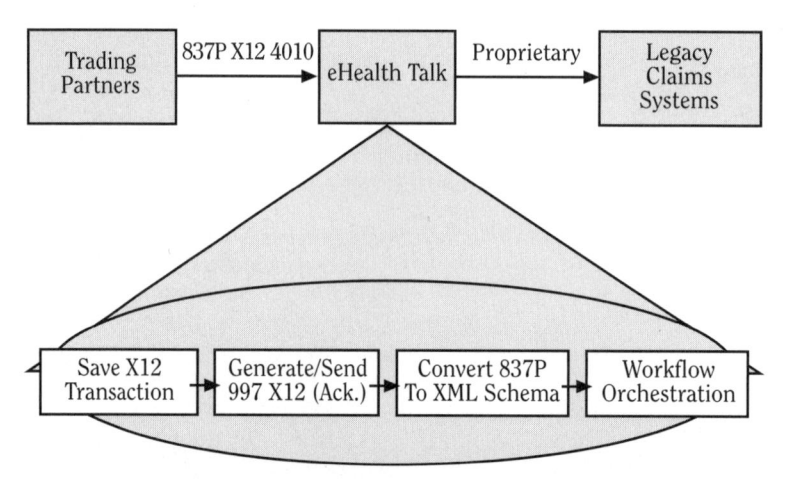

Figure 3-4. *High-level system diagram*

The Implementation Team

For this project, the Healthaxis team was organized as in Figure 3-5.

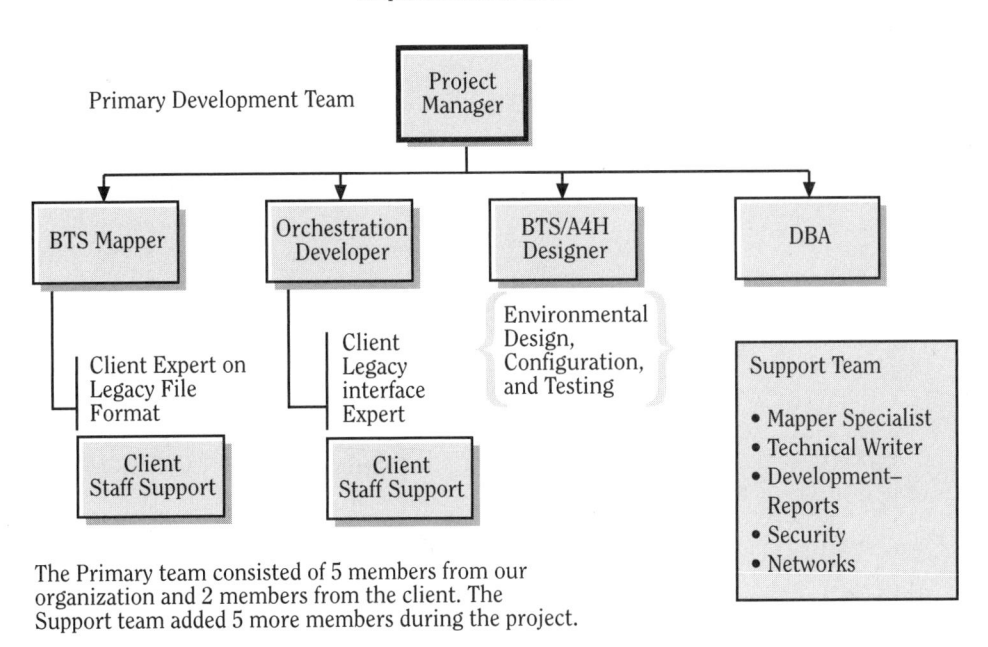

Implementation Team

```
                            Project
Primary Development Team    Manager
       ┌──────────┬─────────┴──────┬─────────────┐
   BTS Mapper  Orchestration    BTS/A4H         DBA
               Developer        Designer
       │           │                │
   Client Expert  Client         Environmental      Support Team
   on Legacy     Legacy         Design,
   File Format   interface      Configuration,   • Mapper Specialist
                 Expert         and Testing      • Technical Writer
   Client        Client                          • Development-
   Staff Support Staff Support                     Reports
                                                 • Security
                                                 • Networks
```

The Primary team consisted of 5 members from our organization and 2 members from the client. The Support team added 5 more members during the project.

Figure 3-5. *Implementation team*

Design Goals with Constraints/Expectations

Setting realistic design goals and managing expectations can make or break a project. These very important steps should never be overlooked, especially when introducing a client to tools as powerful as BizTalk Orchestration. As design goals are being set, you should resist the tendency to include more than you can build.

It is equally important to understand both what your client needs today and what they will need in the future in order to do business. Many of the items included among our design goals came from business plans that the client had already established. Some of the goals and constraints we set for this project are listed below:

- Process 30,000 encounters in 6 hours (3 times the daily total claim volume then current)
- Complete end-to-end transactions for all three 837 transactions
- Integrate to both Imaging and Claims Adjudication Systems
- Provide Data Warehousing for all transactions (Audit)
- Develop complete documentation for all systems
- Train client to be self-sufficient in EDI
- Enhance data to provide Eligibility and Provider lookup

The goals were ambitious but very tightly defined and each could be judged a success or a failure fairly easily. This was beneficial as the project progressed.

Solution Design Document

The next piece to be developed was a solution design document. We specified the solution's Features and Services and had gathered enough information to put together some Usage Scenarios as well. The architecture for the solution was also further defined during this phase. A more detailed picture of the solution came into view during this effort. A diagram of the overall system flow is shown in Figure 3-6.

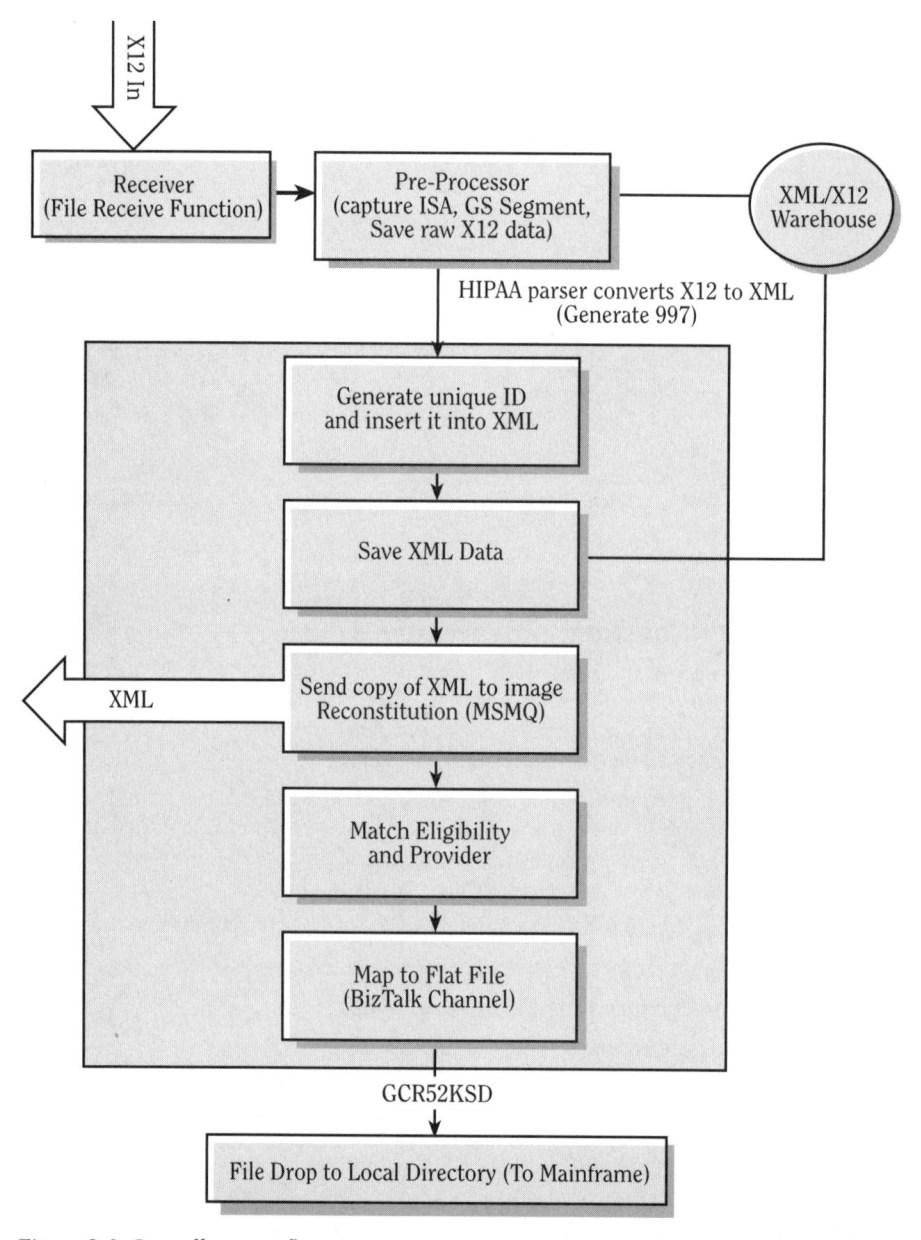

Figure 3-6. *Overall system flow*

Component Specification

Developers and designers have some significant work to do during this phase. Having a good set of standards in place really helps (see the Project Standards section later in this chapter). This is the part of the project where the work of our development teams succeeds or fails. With a significant number of systems interfacing, having a complete and well-defined list of components specified was critical.

Component specification is also where data analysis, both current and historical, became crucial. A big part of this project was building maps from EDI to a legacy file format (flat file). GAP analysis allowed the building of specifications for our development of detailed maps later on. It is difficult to imagine this project succeeding during the development stages if a lot of effort had not been applied here.

Risks Management

Ongoing efforts to identify and mitigate risks on any project can prevent a disaster or an unplanned delay. A continuous effort to manage risks went on during this project. At this point, the risks were evolving from high-level project risks (for example, BizTalk ships late) to very detailed risks (the possibility of SQL XML transaction failure).

Project Standards

We were fortunate to have some very well-established technical standards in place for this project. They included everything from coding conventions to documentation guidelines and source control. Combining these with the OnlyConnect methodology resulted in an excellent base of standards to work from.

Project Plan Constructed

As we approached the development stage, our project manager put together a Detailed Project Plan. This included every aspect of the project, namely:

- Communication Plan
- Testing Plan
- Training Plan
- Development Plan
- Deployment Plan
- Procurement Plan
- Environment Testing (Unit Test, System Test, Model Office, Production)
- Budget Plan
- Capacity Plan

This is where good project management skills really come into play. With the number of deliverables and an aggressive schedule, keeping track of everything was critical.

Development

This stage was easy to spot: our development teams started ordering dinner in, and keyboards were moving. The development teams did what they do best—write code. The development stage was broken down into some important steps, defined below:

- Technology validation (ongoing with this project)

- Proof of concept (First Transaction Set)
- Pre-production testing
- Pilot testing

Technology Validation: Get the First Transaction Working

The delivery of this project included providing end-to-end processing of the three HIPAA claim transactions. As part of our validation plan, we were going to prove the technology by building out one transaction first (the 837 Institutional). This also served as our proof of concept for the rest of the development effort.

One of the most difficult pieces of this effort was the Data Mapping. Building the maps to the legacy system was challenging. Without solid, up-front analysis (GAP), EDI skills, and persistence, building the maps would have taken much longer. To get a sense of the effort involved see Figure 4-4 in Chapter 4.

Additionally, building the Orchestrations representing the system's workflow required a significant amount of work. This effort involved a Data Warehouse, Data Mapping, Maps to the Imaging System, Data Enhancements, and Maps to the Claims Adjudication system. See Figure 4-5 in Chapter 4 for a diagram of the workflow process.

Once the Maps and Workflow (Orchestration) pieces were constructed, we were almost ready to do a proof of concept. Here we hit our first two major risk items of the project.

Problems Found

Two things slowed down the effort when we were ready to begin proof of concept testing. First, because we were using a very early release of the schemas, some of the schema definitions changed. This would have an impact on our maps. Second, we lacked solid test data to run through the system.

Both of these problems were overcome quickly. Solid planning and analysis (GAP) of the data specifications allowed us to make map modifications. Having some solid EDI expertise and great technology partners put us back on track with test data. Good communication and teamwork were very helpful when we encountered these problems.

Finishing the Solution

Once we were able to get the first transaction working, we aimed to duplicate the process for the other two transactions. During this time, a lot of training was going on, with both WPC and Microsoft providing critical training and assistance on EDI and BizTalk. This part of the development process went fairly smoothly.

Pre-Production Testing

After all three transaction sets were complete, we were ready to start hooking all of the pieces together for pre-production processing. The release process included a Unit Test, a Systems Test, and a Model Office environment, all to go through prior to production.

We also involved the client's Imaging and Claims Adjudication processing systems in this phase of testing.

The process started by tying together all of the hardware and software components to make sure that it worked in the actual run-time environment. Because a lot of component testing was done during the proof of concept stage, this part of the process focused mainly on tweaks to environments and code to get everything working properly.

Pilot Testing

Once the environments were working, it was time to test the systems. This included loading valid claims into the systems to evaluate end-to-end processing, high-volume loading to stress-test the systems, and auditing all processes for any anomalies.

Several items were identified for fine tuning at this point, including monitoring frequencies, indexes on SQL tables, and code invocation parameters (COM+).

System documentation and operational turnover plans also were part of the testing phases. Activities in these two areas would go on throughout the deployment phase.

Deployment

With pilot testing complete, it was time to move into production. The following steps were followed:

- Core Technology Deployment
- Site Deployment
- Sign-Off

Core Technology Deployment

Production Equipment and Software were deployed on site at the insurance company. This involved the Operations Staff and IT support teams. Machines were installed and configured to meet datacenter requirements.

Site Deployment

All production code was then loaded and tested for stability and function.

Sign-Off

With deployment of the hardware, software, and operational components, our client proceeded to evaluate system functionality, performance, and stability. After review of the system, the project was signed-off as complete.

Approximately two weeks after sign-off we held a Project Review. There was a lot of satisfaction at how well this project had gone. With new software, tight time schedules, and many interacting teams, everything had come together with very few problems.

Project Review

The Seven Steps to the OnlyConnect Methodology were key factors in the success of this project. No single factor can make a project succeed or fail. For this project, a great team, a great client, and great partners were invaluable. Combining the OnlyConnect Methodology with our project team resulted in a very successful project.

Chapter 4

Technical Deployment Overview

The Microsoft BizTalk Accelerator for HIPAA is occasionally referred to in this book as the *Solution* for health care entities seeking to comply with the terms of HIPAA. But don't be misled by that singular noun, *Solution*. The BizTalk Accelerator is no portable monolith, to be wedged into whatever niche awaits it. The solution it provides is the end result of an interoperating complex of components. Each entity's use of the accelerator will be unique, varying in its particulars just as the workings of a pediatrician's office vary from those of a claims clearinghouse.

The Microsoft BizTalk Accelerator for HIPAA can be applied in such a way that existing business routines continue. The content and appearance of monitor screens will be so consistent with legacy systems that the user is unaware that a change has occurred. Where possible, compliance in which user interfaces remain the same, or change only in small, subtle ways, might be the least disruptive to an organization's functioning because it requires little or no retraining of staff. Alternatively, an enterprise might make the necessity of complying with HIPAA the impetus to adopt improved business practices. The software aspects of the Microsoft Solution, including WPC's document specifications, are designed to ease the transition to health care administration's best practices as HIPAA compliancy is achieved. Either way, the Solution's goal is HIPAA compliancy achieved without interrupting an organization's normal day-to-day operation.

The HIPAA Solution is made of these components:

- OnlyConnect Framework, a blueprint for HIPAA compliance, based on the OnlyConnect Methodology from WPC and the Solution Framework from Microsoft
- Microsoft BizTalk Server 2000
- Microsoft BizTalk Accelerator for HIPAA
- Microsoft SQL Server 2000
- Microsoft Windows 2000
- WPC and Microsoft Consulting Services (MCS) consulting and training
- Independent software vendors and systems integration partners
- The implementing organization's IT staff

All these components were mentioned in this book's Introduction and briefly described in Chapter 3. What follows is a deeper look into the interactions of four of the Solution's technical components, namely:

- Microsoft BizTalk Server 2000
- Microsoft BizTalk Accelerator for HIPAA
- OnlyConnect Gap Analysis Tool
- OnlyConncct FirstPass

Working in Tandem

The BizTalk Server 2000 and the BizTalk Accelerator for HIPAA together form the core of the Solution. The Accelerator includes a HIPAA-specific parser that breaks strings of EDI data down into the smallest parts possible. The parser uses WPC-supplied document specifications to transform incoming X12N HIPAA-formatted data into XML documents. XML (Extensible Markup Language) is a highly flexible format in which data can be easily manipulated. Subsequent processing by BizTalk Server 2000 components transforms the XML documents, using document specifications and maps generated by the OnlyConnect Gap Analysis Tool (GAT), into the file structures required by legacy environments. After the OnlyConnect GAT has forged the necessary links to legacy systems, FirstPass is employed. A testing module, FirstPass is the tool that enables the user to see if the freshly compliant system is ready for field testing.

BizTalk Server 2000

Running under Microsoft Windows 2000, BizTalk Server 2000 uses Microsoft SQL Server 2000 to store information during run-time and for subsequent auditing. BizTalk Server 2000 is composed of six main parts:

- BizTalk Editor
- BizTalk Mapper
- BizTalk Orchestration Designer
- BizTalk Messaging Manager
- BizTalk Document Tracking
- BizTalk Server Administration

BizTalk Editor

The BizTalk Editor is a tool to create, edit, and manage document specifications. These specifications model an XML document structure, or they can be based on industry standards such as X12 or on legacy formats such as the National Standard Format (NSF). The BizTalk Editor enables users to create document specifications based on a template, an existing schema, or in some cases a sample of an XML document. A blank specification can also be the starting point.

In Figure 4-1, the Editor's left panel displays the fields that comprise *Dependent Name* as it appears in an *Eligibility Request Transaction*. The panel to the right displays the properties of the highlighted field, in this case, *Dependent Last Name*.

Within the generic X12 standard, what is expressed as *Individual or Organizational Name* is contained by eleven fields. In X12 EDI terms, this collection of fields is a *Data Segment*, or more simply, a segment. In this implementation of the generic concept of *name*, only six of those eleven fields are used: the first through the fifth fields and the seventh. The Editor displays unused fields preceded by the letters *NU*, indicating they are *Not Used*. In other instances where the name segment is employed, other fields are used. This idea—the generic name segment that is implemented differently according to the business process in which it is used—is a key feature of the X12 family of standards. The HIPAA document specifications within the Accelerator completely describe, from a syntactical perspective, which parts of the generic X12 standard are used for the business process that particular document describes. The used and unused fields and their properties are easily viewed with the Editor's graphical user interface.

Chapter 4 Technical Deployment Overview   57

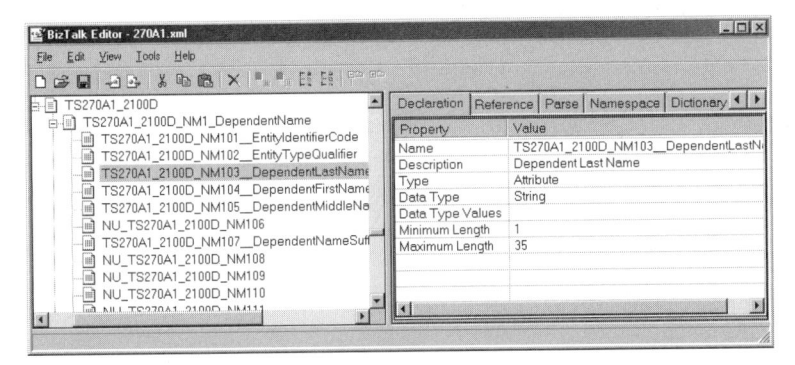

Figure 4-1. *BizTalk Editor displaying the Eligibility Request Document Specification*

BizTalk Mapper

For BizTalk Mapper, document specifications are used as a starting point or as a destination. The Mapper defines the relationship between fields used in one specification and the fields used in another, different specification and makes a map that expresses this relationship. Each map contains an Extensible Stylesheet Language (XSL) construct, called a style sheet, which the BizTalk Server uses to transform an XML document into another structure described by the map. The resulting structure can be another XML document, an industry standard (such as X12) document, or a flat file. Figure 4-2 shows a partial view of a map used to effect the transformation of a transmission that began as X12N HIPAA-formatted data, was parsed into an XML document, and is becoming a document of the legacy system's UB-92/EMC data structure.

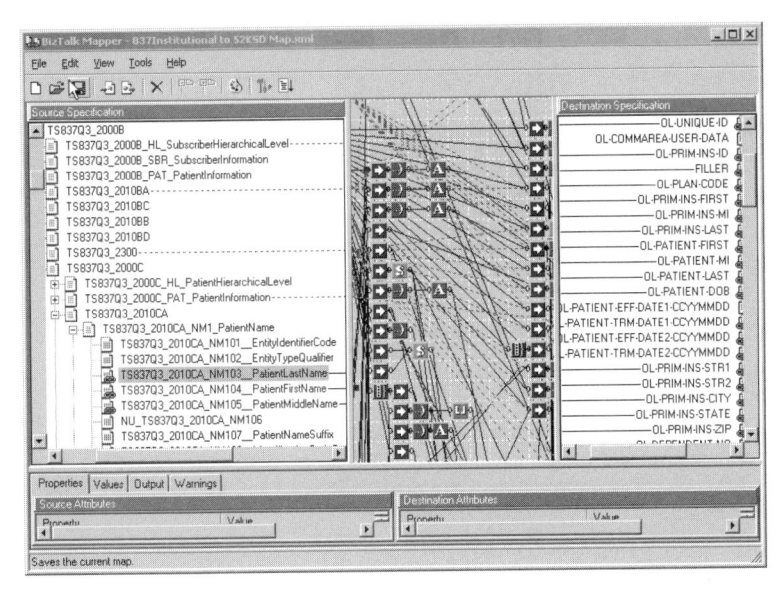

Figure 4-2. *BizTalk Mapper displaying a Map from an incoming Institutional Claim*

The OnlyConnect Gap Analysis Tool generates maps compatible with the BizTalk Mapper to jumpstart transformation of incoming X12N HIPAA-formatted data into legacy data structures. The Mapper can configure the maps to perform a rich array of data manipulations while they transform an XML document to a legacy system flat file. For example, a legacy environment might store a patient's name as *Last Name, First Name, MI*, while that information is contained in the incoming data stream divided into three distinct fields. A Mapper *Functoid* can be configured to concatenate the three fields, add the appropriate commas, and map the resultant string to a single legacy field.

BizTalk Orchestration Designer

The Orchestration Designer (see Figure 4-3) is based on Microsoft's Visio 2000 application. The Designer enables a business analyst to describe a business process—such as the interactions that occur when a health care provider sends a patient to a specialist—by creating drawings that are compiled and run as XLANG schedules. An XLANG schedule binds the process described by the Visio drawing to the applications that execute the business functions. The business functions can be interactive, such as a request for eligibility with a real-time answer, or long-running, such as a claim for a pregnancy coverage from prenatal care through delivery.

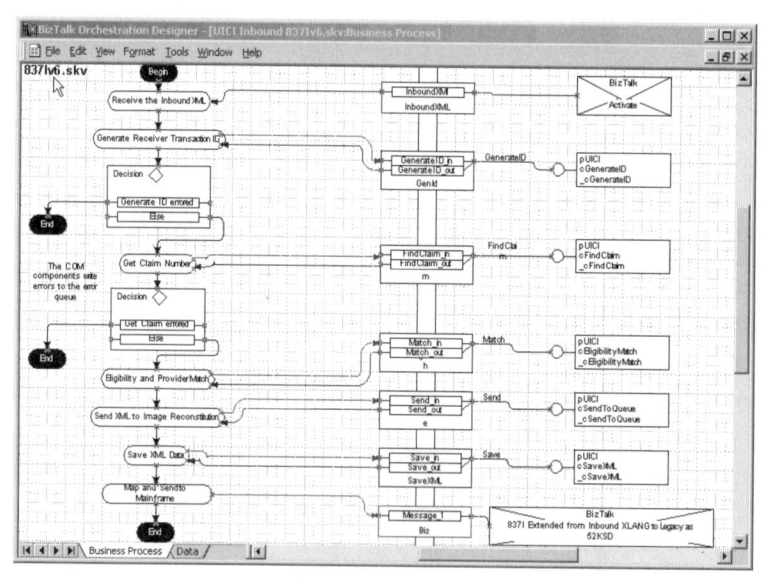

Figure 4-3. *BizTalk Orchestration Designer*

In Figure 4-3, the left panel is where a business analyst draws a representation of a business process. The panel to the right will be used by IT staff, who automate that business process by binding to it the applications that perform those functions.

BizTalk Messaging Manager

The Messaging Manager employs a graphical user interface to accomplish the smooth exchange of documents pertaining to internal applications between an enterprise and its external trading partners. The Messaging Manager is used to create messaging ports that direct how documents are enveloped, secured, and transported to a destination. In addition to ports, the Messaging Manager creates *channels*. A channel designates for a particular document the processing steps to be performed by the BizTalk Server before that document is delivered to its destination.

BizTalk Document Tracking

BizTalk Document Tracking is a Web application that is used to view the progress of documents as they move within an enterprise or to external trading partners. For example, a system administrator can configure the tracking database to view information about source and destination, document type (such as an eligibility request), and relevant dates and times. Document tracking can be configured to display transmissions individually or in batches and to save complete copies of incoming and outgoing documents.

BizTalk Server Administration

There are four main areas of administration:

- Server Administration
    - Configure and manage server groups and servers
    - Configure and manage receive functions
    - Manage queues
- Application Administration
    - Configure and manage the COM+ applications that host XLANG schedules
    - Configure and manage the default XLANG Scheduler application
- Programmatic Administration
    - Configure XLANG system managers, XLANG group managers, XLANG schedule instances, and XLANG ports
- Database Administration
    - Configure, manage, and maintain the following databases: BizTalk Messaging Management, Orchestration Persistence, Tracking, and Shared Queue

The Microsoft BizTalk Accelerator for HIPAA

The Accelerator is comprised of:
- A HIPAA-specific parser (see Figure 4-4).

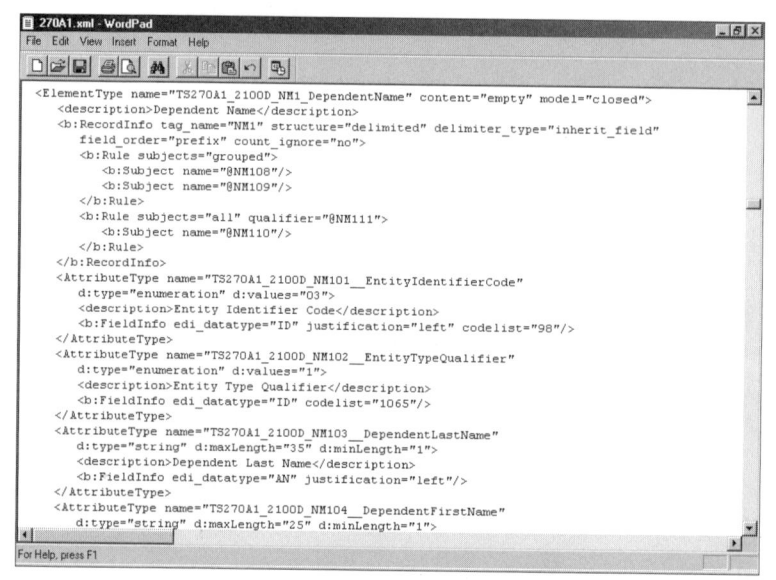

Figure 4-4. *A portion of the Eligibility Request Schema*

- Document specifications for the twelve X12N HIPAA transaction standards in the form of BizTalk Server schemas (see Figure 4-5).

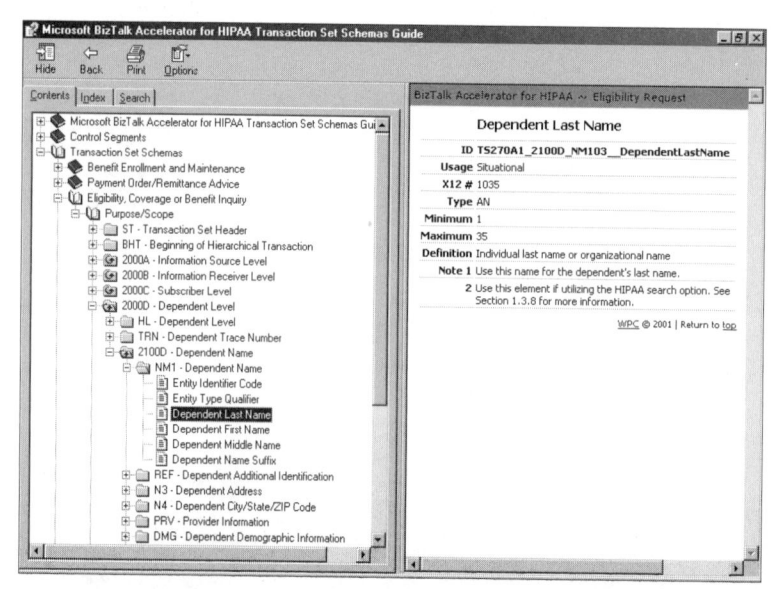

Figure 4-5. *The Help file with Dependent Last Name highlighted from the Eligibility Request*

- A Windows Help file containing all of the technical portions of the X12N HIPAA implementation guides along with explanatory information. Both the schemas and the Help file are generated from their regulation-mandated home, the WPC database.
- Special support for splitting large incoming documents (for example, splitting 100 claims into 100 individual XML claim documents). The splitting feature is for professional, institutional, and dental claims, along with claim payments and benefit enrollment.
- A flexible claims processing sample application that can be configured to either send or receive claims. The sample includes four components:
  - A BizTalk orchestration schedule sample that controls the long-running business process of submitting or receiving claims. The XLANG schedule can be modified with the BizTalk Orchestration Designer to reflect a role within the claim submission and reconciliation process—either provider or payer. In addition, the schedule controls the database used to track and report on individual line items within any given claim.
  - The sample includes components that the schedule uses to perform business functions, like reconciling payments to claims.
  - A SQL Server 2000 database to track, reconcile, and report on the status of individual claim line items.
  - BizTalk Messaging configuration scripts that direct incoming transmissions to the proper document specification and transform the data to XML and then to internal data structures or, conversely, transform internal data into XML and then to trading partners as HIPAA-compliant transmissions.

The 12 X12N HIPAA Implementation Guide Schemas

Covering much of the administrative business surrounding health care claims, the following descriptions provide a brief overview of the business processes and the parties that engage in each transaction.

Benefit Enrollment and Maintenance – 834

The 834 is used to transfer enrollment information from the sponsor of the health care insurance coverage, benefits, or policy to a payer.

The following parties engage in the enrollment process:

- Sponsor
  A sponsor is the party that ultimately pays for the coverage, benefit, or product. A sponsor can be an employer, union, government agency, association, or insurance agency.

- Payer/Insurer
  The payer is the party that pays claims and/or administers the insurance coverage, benefit, or product. A payer can be an insurance company; health maintenance organization (HMO); preferred provider organization (PPO); a government agency, such as Medicare or Civilian Health and Medical Program of the Uniformed Services (CHAMPUS); or another organization contracted by one of these groups.

- Third Party Administrator (TPA)

    A sponsor can elect to contract with a Third Party Administrator (TPA) or other vendor to handle collecting insured member data if the sponsor chooses not to perform this function.

- Subscriber

    The subscriber is an individual eligible for coverage because of his or her association with a sponsor. Examples of subscribers include the following: employees; union members; and individuals covered under government programs, such as Medicare and Medicaid.

- Dependent

    A dependent is an individual who is eligible for coverage because of his or her association with a subscriber. Typically, a dependent is a member of the subscriber's family.

- Insured or Member

    An insured individual or member is a subscriber or dependent who has been enrolled for coverage under an insurance plan. Dependents of a subscriber who have not been individually enrolled for coverage are not included in Insured or Member.

Payment Order/Remittance Advice – 820

The X12N Payroll Deducted and Other Group Premium Payment for Insurance Products Implementation Guide provides standardized data requirements and content to all users of the ANSI ASC X12 Premium Payment Order/Remittance Advice (820) Transaction Set for the purpose of reporting payroll deducted and other group premiums.

For HIPAA, only portions of the complete 820 implementation guide are applicable. The 820 is used when sending premium payments to an insurance company, health care organization, or government agency.

General business functions applicable under HIPAA compliance fall into two categories:

- The first is the use of an Electronic Funds Transfer (EFT) with remittance information carried through the Automated Clearinghouse (ACH) system. The choice of which type of detail, Organization Summary Remittance Detail or Individual Remittance Detail, depends on contract type. Individual Remittance Detail should only be sent for those contractors that require individual remittance information in order to properly apply the premium payments.
- The second function applicable under HIPAA is the use of an EFT or a check to make the payment, with separate Remittance Advice containing either Organization Summary Remittance Detail or Individual Remittance Detail information. The movement of the Remittance Advice is through an 820 transaction that is communicated outside of the banking networks. The choice of which type of detail again depends on contract type.

Health Care Eligibility Request – 270

Until HIPAA, providers of medical services submitted health care eligibility and benefit inquiries by a variety of methods, either on paper, by phone, or electronically.

The information requirements vary depending upon:
- Type of insurance plan
- Type of service performed
- Where the service is performed
- Where the inquiry is initiated
- Where the inquiry is sent

The Health Care Eligibility Request is designed so that the inquiry submitter (information receiver) can determine (a) whether an information source organization (for example, a payer, employer, or HMO) has a particular subscriber or dependent on file, and (b) the health care eligibility and/or benefit information about that subscriber and/or dependent(s).

The 270 is designed to be flexible enough to encompass all the information requirements of various entities. These entities include, but are not limited to:
- Insurance companies
- Health maintenance organizations (HMOs)
- Preferred provider organizations (PPOs)
- Health care purchasers (employers)
- Professional review organizations (PROs)
- Social worker organizations
- Health care providers (physicians, hospitals, laboratories)
- Third-party administrators (TPAs)
- Health care vendors (practice management vendors, billing services)
- Service bureaus
- Government agencies such as Medicare, Medicaid, and Civilian Health and Medical Program of the Uniformed Services (CHAMPUS)

Some submitters do not have ready access to all the information needed to generate an inquiry to a payer. An outside lab or pharmacy that furnishes services to a health care providing institution might need to ask that institution which payer a health care eligibility inquiry or benefit inquiry should be routed to. In this type of situation, a 270 might originate from a provider and be sent to another provider if the inquiry is supported by the receiving provider.

Eligibility, Coverage or Benefit Information – 271

The eligibility or benefit reply information from the information source organization (payer or employer) is contained in the 271 in an Eligibility or Benefit Information (EB) data segment. The information source can also return other information about eligibility and benefits based on its business agreement with the inquiry submitter and available information that it might be able to provide.

The content of the Eligibility, Coverage and Benefit Information transaction set varies depending on the level of data the information source organization makes available.

General requests include:

- Eligibility status (active or not active in the plan)
- Maximum benefits (policy limits)
- Exclusions
- In-plan/out-of-plan benefits
- Coordination of benefits information
- Deductible
- Co-pays

Specific requests include:

- Procedure coverage dates
- Procedure coverage maximum amount(s) allowed
- Deductible amount(s)
- Remaining deductible amount(s)
- Co-insurance amount(s)
- Co-pay amount(s)
- Coverage limitation percentage
- Patient responsibility amount(s)
- Non-covered amount(s)

Health Care Claim: Professional, Institutional, and Dental – 837

The Health Care Claim Transaction (837) is intended to originate with the health care provider or the health care provider's designated agent. It might also originate with payers in an encounter reporting situation. The 837 provides all necessary information to allow the destination payer to at least begin to adjudicate the claim.

Certain terms have been defined to have a specific meaning within the X12N documentation. The following terms are particularly key to understanding and using the other information under this heading:

- **Dependent**

    In the hierarchical loop coding, the dependent code indicates the use of the patient hierarchical loop.

- **Destination Payer**

    The destination payer is the payer who is specified in the Subscriber/Payer loop.

- **Patient**

    The term *patient* is intended to convey the case where the Patient loop is used. In that case, the patient is not the same person as the subscriber, and the patient is a person (for example, a spouse, child, or other) who is covered by the subscriber's insurance plan. However, it also happens that the patient is sometimes the same person as the subscriber. In that case, all information about the patient/subscriber is carried in the Subscriber loop. Every effort has been made to ensure that the meaning of the word *patient* is clear in its specific context.

- **Provider**

  In a generic sense, the provider is the entity that originally submitted the claim/encounter. A provider may also have provided or participated in some aspect of the health care service described in the transaction. Specific types of providers are identified in the transaction set (billing provider, referring provider).

- **Secondary Payer**

  The term *secondary payer* refers to any payer who is not the primary payer. The secondary payer might be the secondary, tertiary, or even quaternary payer.

- **Subscriber**

  The subscriber is the person whose name is listed in the health insurance policy. Other synonymous terms include *member* and *insured*. In some cases the subscriber is the same person as the patient. See the definition of *patient*.

- **Transmission Intermediary**

  A transmission intermediary is any entity that handles the transaction between the provider (originator of the claim/encounter transmission) and the destination payer. The term *intermediary* is not used to convey a specific Medicare contractor type.

Health Care Services Review: Request for Review – 278

The Request for Review and the Response to that Request Transaction Sets cover the following business events:

- Admission certification review request and response
- Referral review request and response
- Health care services certification review request and response
- Extend certification review request and response

This section contains definitions of terms frequently used in the services review transactions, as well as descriptions of the parties that engage in services review transactions.

- **Long-term care**

  Long-term care refers to the range of services typically provided at skilled nursing, intermediate-care, personal care, or elder-care facilities.

- **Patient event**

  Patient event refers to the service or group of services associated with a single episode of care. Examples include the following:

  - An admission to a facility for treatment related to a specific patient condition or diagnosis or related group of diagnoses
  - A referral to a specialty provider for a consult or testing to determine a specific diagnosis and appropriate treatment

- Services to be administered at a patient visit such as chiropractic treatment delivered in a single patient visit. The same treatment can be approved for a series of visits. X12N recommends limiting each request to a single patient event.

- **Requester**

  Requester refers to providers (physicians, medical groups, independent physician associations, facilities, and others) who request authorization or certification for a patient to receive health care services.

- **Service Provider**

  Service provider is the referred-to provider, specialist, specialty entity, group, or facility where the requested services are to be performed.

- **Utilization Management Organization (UMO)**

  UMO refers to insurance companies, health maintenance organizations, preferred provider organizations, health care purchasers, professional review organizations, other providers, and other utilization review entities who receive and respond to requests for authorization or certification. The UMO might or might not be the organization that makes the medical decision on a service review request. The UMO might have a relationship with a payer that calls for the payer to make a decision in certain cases. It is the role of the UMO to forward that request to the payer, receive the response from the payer, and then return the response to the requester. From the requester's perspective, the exchange of information is between the requester and the UMO.

Health Care Claim Status Request – 276

The 276 is used to request the current status of a specified claim(s).

Entities requesting health care claim status include, but are not limited to, the following health care claims adjudication processors:

- Hospitals
- Nursing homes
- Laboratories
- Physicians
- Dentists
- Allied professional groups
- Employers
- Supplemental (other than primary payer)

  Other business partners affiliated with the 276 include:

- Billing services
- Consulting services
- Vendors of systems

- EDI network intermediaries, such as Automated Clearinghouses (ACHs), Value-Added Networks (VANs), and telecommunications services

Health Care Claim Status Response – 277

The 277 transaction set can be used as for the following:
- A solicited response to a health care claim status request (276)
- A notification about health care claim(s) status, including front end acknowledgments
- A request for additional information about a health care claim(s)

Organizations sending the 277 Health Care Claim Status Response include payers, who might be:
- Insurance companies
- Third party administrators (TPAs)
- Service corporations
- State and Federal agencies and their contractors
- Plan purchasers
- Any other entity that processes health care claims

Other business partners affiliated with the 277 include:
- Billing services
- Consulting services
- Vendors of systems
- EDI network intermediaries such as Automated Clearinghouses (ACHs), Value-Added Networks (VANs), and telecommunications services

Health Care Claim Payment/Advice – 835

The 835 is used to send and/or receive Electronic Remittance Advice (ERA) and/or payments. Health care providers receiving the 835 include but are not limited to:
- Hospitals
- Nursing homes
- Laboratories
- Physicians
- Dentists
- Allied professional groups

Organizations sending the 835 include:
- Insurance companies
- Third party administrators
- Service corporations
- State and Federal agencies and their contractors
- Plan purchasers
- Any other entities that process health care reimbursements

Other business partners affiliated with the 835 include:

- Depository Financial Institutions (DFIs)
- Billing services
- Consulting services
- Vendors of systems
- EDI network intermediaries such as Automated Clearinghouses, Value-Added Networks, and telecommunications services

The OnlyConnect Gap Analysis Tool

Whether the selected implementation is to seamlessly recreate an environment familiar to end users so that retraining is not required or to build a new system, a thorough analysis of the legacy system's database structure is necessary. In order to populate a legacy environment with identical or extremely similar data structures, fields that will no longer be populated must first be identified. New fields that must be added to the legacy system must also be identified.

The OnlyConnect Gap Analysis Tool (GAT) compares the HIPAA Implementation Guides with the legacy environment. A Web-based and multi-user tool, GAT allows the simultaneous connecting of multiple legacy environments to multiple HIPAA transaction standards. The tool's analysis is used to identify:

- Legacy fields that will no longer be received from trading partners
- New fields to be added to the legacy environment or to be stored elsewhere if the data is required for sending to trading partners further downstream
- Any discrepancy in data type or field length

The tool's Web page is divided into two frames: the implementation guide frame and the connect frame. The implementation guide frame displays the hierarchical structure of the implementation guide using a tree control. Clicking on the word *CONNECT* causes the connect frame to display the properties of the tree node clicked on and allows the user to identify the location(s) in their legacy environment.

```
□ Patient Hierarchical Level [Loop 2000C] [CONNECT]
    ⊞ Patient Hierarchical Level [Segment] [CONNECT]
    ⊞ Patient Information [Segment] [CONNECT]
    □ Patient Name [Loop 2010CA] [CONNECT]
        □ Patient Name [Segment] [CONNECT]
            ⊞ Entity Identifier Code [Coded Element] [CONNECT]
            ⊞ Entity Type Qualifier [Coded Element] [CONNECT]
            • Patient Last Name [Element] [CONNECT]
            • Patient First Name [Element] [CONNECT]
            • Patient Middle Name [Element] [CONNECT]
            • Patient Name Suffix [Element] [CONNECT]
            ⊞ Identification Code Qualifier [Coded Element] [CONNECT]
            • Patient Primary Identifier [Element] [CONNECT]
        ⊞ Patient Address [Segment] [CONNECT]
        ⊞ Patient City/State/ZIP Code [Segment] [CONNECT]
        ⊞ Patient Demographic Information [Segment] [CONNECT]
        ⊞ Patient Secondary Identification Number [Segment] [CONNECT]
        ⊞ Property and Casualty Claim Number [Segment] [CONNECT]
    ⊞ Claim information [Loop 2300] [CONNECT]
```

Figure 4-6. *OnlyConnect Gap Analysis Tool: Implementation Guide Frame*

Figure 4-6 displays a portion of the *Health Care Claim: Institutional Implementation Guide*—specifically the patient name level as it appears in the Implementation Guide Frame. The relative indentations indicate a parent-child relationship. Different icon colors indicate the status of the connection:

- Black icons indicate that the node will never be connected to the legacy environment.
- Yellow icons indicate that the node has been connected at least once, but it might have additional connections.
- Green indicates that the node has been connected to all possible legacy fields.
- All icons are red at the start of implementation, indicating that the node has not been worked with.

```
       Name Name Last or Organization Name
      Usage Required
    Datatype AN
     Minimum 1
     Maximum 35
   Definition Individual last name or organizational name
     UB-92 1 FL 12
   EMC v.6.0 1 Record Type 20 Field No. 4
```

Figure 4-7. *OnlyConnect Gap Analysis Tool: Connect Frame, Properties*

Figure 4-7 displays a portion of the Connect Frame after the *CONNECT* link is clicked on the node *Patient Last Name*. This property information comes directly from the WPC implementation guide database. In this case, the screen displays the generic X12 name, the healthcare industry usage, X12 data type, minimum and maximum length, definition, and industry cross-references to a UB-92 Form Locator and to the Electronic Media Claim flat file.

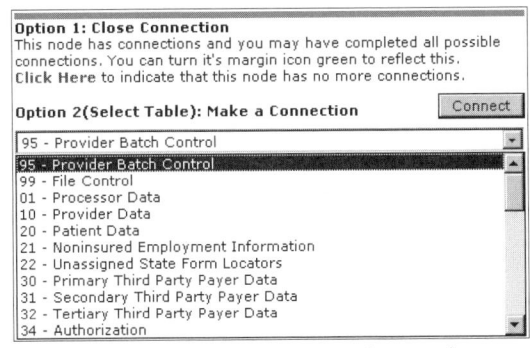

```
Option 1: Close Connection
This node has connections and you may have completed all possible
connections. You can turn it's margin icon green to reflect this.
Click Here to indicate that this node has no more connections.

Option 2(Select Table): Make a Connection        [ Connect ]

95 - Provider Batch Control
95 - Provider Batch Control
99 - File Control
01 - Processor Data
10 - Provider Data
20 - Patient Data
21 - Noninsured Employment Information
22 - Unassigned State Form Locators
30 - Primary Third Party Payer Data
31 - Secondary Third Party Payer Data
32 - Tertiary Third Party Payer Data
34 - Authorization
```

Figure 4-8. *OnlyConnect Gap Analysis Tool: Connect Frame, Connection Options, Pull-Down 1*

The connection options section allows the user either to close the connection, indicating that the node will never be connected, or to indicate that there are no additional connections to other systems for the given node. In this case, the legacy environment is a UB-92/EMC system. The initial pull-down displayed in Figure 4-8 shows all the record types in the legacy database. Selecting a record type—in this case, record type 20, Patient Data—sends a message to the server to populate a replacement pull-down with all of the fields in record type 20 (see Figure 4-9).

HIPAA Solutions

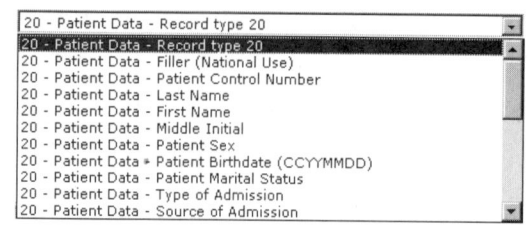

```
20 - Patient Data - Record type 20
20 - Patient Data - Record type 20
20 - Patient Data - Filler (National Use)
20 - Patient Data - Patient Control Number
20 - Patient Data - Last Name
20 - Patient Data - First Name
20 - Patient Data - Middle Initial
20 - Patient Data - Patient Sex
20 - Patient Data - Patient Birthdate (CCYYMMDD)
20 - Patient Data - Patient Marital Status
20 - Patient Data - Type of Admission
20 - Patient Data - Source of Admission
```

Figure 4-9. *OnlyConnect Gap Analysis Tool: Connect Frame, Existing Connections, Pull-Down 2*

Selecting the logical connection *Last Name* creates an entry in the underlying SQL Server 2000 database that is subsequently queried for reporting (see Figure 4-10).

```
If there are current connections for Name Last or Organization
Name, you can click below to edit them.

EMC6 - 20 - Patient Data - Last Name
```

Figure 4-10. *OnlyConnect Gap Analysis Tool: Connect Frame, Existing Connections*

The third area of the connect frame indicates that the selected node is already connected to one or more legacy fields. Clicking on the description of the legacy field displays additional information collected after connection (see Figure 4-11).

```
System Name - Table Name - Column Name
EMC6 - 20 - Patient Data - Last Name

Data Type      Length       Can be Null?
AN             20           yes

Is there a problem?       (•) Yes   ( ) No
Is the data type ok?      (•) Yes   ( ) No
Is the data length ok?    ( ) Yes   (•) No
Can this field be null?   (•) Yes   ( ) No

The HIPAA implementation guides indicate that we may
receive last names longer than 20 characters.

[ Update Connection ]         [ Delete Connection ]
```

Figure 4-11. *OnlyConnect Gap Analysis Tool: Connect Frame, Connection Detail*

Following a connection, or when an existing connection is clicked, the connection detail form is displayed. This form allows the user to store additional information in the database, including notes.

Any existing system that needs to be fed from BizTalk requires a document specification. The BizTalk Editor can be used to create XML, positional, or delimited flat file specifications for legacy systems, or the GAT can be used to generate them. The GAT can also generate maps compatible with the BizTalk Mapper that greatly reduce the time it takes to deploy an application. Updates to the GAT as the implementation guides change assure that an unbroken path to compliance will continue.

OnlyConnect FirstPass

The OnlyConnect Methodology describes seven steps that, when correctly followed, result in HIPAA transaction standard compliancy. The sixth step involves testing outgoing X12N HIPAA-formatted data to ensure compliancy. OnlyConnect FirstPass is a stand-alone Windows application that accepts X12 data, analyzes the data stream for adherence to X12 syntax and other requirements specified in the HIPAA Implementation Guides (IG), and produces an error report. If no errors exist, the generating application is deemed ready for field testing.

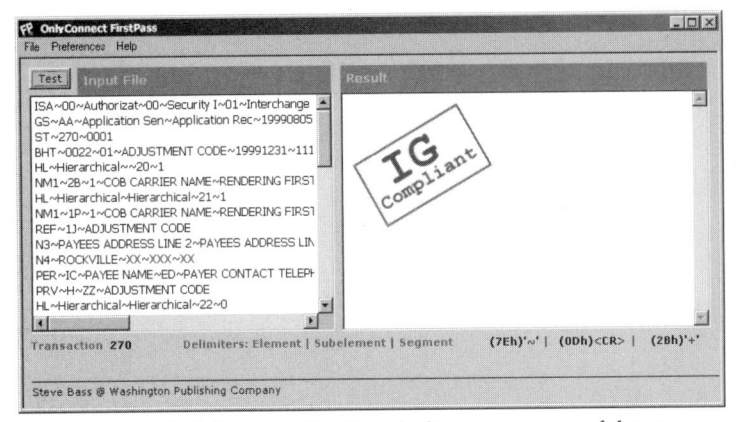

Figure 4-12.   *OnlyConnect FirstPass indicating a successful test*

In Figure 4-12, the panel to the left displays the test file and the panel to the right displays the test result. Figure 4-13 shows the same transmission after clicking inside the left panel and deleting the eighth field in the NM1 segment. Clicking the Test button retests the transmission and reveals two errors. The first is an X12 syntax error indicating that if the ninth element is used, the eighth is required. Scrolling the *Results Pane* upward reveals an IG error; specifically, that the eighth field is required by this implementation. In addition, the segment in error is highlighted in the left panel.

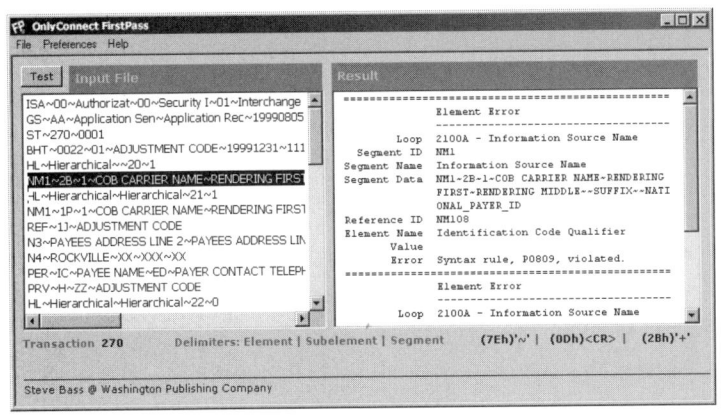

Figure 4-13.   *OnlyConnect FirstPass displaying an error report*

The tools described in this section are designed to empower staff members to get a handle on HIPAA and deal with it. With a well-thought-out plan for implementation in place, whether consultants were used for part of the process or not, an enterprise's pre-implementation employees will not have to learn a lot of hard-to-understand applications just to keep doing business as usual. With their understanding of existing systems and business processes still useful, they are now enabled to send, receive, and manage HIPAA material.

Staff knows where data is stored, what the data is used for, and how it moves from one step to another both inside and outside the enterprise. The Microsoft BizTalk Accelerator for HIPAA Solution, combined with the OnlyConnect FirstPass, gives staff the most complete set of tools to achieve the savings promised by HIPAA when the transaction standards are in full use. For additional information and updated information as data-transaction standards change, visit the WPC Web site at *http://www.wpc-edi.com*.

Chapter 5

The New Health Care Economy: A Vision of Fundamental Change

Technology Empowering Consumers

When the Health Insurance Portability and Accountability Act moves the industry beyond planning to compliance, its principal effect—that administrative information will be exchanged electronically in a single, standard way—has the potential to improve aspects of health care far more substantive than administration. As a unifying force, HIPAA's impact could eventually extend to how physicians and other caregivers provide care.

The simplification of procedures for obtaining care and for reaching insurers that HIPAA entails will allow consumers to participate more fully in the management of their own care. With the red tape associated with insurance claims drastically cut back, exploring the options of a policy—or even options for treatment—will be less daunting for patients. Once the administrative side of health care is less mysterious, patients stand to have more to say about the cost of care. Payers and providers will be more apt to hear those voices when consumers select health care and insurance as they would buy a new car or manage their money: searching for value and a good return on their investment.

As the changes occurring with HIPAA converge with trends in information technology (IT) and scientific research, dramatic improvements in health care quality and broader access to that improved care—at a reasonable cost—are possible. Rising consumerism, burgeoning technology, and the spreading accordance of disparate groups in shared standards are forces for change not just in health care but in other vital areas such as education and commerce.

The HIPAA transaction standards will function as a catalyst for such change. Their use will produce a comprehensive body of information that has never existed before. Emanating from the points of care, the information expressed in the administrative transaction sets will impeccably reflect health care in the United States. This unfiltered perspective will drive changes in policy and practice.

Inequities in the quality and dissemination of care will be exposed and the factors they are based on will be traceable. The technology enabling these administrative transactions also assures better clinical information and the efficacy of its reporting. This is the content which will influence future research.

As soon as this technology is functioning, patients will notice differences in how they obtain and pay for health care. The time-consuming pre-HIPAA process of obtaining a referral made health insurance companies faceless gate-keepers, capable of blocking or delaying access to particular forms of medical care. When such authorizations are effected electronically, the consumer of care will no longer act as a paper-clutching suppliant whose patience is tested by the process.

Aspects of the impact of HIPAA—the effect of standards, changes that will improve administrative process and reduce workflow—have been thoroughly explored in previous chapters. The focus of this chapter is how technology and the emergence of consumerism will combine with the effects of HIPAA compliance to bring about fundamental reform yet to reach the health care market.

Microsoft's contribution, BizTalk Accelerator for HIPAA, is aimed at helping health care organizations comply with transaction requirements. But the Accelerator's capabilities go way beyond the initial requirement of HIPAA transaction set compliance. The BizTalk Accelerator will provide continuing value as future schema updates are quickly implemented. If a regulating government agency requires an audit, the Accelerator will provide Solution users with documentation that makes their actions transparent. Organizations that provide care will discover ways to capitalize on the breadth of its features.

The industry expertise of Washington Publishing Company, compounded with the implementation expertise of global systems integrators, further leveraged by the participation of product-savvy Microsoft, has produced a product that does what it was designed to do: reduce the time and risk associated with HIPAA compliance. Health care organizations that use it will realize a significant return on their investment.

The Health Care Landscape

The BizTalk platform that the Accelerator for HIPAA is built upon enables entities complying with HIPAA to apply its features to other, more traditional e-commerce–based requirements: precisely, the obtaining of supplies and, as needed, banking interfaces, HL7 applications, functions called for by NCPDP, and many others. Organizations that take more than HIPAA into consideration when building a Solution will benefit from the investment beyond the mandated HIPAA transactions sets, and they will be poised to accommodate future requirements of HIPAA.

With the passage of time, organizations will develop uses for the Accelerator for HIPAA. It can be a partner in creativity, helping to streamline processes and improve quality without increasing costs. The number of staff members might be reduced, or their efforts redirected, thanks to real-time electronic patient referrals and eligibility request processing. In the process of balancing the books, organizations can create cost-benefit analyses. By following claims from start to finish, they will cut the time spent in accounts receivable. The Microsoft BizTalk Accelerator for HIPAA can draw upon platforms in use today and others that are not yet conceived because it has the versatility to be XML- and SOAP-capable and to integrate with legacy systems. New technologies straining for definition such as ebXML won't require Solution users to retool.

Forward-thinking health care executives will discover ways to use what HIPAA will have wrought to spark positive change across their enterprises.

Within today's U.S. health care industry, four domains furnish economic and business catalysts for change in how health care is funded and delivered. They are:

- Providers, including myriad health delivery organizations and physicians;
- Payers, such as insurance companies and public agencies that fund care;
- Manufacturers, such as the makers of devices, whose interest in innovation is sparked by the need for markets to buy what they create; and

- Employers, whose stake in the health of the vast American workforce can hardly be underestimated.

An emergent fifth driving force for fundamental improvement is the empowered consumer of health care services. A look at the dynamics of each of these domains and how they envision the future of health care follows.

Provider Organizations and Physicians

The core of the current health care delivery system in the U.S. is formed by care-providing entities: organizations that own and manage hospitals, clinics, and other care-delivery settings; retail pharmacies; stand-alone clinics; long-term care facilities; laboratories and other testing facilities; home health agencies; and facilities for patient education. These types of organizations provide support and facilities for individual physicians, nurses, therapists, and practitioners of every kind. Comprising the foundation of American health care, many of these types of organizations have historically been public sector entities—municipal and county-owned facilities—or not-for-profit organizations. Some for-profit organizations function within this domain by obtaining capital from commercial capital markets; however, the vast majority of health care organizations fund investments in two ways: with the earnings they generate, and through long-term bonds. One result of this has been an environment where the capital available to invest in information systems technology has, on average, rarely exceeded 3% of an entity's total annual spending. Boards of directors of these provider organizations must routinely decide how to spend scarce resources, and funding a new information technology infrastructure doesn't compete well against such patient-centered investments as a new emergency room or CAT scanner. The business of health care gives priority to patient needs that are more urgent than improving administrative systems and to providing services that insurance companies will pay for.

The business model for provider organizations depends on patients having health insurance—to be already participating, when they enter a care providing facility, in a system that pays for services yet to be delivered. This business model requires providers to charge as much as they can for their services so that they, and the care organizations they are a part of, can keep as much of the revenue as possible. Revenue is generated when inpatient beds are filled and outpatient facilities have plenty of sick people needing treatment.

In the past two decades the business model called *capitation* has emerged, wherein a defined population pays a fixed (or *capped*) amount per person annually to cover the costs of care providers to keep them healthy. Provider organizations commonly known as health maintenance organizations (HMOs) have made many sound attempts to adapt this model. Very few of these attempts have been successful. HMOs lacked, and continue to lack, the accurate information needed to determine the true costs of delivering services and to anticipate the rate at which those services will be consumed. In addition, IT systems were designed, with few exceptions, around the efficient delivery of care in inpatient settings, which is the predominant focus of the provider community. Therefore, the informational needs of capitation systems were, and continue to be, woefully underserved. Investment in systems that improve the prevention and diagnosis of medical conditions and promote early intervention with the intent to avoid or minimize inpatient care and outpatient surgery is meager compared with amounts devoted to crisis-driven treatment.

An examination of how people manage their cholesterol levels is an example of this. People who have elevated cholesterol levels can avoid painful and life-threatening cardiac events—requiring surgery and other expensive and invasive interventions—by properly managing their condition. This is accomplished through altering diet, engaging in exercise, taking proper medication, and regularly being examined by a care provider familiar with the patient. But surveys of health care executives throughout the past 10 years found that most of their organizations delivered no programs to help patients lower cholesterol levels through these behavior changes. The system affords no fee for such services. However, the same institutions almost invariably had cardiac surgery programs, which are among the most profitable programs in the health care delivery system. It appears that consumers cannot depend on health care organizations to help them manage this condition non-invasively, avoiding surgery or serious health impairment, because of a lack of monetary incentives for providers.

That fostering health is, at least in this example, not the primary function of the system but subordinate to generating profits seems amply demonstrated. The best interests of a patient too often are on the losing side when they conflict with the best monetary interests of care providers. But as health care providing organizations comply with HIPAA, a unique opportunity arises. The same data that comprises a health care claim potentially constitutes treatment reporting—the very thing that HMOs, and other approaches that stress prevention, have lacked. When the HIPAA standards are commonly used, a portrait of American health care will emerge from that data like a mosaic image emerges from uncounted tiny tiles. Administrative transaction sets can furnish the way to recreate the health care landscape in accordance with the best motives of providers and the best results for consumers.

The Small Health Care Provider

In the U.S., the hundreds of thousands of physicians who practice medicine in small groups or in solo practices follow a business model that, like the one that predominates among larger groups of care providers, is based on getting the highest remuneration for services possible. But this group also is not compensated if its members deliver services that prevent illness, provide early diagnosis, or otherwise help patients avoid more serious health conditions that would require a greater, more costly, degree of intervention. These physicians have even less capital to invest in IT. The current lack of standards for the small, local physician's office means that the accounts receivable (AR) cycle for a commercial claim can be as high as 120 days. Such practices do not have the tools to allow them to use information to improve their delivery of services and have no business incentive to develop them, so services that would prevent hospitalization and invasive interventions are not developed by physicians. Because this group of care providers—physicians in small practices—is responsible for 80% of health care consumption (determined by the volume of supplies they order), they hold the key to fundamental change, but they are not presently expected to use it. HIPAA, as it is currently defined, will have a great, positive impact on this sector of the provider domain by shortening the AR cycle. The standard data set will enable the small office to generate standard financial reports, as well as patient demographic information, with ease.

In these ways and others, the establishment of the standard data set will change and empower the provider community. These changes will also benefit the emerging fifth domain—patients, redefined as health care consumers.

Payers

Hundreds of organizations in the U.S. write health care insurance policies and manage those policies, facilitate payment for services covered by those policies, or both. In the case of the growing number of companies that are self-insured, these organizations provide administrative services, contracting with providers to secure favorable pricing. The business model for payers is to retain as much capital—whether it is generated by the premiums paid by policy holders or by the administrative fees employers pay—as possible. Payer entities accomplish this by strict, efficient management of authorizations and of payments for services. HIPAA presents an immediate opportunity for the payer domain to reduce costs and increase value by forcing the standardization of the core transactions.

Paradoxically, HIPAA also presents a threat to the payer sector. The same transactions from which payer entities draw compensation also benefit the provider community, creating a yin/yang effect that ultimately will benefit the health care consumer.

The consumer is on both sides of the equation: as the central figure in the HIPAA-revised health insurance dynamic, and as the constituent of the emergent fifth domain fostering reform.

An example of this dual status vested in patients (health care consumers) is illustrated by the *request for eligibility* transaction set. Effecting a fundamental transaction used across the continuum of health care services, this set of data elements will be essential to physicians and other individual caregivers, large provider organizations, and retail pharmacies, among others. Once a patient-consumer's eligibility verification has been done, the care provider's Solution IT "knows" what that consumer is entitled to, and the provider will be able to serve the consumer with alacrity. The payer will benefit by being required to process only the claims that are legitimate. The promise of cost reduction and administrative simplification is not the bottom line of this transaction's salutary effects. When executives affiliated with paying entities describe the biggest business challenges they face, they frequently focus on the management of care for that portion of their covered populations receiving the most services because of acute or chronic health conditions. Often, this group is a small percentage of the total number of lives.

When do consumers need to communicate with the payer community? Normally, this happens when the consumer is compromised in some way. One example is a life-altering event, such as a diagnosis of cancer. The key to effective management of this set of consumers is the frequent delivery of care at the physician office level. The referral transaction is a good example of a data set employed in such a circumstance. The patient's visit with a primary care provider where a life-changing diagnosis is made will prompt a standard transaction between the primary care provider and the payer that will expedite treatment and referral. Because of the HIPAA transaction sets, the insured consumer's rapid access to care will be experienced as a positive, even salutary, response from the payer community. But in the pre-HIPAA environment, the tools needed by physicians and their care-giving teams to secure this correct, timely—and, perhaps, life-saving—payer response are unlikely to be as available because of the lack of a single, mandatory electronic standard for communicating vital administrative data. The benefits of HIPAA compliance—for the parties occupying all domains involved—could not be more starkly illustrated.

Device Manufacturers

A subject that was touched on earlier in this chapter, health care device manufacturers as sources of medical innovation, deserves more detailed examination. Positive change in health care delivery that originates in the life sciences sector includes not only those companies that research, design, and make medical devices but those that make new drugs and treatments available. The business model for these firms requires long term investment in research and development (R&D), followed by rapid innovation so that they have time to market new devices and realize the profits that make R&D possible. The success of this sector of the health care economy is based on compressing the time involved in fundamental research, obtaining the approval of regulatory agencies, and market introduction. The key to successful compression of these events is information: data, the accuracy of which must be completely reliable, managed to support the development-and-approval life cycle. Life sciences executives state that the key to their competitive advantage is the interaction between care-providing teams (including physicians) and the patients they treat. It is in this interaction that clinical trials are undertaken, samples introduced, and the post-approval demand created. The business model for creating and delivering products based on the life sciences requires tools capable of automatically capturing health care information as it originates, at the point of care. Again, the mandated HIPAA standards are a basis for accomplishing a task with implications for the future of this domain. A new, greater level of integration of treatment data with research will significantly impact the health care landscape. Currently, no standard method of reporting breast cancer treatment efficacy is in place. With various treatment sources reporting their results by disparate means, contradictory treatment methods proliferate.

Clinical trials necessarily include participants—and investigators—from a broad range of geographic, linguistic, and cultural backgrounds. Differing regulatory environments are also represented. The challenge of creating and deploying tools that effectively automate information capture in such a diverse landscape is formidable. From a physician's point of view, the fewer patients in a clinical trial, the more reluctant a caregiver will be to adopt a treatment based on a trial's encouraging results, even with supporting trials conducted by different firms. Care providers cannot adopt a tool set that is unique to a particular trial. The learning curves of researchers are steep, and the management processes concerned with multiple computers and other devices are difficult. The rewards for effective, automated collection and management of clinical trial data will be enormous, in both economic and human terms. Executives in this sector of the health care industry are looking for ways to bring better tools into the clinical trial process. HIPAA, and future HIPAA initiatives, will pave the way for a harmonization of clinical information. The potential beneficiaries of improved R&D that produce a breakthrough are all consumers who share that diagnosis. This is new use of health care data, made possible by the standardization of such data. Not yet fully explored, it has the potential to be the most influential.

Private Sector Employers, Public Sector Agencies: Funding Health Care

Many discussions of the health care economy focus on providers, often physicians; payers, whether insurance companies, government agencies, or both; and research and development. Each of these plays an important role in the development of the current health care system and in the development of the current state of information technology. During the past 25 years, the cost of health care has grown tremendously. The real financial burden for this increase in spending has been on employers with health plans as part of their employee benefits packages.

The tax burden shared by U.S. residents for health care services paid for by the public sector is increasing dramatically. The cost of health plan benefits to private sector employers is often the largest component of an employee benefits package, with annual inflation. Employers are increasingly looking for ways to maintain high levels of benefits and manage the cost of these benefits while maintaining high employee satisfaction. Efforts to work with payers and providers, while yielding some positive results, have not improved quality or appreciably lowered costs. This is mostly because of the lack of a standard data set.

Under the provisions of HIPAA, health care plans are portable—from employer to employer—and might be convertible to a non-employer program, if an assortment of financial services firms compete aggressively for this new market. These are core dynamics in creating catalysts to fulfill the vision of the new health economy. Clearly, employers have incentives to deliver benefits that attract and retain a quality work force while simultaneously controlling the cost of those valuable benefits. Employers have learned that making sure employees gain access to high quality services from appropriate health care providers, when needed, is integral to employee health and satisfaction. Employers have also recognized that, in health care management, the key interaction for cost control is between the care provider and the employee.

Vision for a New Health Care Economy

At the core of this vision of a new health care economy is empowerment of the physician-caregiver team and the consumer. It is the interaction between these that really delivers. Both the caregiver and the consumer make informed decisions that optimize the delivery of care and the management of its costs. This vision has five technical components at its core:

- Technology that integrates information capture and management
- Technology that is accessible at the individual caregiver level
- Technology that is delivered in flexible and extendable business models
- Technology that enables consumers to control their medical records
- Technology that adapts to, and can be integrated with, current processes but is open-ended to support the innovation that brings new processes

The HIPAA transaction set standards serve as a catalyst to this vision in one simple but incredibly powerful way. By standardizing key transactions that emanate from the point of care, caregivers are enabled to communicate in a common language supportable by cost-effective technology. The critical tools that have so long eluded the health care industry, and for which payers and providers have lacked either the incentive or the ability to provide, will be acquired in the same way health care practices now purchase cell phone service.

A closer look at the vision's five components will illustrate how close it is to realization as the foundation of the new health care economy.

Integration of Information Capture and Management

For all the many attempts throughout the past fifteen years to define and deliver an electronic patient record, today the most common record-keeping system in physician offices is the hand-written paper chart. Information needed during a physician-patient encounter is usually not included in common descriptions of an electronic patient record. Data necessary for clinical decision-making is often the data most recently acquired. Applications that use standard development tools are now reaching the market. They will provide for digital data capture. The physical tools for capture are often a mouse, keyboard, or stylus, but current applications for direct dictation capture, as well as data capture from digital blood pressure cuffs, weight scales, and other common measuring and recording instruments, are extant.

Accessible Technology

With the dramatic expansion of computer processor power and the proliferation of "smart devices," the clinical caregiver can choose from among many computer forms. Devices range from cell phones that function as computers to computers that have the features of a cell phone. Tablet PCs weighing less than 2.5 pounds perform superbly, and at costs that put incredible computing power and wireless network capability within the reach of most physician office budgets. With storage capacity exceeding 2 gigabytes (GB) in a hand-held wireless computer, constant connectivity to large servers is not needed. Redundant local storage and Internet connectivity impart to even remote office locations access to rich, Web-based data stores, while maintaining secure records close to the point of care.

Flexible Technology

Converging with the availability of computing platforms and digital charting applications, new business models are being established, some of which look more like cell phone subscriptions than traditional IT investments. These business models allow users to benefit from the large capital investments that have been made in Internet connectivity and hosted Web services. Their capital costs are distributed among large groups of business users, lowering the individual burden to a monthly service fee. The telecommunication model serves as a useful framework. Voice mail that is hosted by the user's local carrier exemplifies this decentralization. Small- and medium-sized businesses pay a monthly fee to a service, such as bCentral from MSN, for core business applications, e-mail, and Web services. Applications focused on the caregiver are following this model, reducing or eliminating the need for large capital investment.

The real innovation is in the proliferating ways that services can be structured. They are adaptable to the needs of the user. Effective self-provisioning is being enabled through powerful customer relations tools: the user decides what and how much to purchase, expanding their use of services when circumstances warrant it. A physician might decide to add real-time notification for all patients having a claim requiring one or two data elements to be auto-adjudicated. This way, the physician is not hampered by AR problems that could be solved with one or two simple data elements, or by questions answered at or near the patient encounter. A care provider might subscribe to instant notification accomplished by Web phone, wireless PDA, or office tablet PC, for those patients for whom critical lab results are pending. What makes this capability incredibly powerful is that individual providers can purchase these systems independent of provider organizations and payers. They maintain a sense of control and autonomy that allows them to practice medicine in the manner they choose.

Consumer-Enabling Technology

The critical counterpart of caregiver digital record creation and management is the consumer controlled medical record. Cornerstone of consumer empowerment, medical encounter information is recorded in a form that is easy to present and understand. These tools allow for data to be submitted by such caregivers as pharmacists, physicians, and nurses, as well as allowing data to be consumer-generated. Each data entry is logged by source, keeping care providers' record information distinct from consumer-entered information. The key enabler is a record system that uses the Internet and Web services to create and store information. An attribute of this type of system is the ability for consumers to maintain access to their record. The system will allow users to grant access to a specific set of data and not others, or allow access on a one-time basis of limited time duration or on an ongoing basis until access is revoked. A consumer-controlled medical record will likely be a monthly subscription service model. Current models have a monthly cost per user of under $4.00. Both payers and employers are sponsoring these systems, recognizing that the value of maintaining a core consumer medical record is incredibly high when the effect on medical costs is considered.

Adaptable Technology

One of the major challenges facing commercial developers of applications is to create great software and provide ongoing enhancements and new features that users will want. Web services like those previously described allow for the exploitation of powerful smart devices while leveraging the Internet to serve up applications that are refreshed as often as they need to be. The HIPAA Solution from Microsoft and Washington Publishing Company is responsive to its environment: it uses technology that adapts to, and can be integrated with, current processes but is open-ended to support innovation that brings new processes.

Once health caregivers and consumers are able to re-establish the physician/patient relationship, enabled by a digital medical record that both can use to manage care, it is hard to predict what either user will want next. This new, standards-based framework will deliver rapid innovations in application features and services that will respond to these new requirements.

The New Healthscape

The HIPAA standards, once they become the means of administering health care throughout the United States, will bring major improvements, some appreciable right away and others requiring months or years to come to fruition.

Health care providers will soon feel a great sense of relief and release as the unfairly burdensome clerical requirements they have borne are lightened by administrative simplification. Much of that relief, coming to health care entities large and small, will be monetary and might make the difference between fiscal health and operating at a deficit—or ceasing to operate at all.

Payers of the cost of health care will be more accountable for their actions. Their responsibilities more clearly defined, they will forge a new, less adversarial relationship with the people they serve.

The consumers of health care—patients—will find that health insurance is no longer contingent on remaining with the same employer. Care will be easier to obtain and health insurance claims will be paid faster.

But the most significant potential result of the HIPAA standards is a long-term effect. The data that will exist in them—owned by the individuals it describes but separated from their identities—must be used to improve treatments throughout all facets of medicine. With current information technology applied to the richest, most complete health care database ever, the eventual and continuing result will be nothing less than improved national health.

Appendix A

What Is the Federal Register?

The *Federal Register* is a legal newspaper published every business day by the National Archives and Records Administration (NARA). It contains Federal agency regulations; proposed rules and notices; and Executive orders, proclamations, and other Presidential documents. The *Federal Register* informs citizens of their rights and obligations and provides access to a wide range of Federal benefits and opportunities for funding. NARA's Office of the Federal Register prepares the *Federal Register* for publication in partnership with the Government Printing Office (GPO), which distributes it in paper, on microfiche, and on the World Wide Web.

Each issue of the *Federal Register* is organized into four categories:

- Presidential Documents, including Executive orders and proclamations;
- Rules and Regulations, including policy statements and interpretations of rules;
- Proposed Rules, including petitions for rulemaking and other advance proposals; and
- Notices, including scheduled hearings and meetings open to the public, grant applications, and administrative orders.

Documents published in the *Federal Register* as rules and proposed rules include citations to the *Code of Federal Regulations* (CFR) to refer readers to the CFR parts affected. The CFR contains the complete and official text of agency regulations organized into fifty titles covering broad subject areas. The CFR is updated and published once a year in print, fiche, and on-line formats.

The Final HIPAA Rule for Transaction and Code Set Standards was published in the *Federal Register* on August 17, 2000. The complete text includes a lengthy *Preamble* along with the *Regulation*. The *Preamble* summarizes and provides comments to questions raised during the required 60-day comment period that follows a Notice of Proposed Rulemaking (NPRM). Both the *Preamble* and the *Regulation* were made available as a Portable Document Format (PDF) file and are still available at: *www.hipaa-dsmo.org/txfinal.pdf*. The following text of just the *Regulation* is reproduced below for the convenience of the reader. It can also be found on the Internet at: *aspe.dhhs.gov/admnsimp/final/txfin01.htm*.

The Final HIPAA Rule for Transaction and Code Set Standards

List of Subjects in 45 CFR

Part 160

Electronic transactions, Health, Health care, Health facilities, Health insurance, Health records, Medicaid, Medical research, Medicare, Reporting and recordkeeping requirements.

Part 162

Administrative practice and procedure, Electronic transactions, Health facilities, Health insurance, Hospitals, Incorporation by reference, Medicare, Medicaid, Reporting and recordkeeping requirements.

For the reasons set forth in the preamble, 45 CFR subtitle A, subchapter C, is added to read as follows:

SUBCHAPTER C – ADMINISTRATIVE DATA STANDARDS AND RELATED REQUIREMENTS

PART 160 – GENERAL ADMINISTRATIVE REQUIREMENTS

Subpart A – General Provisions

Sec.

160.101 Statutory basis and purpose.

160.102 Applicability.

160.103 Definitions.

160.104 Modifications.

Subpart B – [RESERVED]

Authority: Secs. 1171 through 1179 of the Social Security Act (42 U.S.C. 1320d - 1320d-8), as added by sec. 262 of Pub. L. 104-191, 110 Stat. 2021-2031, and sec. 264 of Pub. L. 104-191, 110 Stat. 2033-2034 (42 U.S.C. 1320d-2 (note)).

Subpart A – General Provisions

§ 160.101 Statutory basis and purpose.

The requirements of this subchapter implement sections 1171 through 1179 of the Social Security Act (the Act), as added by section 262 of Public Law 104-191, and section 264 of Public Law 104-191.

§ 160.102 Applicability.

Except as otherwise provided, the standards, requirements, and implementation specifications adopted under this subchapter apply to the following entities:

(a) A health plan.

(b) A health care clearinghouse.

(c) A health care provider who transmits any health information in electronic form in connection with a transaction covered by this subchapter.

§ 160.103 Definitions.

Except as otherwise provided, the following definitions apply to this subchapter:

Act means the Social Security Act.

ANSI stands for the American National Standards Institute.

Business associate means a person who performs a function or activity regulated by this subchapter on behalf of a covered entity, as defined in this section. A *business associate* may be a *covered entity*. Business associate excludes a person who is part of the covered entity's workforce as defined in this section.

Compliance date means the date by which a covered entity must comply with a standard, implementation specification, or modification adopted under this subchapter.

Covered entity means one of the following:

(1) A health plan.

(2) A health care clearinghouse.

(3) A health care provider who transmits any health information in electronic form in connection with a transaction covered by this subchapter.

Group health plan (also see definition of *health plan* in this section) means an employee welfare benefit plan (as defined in section 3(1) of the Employee Retirement Income Security Act of 1974 (ERISA)(29 U.S.C. 1002(1)), including insured and self-insured plans, to the extent that the plan provides medical care, as defined in section 2791(a)(2) of the Public Health Service (PHS) Act, 42 U.S.C. 300gg-91(a)(2), including items and services paid for as medical care, to employees or their dependents directly or through insurance, reimbursement, or otherwise, that—

(1) Has 50 or more participants (as defined in section 3(7) of ERISA, 29 U.S.C. 1002(7)); or

(2) Is administered by an entity other than the employer that established and maintains the plan.

HCFA stands for Health Care Financing Administration within the Department of Health and Human Services.

HHS stands for the Department of Health and Human Services.

Health care means care, services, or supplies furnished to an individual and related to the health of the individual. *Health care* includes the following:

(1) Preventive, diagnostic, therapeutic, rehabilitative, maintenance, or palliative care; counseling; service; or procedure with respect to the physical or mental condition, or functional status, of an individual or affecting the structure or function of the body.

(2) Sale or dispensing of a drug, device, equipment, or other item in accordance with a prescription.

(3) Procurement or banking of blood, sperm, organs, or any other tissue for administration to individuals.

Health care clearinghouse means a public or private entity that does either of the following (Entities, including but not limited to, billing services, repricing companies, community health management information systems or community health information systems, and "value-added" networks and switches are *health care clearinghouses* for purposes of this subchapter if they perform these functions.):

(1) Processes or facilitates the processing of information received from another entity in a nonstandard format or containing nonstandard data content into standard data elements or a standard transaction.

(2) Receives a standard transaction from another entity and processes or facilitates the processing of information into nonstandard format or nonstandard data content for a receiving entity.

Health care provider means a provider of services as defined in section 1861(u) of the Act, 42 U.S.C. 1395x(u), a provider of medical or other health services as defined in section 1861(s) of the Act, 42 U.S.C. 1395x(s), and any other person or organization who furnishes, bills, or is paid for health care in the normal course of business.

Health information means any information, whether oral or recorded in any form or medium, that—

(1) Is created or received by a health care provider, health plan, public health authority, employer, life insurer, school or university, or health care clearinghouse; and

(2) Relates to the past, present, or future physical or mental health or condition of an individual; the provision of health care to an individual; or the past, present, or future payment for the provision of health care to an individual.

Health insurance issuer (as defined in section 2791(b) of the PHS Act, 42 U.S.C. 300gg- 91(b)(2), and used in the definition of *health plan* in this section) means an insurance company, insurance service, or insurance organization (including an HMO) that is licensed to engage in the business of insurance in a State and is subject to State law that regulates insurance. Such term does not include a group health plan.

Health maintenance organization (HMO) (as defined in section 2791 of the PHS Act, 42 U.S.C. 300gg-91(b)(3), and used in the definition of *health plan* in this section) means a Federally qualified HMO, an organization recognized as an HMO under State law, or a similar organization regulated for solvency under State law in the same manner and to the same extent as such an HMO.

Health plan means an individual or group plan that provides, or pays the cost of, medical care (as defined in section 2791(a)(2) of the PHS Act, 42 U.S.C. 300gg-91(a)(2)). *Health plan* includes, when applied to government funded programs, the components of the government agency administering the program. *Health plan* includes the following, singly or in combination:

(1) A group health plan, as defined in this section.

(2) A health insurance issuer, as defined in this section.

(3) An HMO, as defined in this section.

(4) Part A or Part B of the Medicare program under title XVIII of the Act.

(5) The Medicaid program under title XIX of the Act, 42 U.S.C. 1396 et. seq.

(6) An issuer of a Medicare supplemental policy (as defined in section 1882(g)(1) of the Act, 42 U.S.C. 1395ss(g)(1)).

(7) An issuer of a long-term care policy, excluding a nursing home fixed-indemnity policy.

(8) An employee welfare benefit plan or any other arrangement that is established or maintained for the purpose of offering or providing health benefits to the employees of two or more employers.

(9) The health care program for active military personnel under title 10 of the United States Code.

(10) The veterans health care program under 38 U.S.C. chapter 17.

(11) The Civilian Health and Medical Program of the Uniformed Services (CHAMPUS), as defined in 10 U.S.C. 1072(4).

(12) The Indian Health Service program under the Indian Health Care Improvement Act (25 U.S.C. 1601 et seq.).

(13) The Federal Employees Health Benefit Program under 5 U.S.C. 8902 et seq.

(14) An approved State child health plan under title XXI of the Act, providing benefits that meet the requirements of section 2103 of the Act, 42 U.S.C. 1397 et. seq.

(15) The Medicare + Choice program under part C of title XVIII of the Act, 42 U.S.C. 1395w-21 through 1395w-28.

(16) Any other individual or group plan, or combination of individual or group plans, that provides or pays for the cost of medical care (as defined in section 2791(a)(2) of the PHS Act, 42 U.S.C. 300gg-91(a)(2)).

Implementation specification means the specific instructions for implementing a standard.

Modify or *modification* refers to a change adopted by the Secretary, through regulation, to a standard or an implementation specification.

Secretary means the Secretary of Health and Human Services or any other officer or employee of the Department of Health and Human Services to whom the authority involved has been delegated.

Small health plan means a health plan with annual receipts of $5 million or less.

Standard means a prescribed set of rules, conditions, or requirements describing the following information for products, systems, services, or practices:

(1) Classification of components.

(2) Specification of materials, performance, or operations.

(3) Delineation of procedures.

Standard setting organization (SSO) means an organization accredited by the American National Standards Institute that develops and maintains standards for information transactions or data elements, or any other standard that is necessary for, or will facilitate the implementation of, this part.

State refers to one of the following:

(1) For health plans established or regulated by Federal law, *State* has the meaning set forth in the applicable section of the United States Code for each health plan.

(2) For all other purposes, *State* means the United States, the District of Columbia, the Commonwealth of Puerto Rico, the Virgin Islands, and Guam.

Trading partner agreement means an agreement related to the exchange of information in electronic transactions, whether the agreement is distinct or part of a larger agreement, between each party to the agreement. (For example, a trading partner agreement may specify, among other things, the duties and responsibilities of each party to the agreement in conducting a standard transaction.)

Transaction means the exchange of information between two parties to carry out financial or administrative activities related to health care. It includes the following types of information exchanges:

(1) Health care claims or equivalent encounter information.

(2) Health care payment and remittance advice.

(3) Coordination of benefits.

(4) Health care claim status.

(5) Enrollment and disenrollment in a health plan.

(6) Eligibility for a health plan.

(7) Health plan premium payments.

(8) Referral certification and authorization.

(9) First report of injury.

(10) Health claims attachments.

(11) Other transactions that the Secretary may prescribe by regulation.

Workforce means employees, volunteers, trainees, and other persons under the direct control of a covered entity, whether or not they are paid by the covered entity.

§ 160.104 Modifications.

(a) Except as provided in paragraph (b) of this section, the Secretary may adopt a modification to a standard or implementation specification adopted under this subchapter no more frequently than once every 12 months.

(b) The Secretary may adopt a modification at any time during the first year after the standard or implementation specification is initially adopted, if the Secretary determines that the modification is necessary to permit compliance with the standard.

(c) The Secretary establishes the compliance date for any standard or implementation specification modified under this section.

(1) The compliance date for a modification is no earlier than 180 days after the effective date of the final rule in which the Secretary adopts the modification.

(2) The Secretary may consider the extent of the modification and the time needed to comply with the modification in determining the compliance date for the modification.

(3) The Secretary may extend the compliance date for small health plans, as the Secretary determines is appropriate.

Subpart B [RESERVED]

PART 162 – ADMINISTRATIVE REQUIREMENTS

Subpart A – General Provisions
Sec.
162.100 Applicability.
162.103 Definitions.

Subparts B – H [RESERVED]

Subpart I – General Provisions for Transactions
162.900 Compliance dates of the initial implementation of the code sets and transaction standards.
162.910 Maintenance of standards and adoption of modifications and new standards.
162.915 Trading partner agreements.
162.920 Availability of implementation specifications.
162.923 Requirements for covered entities.
162.925 Additional requirements for health plans.
162.930 Additional rules for health care clearinghouses.
162.940 Exceptions from standards to permit testing of proposed modifications.

Subpart J – Code Sets
162.1000 General requirements.
162.1002 Medical data code sets.
162.1011 Valid code sets.

Subpart K – Health Care Claims or Equivalent Encounter Information
162.1101 Health care claims or equivalent encounter information transaction.
162.1102 Standards for health care claims or equivalent encounter information.

Subpart L – Eligibility for a Health Plan
162.1201 Eligibility for a health plan transaction.
162.1202 Standards for eligibility for a health plan.

Subpart M – Referral Certification and Authorization
162.1301 Referral certification and authorization transaction.
162.1302 Standard for referral certification and authorization.

Subpart N – Health Care Claim Status
162.1401 Health care claim status transaction.
162.1402 Standard for health care claim status.

Subpart O – Enrollment and Disenrollment in a Health Plan
162.1501 Enrollment and disenrollment in a health plan transaction.
162.1502 Standard for enrollment and disenrollment in a health plan.

Subpart P – Health Care Payment and Remittance Advice
162.1601 Health care payment and remittance advice transaction.
162.1602 Standards for health care payment and remittance advice.

Subpart Q – Health Plan Premium Payments
162.1701 Health plan premium payments transaction.
162.1702 Standard for health plan premium payments.

Subpart R – Coordination of Benefits
162.1801 Coordination of benefits transaction.
162.1802 Standards for coordination of benefits.

Authority: Secs. 1171 through 1179 of the Social Security Act (42 U.S.C. 1320d - 1320d-8), as added by sec. 262 of Pub. L. 104-191, 110 Stat. 2021-2031, and sec. 264 of Pub. L. 104-191, 110 Stat. 2033-2034 (42 U.S.C. 1320d-2 (note)).

Subpart A – General Provisions

§162.100 Applicability.

Covered entities (as defined in §160.103 of this subchapter) must comply with the applicable requirements of this part.

§162.103 Definitions.

For purposes of this part, the following definitions apply:

Code set means any set of codes used to encode data elements, such as tables of terms, medical concepts, medical diagnostic codes, or medical procedure codes. A *code set* includes the codes and the descriptors of the codes.

Code set maintaining organization means an organization that creates and maintains the code sets adopted by the Secretary for use in the transactions for which standards are adopted in this part.

Data condition means the rule that describes the circumstances under which a covered entity must use a particular data element or segment.

Data content means all the data elements and code sets inherent to a transaction, and not related to the format of the transaction. Data elements that are related to the format are not *data content*.

Data element means the smallest named unit of information in a transaction.

Data set means a semantically meaningful unit of information exchanged between two parties to a transaction.

Descriptor means the text defining a code.

Designated standard maintenance organization (DSMO) means an organization designated by the Secretary under §162.910(a).

Direct data entry means the direct entry of data (for example, using dumb terminals or Web browsers) that is immediately transmitted into a health plan's computer.

Electronic media means the mode of electronic transmission. It includes the Internet (wide-open), Extranet (using Internet technology to link a business with information only accessible to collaborating parties), leased lines, dial-up lines, private networks, and those transmissions that are physically moved from one location to another using magnetic tape, disk, or compact disk media.

Format refers to those data elements that provide or control the enveloping or hierarchical structure, or assist in identifying data content of, a transaction.

HCPCS stands for the Health [Care Financing Administration] Common Procedure Coding System.

Maintain or *maintenance* refers to activities necessary to support the use of a standard adopted by the Secretary, including technical corrections to an implementation specification, and enhancements or expansion of a code set. This term excludes the activities related to the adoption of a new standard or implementation specification, or modification to an adopted standard or implementation specification.

Maximum defined data set means all of the required data elements for a particular standard based on a specific implementation specification.

Segment means a group of related data elements in a transaction.

Standard transaction means a transaction that complies with the applicable standard adopted under this part.

Subparts B – H [RESERVED]

Subpart I – General Provisions for Transactions

§162.900 – Compliance dates of the initial implementation of the code sets and transaction standards.

(a) Health care providers. A covered health care provider must comply with the applicable requirements of subparts I through N of this part no later than October 16, 2002.

(b) Health plans. A health plan must comply with the applicable requirements of subparts I through R of this part no later than one of the following dates:

(1) Health plans other than small health plans—October 16, 2002.

(2) Small health plans—October 16, 2003.

(c) Health care clearinghouses. A health care clearinghouse must comply with the applicable requirements of subparts I through R of this part no later than October 16, 2002.

§162.910 Maintenance of standards and adoption of modifications and new standards.

(a) Designation of DSMOs.

(1) The Secretary may designate as a DSMO an organization that agrees to conduct, to the satisfaction of the Secretary, the following functions:

(i) Maintain standards adopted under this subchapter.

(ii) Receive and process requests for adopting a new standard or modifying an adopted standard.

(2) The Secretary designates a DSMO by notice in the *Federal Register.*

(b) Maintenance of standards. Maintenance of a standard by the appropriate DSMO constitutes maintenance of the standard for purposes of this part, if done in accordance with the processes the Secretary may require.

(c) Process for modification of existing standards and adoption of new standards. The Secretary considers a recommendation for a proposed modification to an existing standard, or a proposed new standard, only if the recommendation is developed through a process that provides for the following:

(1) Open public access.

(2) Coordination with other DSMOs.

(3) An appeals process for each of the following, if dissatisfied with the decision on the request:

(i) The requestor of the proposed modification.

(ii) A DSMO that participated in the review and analysis of the request for the proposed modification, or the proposed new standard.

(4) Expedited process to address content needs identified within the industry, if appropriate.

(5) Submission of the recommendation to the National Committee on Vital and Health Statistics (NCVHS).

§162.915 Trading partner agreements.

A covered entity must not enter into a trading partner agreement that would do any of the following:

(a) Change the definition, data condition, or use of a data element or segment in a standard.

(b) Add any data elements or segments to the maximum defined data set.

(c) Use any code or data elements that are either marked "not used" in the standard's implementation specification or are not in the standard's implementation specification(s).

(d) Change the meaning or intent of the standard's implementation specification(s).

§162.920 Availability of implementation specifications.

(a) Access to implementation specifications. A person or organization may request copies (or access for inspection) of the implementation specifications for a standard described in subparts K through R of this part by identifying the standard by name, number, and version. The implementation specifications are available as follows:

(1) ASC X12N specifications. The implementation specifications for ASC X12N standards may be obtained from the Washington Publishing Company, PMB 161, 5284 Randolph Road, Rockville, MD, 20852-2116; telephone 301-949-9740; and FAX: 301-949-9742. They are also available through the Washington Publishing Company on the Internet at *http://www.wpc-edi.com*. The implementation specifications are as follows:

(i) The ASC X12N 837 – Health Care Claim: Dental, Version 4010, May 2000, Washington Publishing Company, 004010X097, as referenced in §§162.1102 and 162.1802.

(ii) The ASC X12N 837 – Health Care Claim: Professional, Volumes 1 and 2, Version 4010, May 2000, Washington Publishing Company, 004010X098, as referenced in §§162.1102 and 162.1802.

(iii) The ASC X12N 837 – Health Care Claim: Institutional, Volumes 1 and 2, Version 4010, May 2000, Washington Publishing Company, 004010X096, as referenced in §§162.1102 and 162.1802.

(iv) The ASC X12N 270/271 – Health Care Eligibility Benefit Inquiry and Response, Version 4010, May 2000, Washington Publishing Company, 004010X092, as referenced in §162.1202.

(v) The ASC X12N 278 – Health Care Services Review – Request for Review and Response, Version 4010, May 2000, Washington Publishing Company, 004010X094, as referenced in §162.1302.

(vi) The ASC X12N 276/277 – Health Care Claim Status Request and Response, Version 4010, May 2000, Washington Publishing Company, 004010X093, as referenced in §162.1402.

(vii) The ASC X12N 834 – Benefit Enrollment and Maintenance, Version 4010, May 2000, Washington Publishing Company, 004010X095, as referenced in §162.1502.

(viii) The ASC X12N 835 – Health Care Claim Payment/Advice, Version 4010, May 2000, Washington Publishing Company, 004010X091, as referenced in §162.1602.

(ix) The ASC X12N 820 – Payroll Deducted and Other Group Premium Payment for Insurance Products, Version 4010, May 2000, Washington Publishing Company, 004010X061, as referenced in §162.1702.

(2) Retail pharmacy specifications. The implementation specifications for all retail pharmacy standards may be obtained from the National Council for Prescription Drug Programs (NCPDP), 4201 North 24th Street, Suite 365, Phoenix, AZ, 85016; telephone 602-957-9105; and FAX 602-955-0749. It may also be obtained through the Internet at http://www.ncpdp.org. The implementation specifications are as follows:

(i) The Telecommunication Standard Implementation Guide, Version 5 Release 1, September 1999, National Council for Prescription Drug Programs, as referenced in §§162.1102, 162.1202, 162.1602, and 162.1802.

(ii) The Batch Standard Batch Implementation Guide, Version 1 Release 0, February 1, 1996, National Council for Prescription Drug Programs, as referenced in §§162.1102, 162.1202, 162.1602, and 162.1802.

(b) Incorporations by reference. The Director of the Office of the Federal Register approves the implementation specifications described in paragraph (a) of this section for incorporation by reference in subparts K through R of this part in accordance with 5 U.S.C. 552(a) and 1 CFR part 51. A copy of the implementation specifications may be inspected at the Office of the Federal Register, 800 North Capitol Street, NW, Suite 700, Washington, DC.

§162.923 Requirements for covered entities.

(a) General rule. Except as otherwise provided in this part, if a covered entity conducts with another covered entity (or within the same covered entity), using electronic media, a transaction for which the Secretary has adopted a standard under this part, the covered entity must conduct the transaction as a standard transaction.

(b) Exception for direct data entry transactions. A health care provider electing to use direct data entry offered by a health plan to conduct a transaction for which a standard has been adopted under this part must use the applicable data content and data condition requirements of the standard when conducting the transaction. The health care provider is not required to use the format requirements of the standard.

(c) Use of a business associate. A covered entity may use a business associate, including a health care clearinghouse, to conduct a transaction covered by this part. If a covered entity chooses to use a business associate to conduct all or part of a transaction on behalf of the covered entity, the covered entity must require the business associate to do the following:

(1) Comply with all applicable requirements of this part.

(2) Require any agent or subcontractor to comply with all applicable requirements of this part.

§162.925 Additional requirements for health plans.

(a) General rules.

(1) If an entity requests a health plan to conduct a transaction as a standard transaction, the health plan must do so.

(2) A health plan may not delay or reject a transaction, or attempt to adversely affect the other entity or the transaction, because the transaction is a standard transaction.

(3) A health plan may not reject a standard transaction on the basis that it contains data elements not needed or used by the health plan (for example, coordination of benefits information).

(4) A health plan may not offer an incentive for a health care provider to conduct a transaction covered by this part as a transaction described under the exception provided for in §162.923(b).

(5) A health plan that operates as a health care clearinghouse, or requires an entity to use a health care clearinghouse to receive, process, or transmit a standard transaction may not charge fees or costs in excess of the fees or costs for normal telecommunications that the entity incurs when it directly transmits, or receives, a standard transaction to, or from, a health plan.

(b) Coordination of benefits. If a health plan receives a standard transaction and coordinates benefits with another health plan (or another payer), it must store the coordination of benefits data it needs to forward the standard transaction to the other health plan (or other payer).

(c) Code sets. A health plan must meet each of the following requirements:

(1) Accept and promptly process any standard transaction that contains codes that are valid, as provided in subpart J of this part.

(2) Keep code sets for the current billing period and appeals periods still open to processing under the terms of the health plan's coverage.

§162.930 Additional rules for health care clearinghouses.

When acting as a business associate for another covered entity, a health care clearinghouse may perform the following functions:

(a) Receive a standard transaction on behalf of the covered entity and translate it into a nonstandard transaction (for example, nonstandard format and/or nonstandard data content) for transmission to the covered entity.

(b) Receive a nonstandard transaction (for example, nonstandard format and/or nonstandard data content) from the covered entity and translate it into a standard transaction for transmission on behalf of the covered entity.

§162.940 Exceptions from standards to permit testing of proposed modifications.

(a) Requests for an exception. An organization may request an exception from the use of a standard from the Secretary to test a proposed modification to that standard. For each proposed modification, the organization must meet the following requirements:

(1) Comparison to a current standard. Provide a detailed explanation, no more than 10 pages in length, of how the proposed modification would be a significant improvement to the current standard in terms of the following principles:

(i) Improve the efficiency and effectiveness of the health care system by leading to cost reductions for, or improvements in benefits from, electronic health care transactions.

(ii) Meet the needs of the health data standards user community, particularly health care providers, health plans, and health care clearinghouses.

(iii) Be uniform and consistent with the other standards adopted under this part and, as appropriate, with other private and public sector health data standards.

(iv) Have low additional development and implementation costs relative to the benefits of using the standard.

(v) Be supported by an ANSI-accredited SSO or other private or public organization that would maintain the standard over time.

(vi) Have timely development, testing, implementation, and updating procedures to achieve administrative simplification benefits faster.

(vii) Be technologically independent of the computer platforms and transmission protocols used in electronic health transactions, unless they are explicitly part of the standard.

(viii) Be precise, unambiguous, and as simple as possible.

(ix) Result in minimum data collection and paperwork burdens on users.

(x) Incorporate flexibility to adapt more easily to changes in the health care infrastructure (such as new services, organizations, and provider types) and information technology.

(2) Specifications for the proposed modification. Provide specifications for the proposed modification, including any additional system requirements.

(3) Testing of the proposed modification. Provide an explanation, no more than 5 pages in length, of how the organization intends to test the standard, including the number and types of health plans and health care providers expected to be involved in the test, geographical areas, and beginning and ending dates of the test.

(4) Trading partner concurrences. Provide written concurrences from trading partners who would agree to participate in the test.

(b) Basis for granting an exception. The Secretary may grant an initial exception, for a period not to exceed 3 years, based on, but not limited to, the following criteria:

(1) An assessment of whether the proposed modification demonstrates a significant improvement to the current standard.

(2) The extent and length of time of the exception.

(3) Consultations with DSMOs.

(c) Secretary's decision on exception. The Secretary makes a decision and notifies the organization requesting the exception whether the request is granted or denied.

(1) Exception granted. If the Secretary grants an exception, the notification includes the following information:

(i) The length of time for which the exception applies.

(ii) The trading partners and geographical areas the Secretary approves for testing.

(iii) Any other conditions for approving the exception.

(2) Exception denied. If the Secretary does not grant an exception, the notification explains the reasons the Secretary considers the proposed modification would not be a significant improvement to the current standard and any other rationale for the denial.

(d) Organization's report on test results. Within 90 days after the test is completed, an organization that receives an exception must submit a report on the results of the test, including a cost-benefit analysis, to a location specified by the Secretary by notice in the *Federal Register.*

(e) Extension allowed. If the report submitted in accordance with paragraph (d) of this section recommends a modification to the standard, the Secretary, on request, may grant an extension to the period granted for the exception.

Subpart J – Code Sets

§162.1000 General requirements.

When conducting a transaction covered by this part, a covered entity must meet the following requirements:

(a) Medical data code sets. Use the applicable medical data code sets described in §162.1002 as specified in the implementation specification adopted under this part that are valid at the time the health care is furnished.

(b) Nonmedical data code sets. Use the nonmedical data code sets as described in the implementation specifications adopted under this part that are valid at the time the transaction is initiated.

§162.1002 Medical data code sets.

The Secretary adopts the following code set maintaining organization's code sets as the standard medical data code sets:

(a) International Classification of Diseases, 9th Edition, Clinical Modification, (ICD-9-CM), Volumes 1 and 2 (including The Official ICD-9-CM Guidelines for Coding and Reporting), as maintained and distributed by HHS, for the following conditions:

(1) Diseases.

(2) Injuries.

(3) Impairments.

(4) Other health problems and their manifestations.

(5) Causes of injury, disease, impairment, or other health problems.

(b) International Classification of Diseases, 9th Edition, Clinical Modification, Volume 3 Procedures (including The Official ICD-9-CM Guidelines for Coding and Reporting), as maintained and distributed by HHS, for the following procedures or other actions taken for diseases, injuries, and impairments on hospital inpatients reported by hospitals:

(1) Prevention.

(2) Diagnosis.

(3) Treatment.

(4) Management.

(c) National Drug Codes (NDC), as maintained and distributed by HHS, in collaboration with drug manufacturers, for the following:

(1) Drugs.

(2) Biologics.

(d) Code on Dental Procedures and Nomenclature, as maintained and distributed by the American Dental Association, for dental services.

(e) The combination of Health Care Financing Administration Common Procedure Coding System (HCPCS), as maintained and distributed by HHS, and Current Procedural Terminology, Fourth Edition (CPT-4), as maintained and distributed by the American Medical Association, for physician services and other health care services. These services include, but are not limited to, the following:

(1) Physician services.

(2) Physical and occupational therapy services.

(3) Radiologic procedures.

(4) Clinical laboratory tests.

(5) Other medical diagnostic procedures.

(6) Hearing and vision services.

(7) Transportation services including ambulance.

(f) The Health Care Financing Administration Common Procedure Coding System (HCPCS), as maintained and distributed by HHS, for all other substances, equipment, supplies, or other items used in health care services. These items include, but are not limited to, the following:

(1) Medical supplies.

(2) Orthotic and prosthetic devices.

(3) Durable medical equipment.

§162.1011 Valid code sets.

Each code set is valid within the dates specified by the organization responsible for maintaining that code set.

Subpart K – Health Care Claims or Equivalent Encounter Information

§162.1101 Health care claims or equivalent encounter information transaction.

The health care claims or equivalent encounter information transaction is the transmission of either of the following:

(a) A request to obtain payment, and the necessary accompanying information from a health care provider to a health plan, for health care.

(b) If there is no direct claim, because the reimbursement contract is based on a mechanism other than charges or reimbursement rates for specific services, the transaction is the transmission of encounter information for the purpose of reporting health care.

§162.1102 Standards for health care claims or equivalent encounter information.

The Secretary adopts the following standards for the health care claims or equivalent encounter information transaction:

(a) Retail pharmacy drug claims. The National Council for Prescription Drug Programs (NCPDP) Telecommunication Standard Implementation Guide, Version 5 Release 1, September 1999, and equivalent NCPDP Batch Standard Batch Implementation Guide, Version 1 Release 0, February 1, 1996. The implementation specifications are available at the addresses specified in §162.920(a)(2).

(b) Dental Health Care Claims. The ASC X12N 837 – Health Care Claim: Dental, Version 4010, May 2000, Washington Publishing Company, 004010X097. The implementation specification is available at the addresses specified in §162.920(a)(1).

(c) Professional Health Care Claims. The ASC X12N 837 – Health Care Claim: Professional, Volumes 1 and 2, Version 4010, May 2000, Washington Publishing Company, 004010X098. The implementation specification is available at the addresses specified in §162.920(a)(1).

(d) Institutional Health Care Claims. The ASC X12N 837 – Health Care Claim: Institutional, Volumes 1 and 2, Version 4010, May 2000, Washington Publishing Company, 004010X096. The implementation specification is available at the addresses specified in §162.920(a)(1).

Subpart L – Eligibility for a Health Plan

§162.1201 Eligibility for a health plan transaction.

The eligibility for a health plan transaction is the transmission of either of the following:

(a) An inquiry from a health care provider to a health plan, or from one health plan to another health plan, to obtain any of the following information about a benefit plan for an enrollee:

(1) Eligibility to receive health care under the health plan.

(2) Coverage of health care under the health plan.

(3) Benefits associated with the benefit plan.

(b) A response from a health plan to a health care provider's (or another health plan's) inquiry described in paragraph (a) of this section.

§162.1202 Standards for eligibility for a health plan.

The Secretary adopts the following standards for the eligibility for a health plan transaction:

(a) Retail pharmacy drugs. The NCPDP Telecommunication Standard Implementation Guide, Version 5 Release 1, September 1999, and equivalent NCPDP Batch Standard Batch Implementation Guide, Version 1 Release 0, February 1, 1996. The implementation specifications are available at the addresses specified in §162.920(a)(2).

(b) Dental, professional, and institutional. The ASC X12N 270/271 – Health Care Eligibility Benefit Inquiry and Response, Version 4010, May 2000, Washington Publishing Company, 004010X092. The implementation specification is available at the addresses specified in §162.920(a)(1).

Subpart M – Referral Certification and Authorization

§162.1301 Referral certification and authorization transaction.

The referral certification and authorization transaction is any of the following transmissions:

(a) A request for the review of health care to obtain an authorization for the health care.

(b) A request to obtain authorization for referring an individual to another health care provider.

(c) A response to a request described in paragraph (a) or paragraph (b) of this section.

§162.1302 Standard for Referral certification and authorization.

The Secretary adopts the ASC X12N 278 – Health Care Services Review—Request for Review and Response, Version 4010, May 2000, Washington Publishing Company, 004010X094 as the standard for the referral certification and authorization transaction. The implementation specification is available at the addresses specified in §162.920(a)(1).

Subpart N – Health Care Claim Status

§162.1401 Health care claim status transaction.

A health care claim status transaction is the transmission of either of the following:

(a) An inquiry to determine the status of a health care claim.

(b) A response about the status of a health care claim.

§162.1402 Standard for health care claim status.

The Secretary adopts the ASC X12N 276/277 Health Care Claim Status Request and Response, Version 4010, May 2000, Washington Publishing Company, 004010X093 as the standard for the health care claim status transaction. The implementation specification is available at the addresses specified in §162.920(a)(1).

Subpart O – Enrollment and Disenrollment in a Health Plan

§162.1501 Enrollment and disenrollment in a health plan transaction.

The enrollment and disenrollment in a health plan transaction is the transmission of subscriber enrollment information to a health plan to establish or terminate insurance coverage.

§162.1502 Standard for enrollment and disenrollment in a health plan.

The Secretary adopts the ASC X12N 834 – Benefit Enrollment and Maintenance, Version 4010, May 2000, Washington Publishing Company, 004010X095 as the standard for the enrollment and disenrollment in a health plan transaction. The implementation specification is available at the addresses specified in §162.920(a)(1).

Subpart P – Health Care Payment and Remittance Advice

§162.1601 Health care payment and remittance advice transaction.

The health care payment and remittance advice transaction is the transmission of either of the following for health care:

(a) The transmission of any of the following from a health plan to a health care provider's financial institution:

(1) Payment.

(2) Information about the transfer of funds.

(3) Payment processing information.

(b) The transmission of either of the following from a health plan to a health care provider:

(1) Explanation of benefits.

(2) Remittance advice.

§162.1602 Standards for health care payment and remittance advice.

The Secretary adopts the following standards for the health care payment and remittance advice transaction:

(a) Retail pharmacy drug claims and remittance advice. The NCPDP Telecommunication Standard Implementation Guide, Version 5 Release 1, September 1999, and equivalent NCPDP Batch Standard Batch Implementation Guide, Version 1 Release 0, February 1, 1996. The implementation specifications are available at the addresses specified in §162.920(a)(2).

(b) Dental, professional, and institutional health care claims and remittance advice. The ASC X12N 835 – Health Care Claim Payment/Advice, Version 4010, May 2000, Washington Publishing Company, 004010X091. The implementation specification is available at the addresses specified in §162.920(a)(1).

Subpart Q – Health Plan Premium Payments

§162.1701 Health plan premium payments transaction.

The health plan premium payment transaction is the transmission of any of the following from the entity that is arranging for the provision of health care or is providing health care coverage payments for an individual to a health plan:

(a) Payment.

(b) Information about the transfer of funds.

(c) Detailed remittance information about individuals for whom premiums are being paid.

(d) Payment processing information to transmit health care premium payments including any of the following:

(1) Payroll deductions.

(2) Other group premium payments.

(3) Associated group premium payment information.

§162.1702 Standard for health plan premium payments.

The Secretary adopts the ASC X12N 820 – Payroll Deducted and Other Group Premium Payment for Insurance Products, Version 4010, May 2000, Washington Publishing Company, 004010X061 as the standard for the health plan premium payments transaction. The implementation specification is available at the addresses specified in §162.920(a)(1).

Subpart R – Coordination of Benefits

§162.1801 Coordination of benefits transaction.

The coordination of benefits transaction is the transmission from any entity to a health plan for the purpose of determining the relative payment responsibilities of the health plan, of either of the following for health care:

(a) Claims.

(b) Payment information.

§162.1802 Standards for coordination of benefits.

The Secretary adopts the following standards for the coordination of benefits information transaction:

(a) Retail pharmacy drug claims. The NCPDP Telecommunication Standard Implementation Guide, Version 5 Release 1, September 1999, and equivalent NCPDP Batch Standard Batch Implementation Guide, Version 1 Release 0, February 1, 1996. The implementation specifications are available at the addresses specified in §162.920(a)(2).

(b) Dental claims. The ASC X12N 837 – Health Care Claim: Dental, Version 4010, May 2000, Washington Publishing Company, 004010X097. The implementation specification is available at the addresses specified in §162.920(a)(1).

(c) Professional health care claims. The ASC X12N 837 – Health Care Claim: Professional, Volumes 1 and 2, Version 4010, May 2000, Washington Publishing Company, 004010X098. The implementation specification is available at the addresses specified in §162.920(a)(1).

(d) Institutional health care claims. The ASC X12N 837 – Health Care Claim: Institutional, Volumes 1 and 2, Version 4010, May 2000, Washington Publishing Company, 004010X096. The implementation specification is available at the addresses specified in §162.920(a)(1).

Authority: Secs. 1171 through 1179 of the Social Security Act (42 U.S.C. 1320d - 1320d-8), as added by sec. 262 of Public Law 104-191, 110 Stat. 2021-2031, and sec. 264 of Pub. L. 104-191, 110 Stat. 2033-2034 (42 U.S.C. 1320d-2 (note)).

(Catalog of Federal Domestic Assistance Program No. 93.774, Medicare—Supplementary Medical Insurance Program)

Dated: July 25, 2000
Donna Shalala
Secretary
    BILLING CODE 4120-01

Timeline

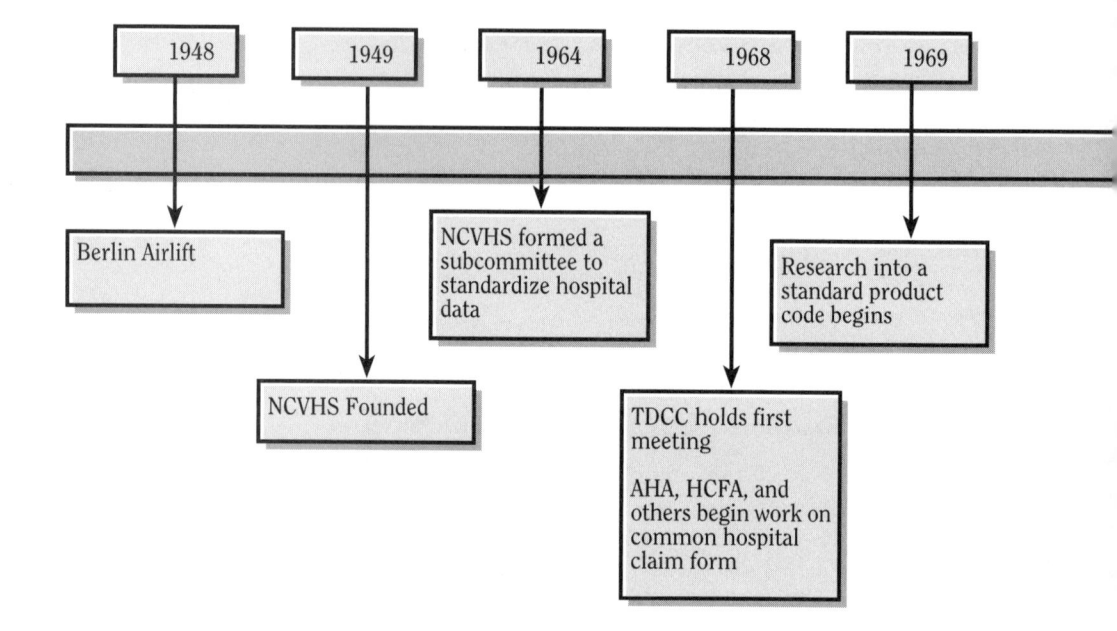

- **1948**: Berlin Airlift
- **1949**: NCVHS Founded
- **1964**: NCVHS formed a subcommittee to standardize hospital data
- **1968**: TDCC holds first meeting

  AHA, HCFA, and others begin work on common hospital claim form
- **1969**: Research into a standard product code begins

Timeline

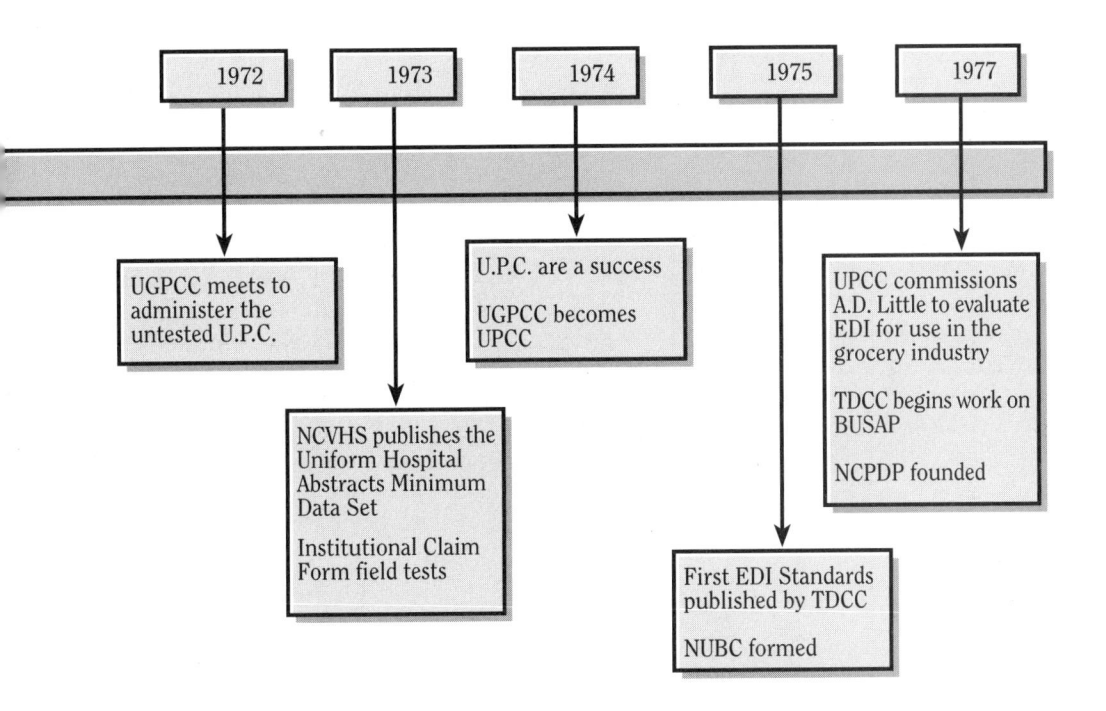

1972 — UGPCC meets to administer the untested U.P.C.

1973 — NCVHS publishes the Uniform Hospital Abstracts Minimum Data Set

Institutional Claim Form field tests

1974 — U.P.C. are a success

UGPCC becomes UPCC

1975 — First EDI Standards published by TDCC

NUBC formed

1977 — UPCC commissions A.D. Little to evaluate EDI for use in the grocery industry

TDCC begins work on BUSAP

NCPDP founded

continued

continued

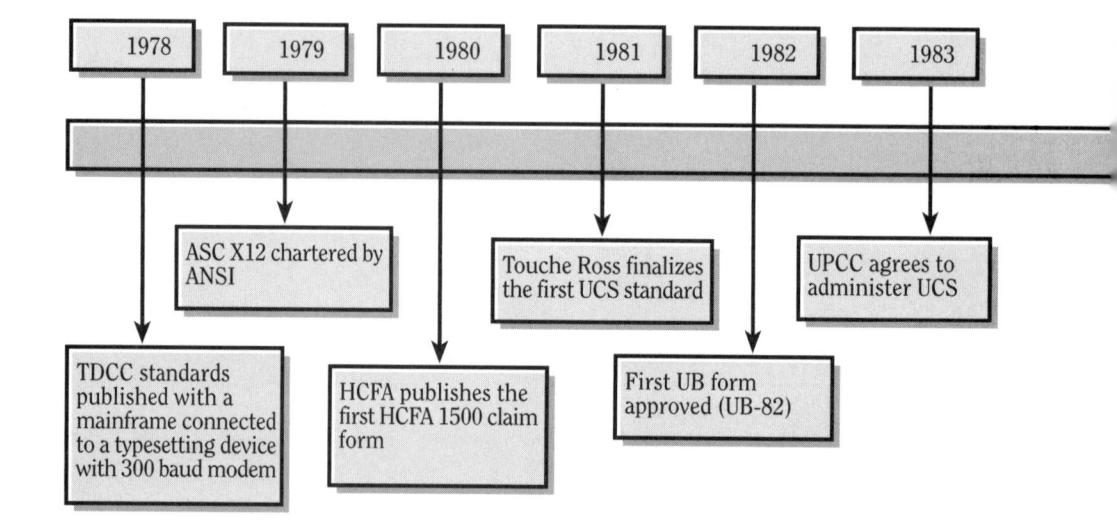

| 1978 | 1979 | 1980 | 1981 | 1982 | 1983 |

- **1978**: TDCC standards published with a mainframe connected to a typesetting device with 300 baud modem
- **1979**: ASC X12 chartered by ANSI
- **1980**: HCFA publishes the first HCFA 1500 claim form
- **1981**: Touche Ross finalizes the first UCS standard
- **1982**: First UB form approved (UB-82)
- **1983**: UPCC agrees to administer UCS

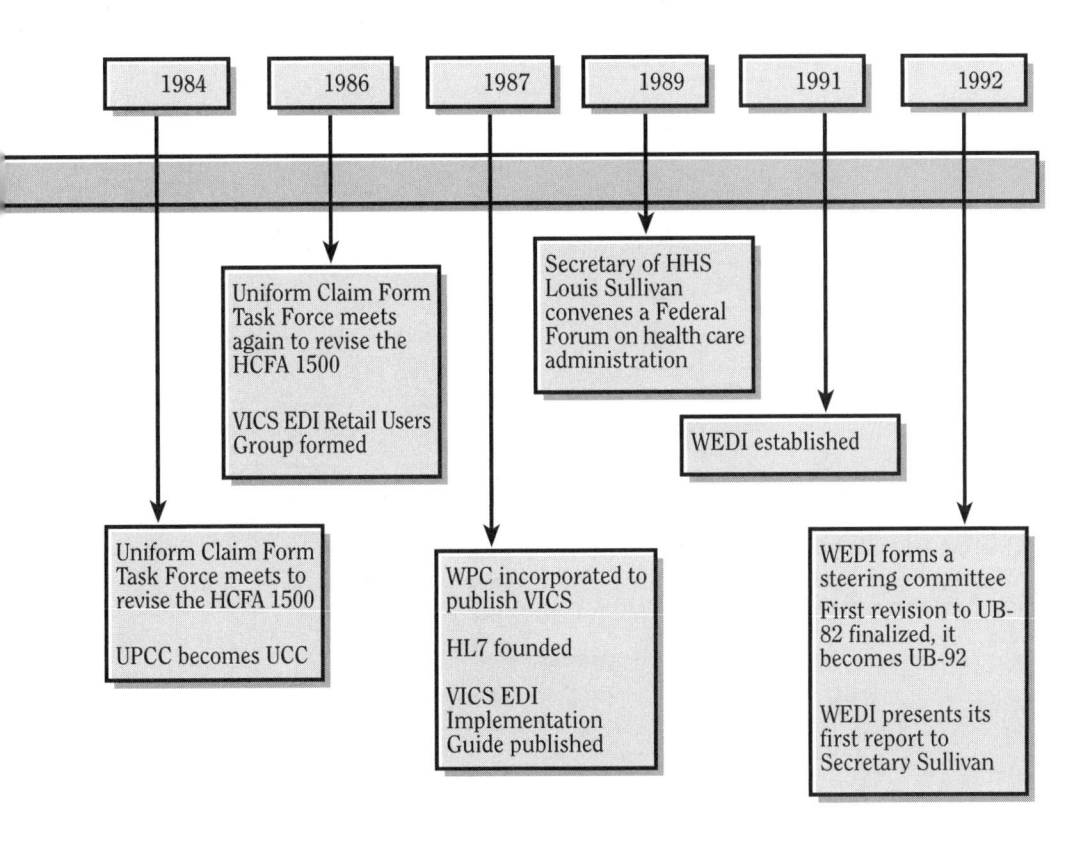

Timeline

1984
- Uniform Claim Form Task Force meets to revise the HCFA 1500
- UPCC becomes UCC

1986
- Uniform Claim Form Task Force meets again to revise the HCFA 1500
- VICS EDI Retail Users Group formed

1987
- WPC incorporated to publish VICS
- HL7 founded
- VICS EDI Implementation Guide published

1989
- Secretary of HHS Louis Sullivan convenes a Federal Forum on health care administration

1991
- WEDI established

1992
- WEDI forms a steering committee
- First revision to UB-82 finalized, it becomes UB-92
- WEDI presents its first report to Secretary Sullivan

continued

continued

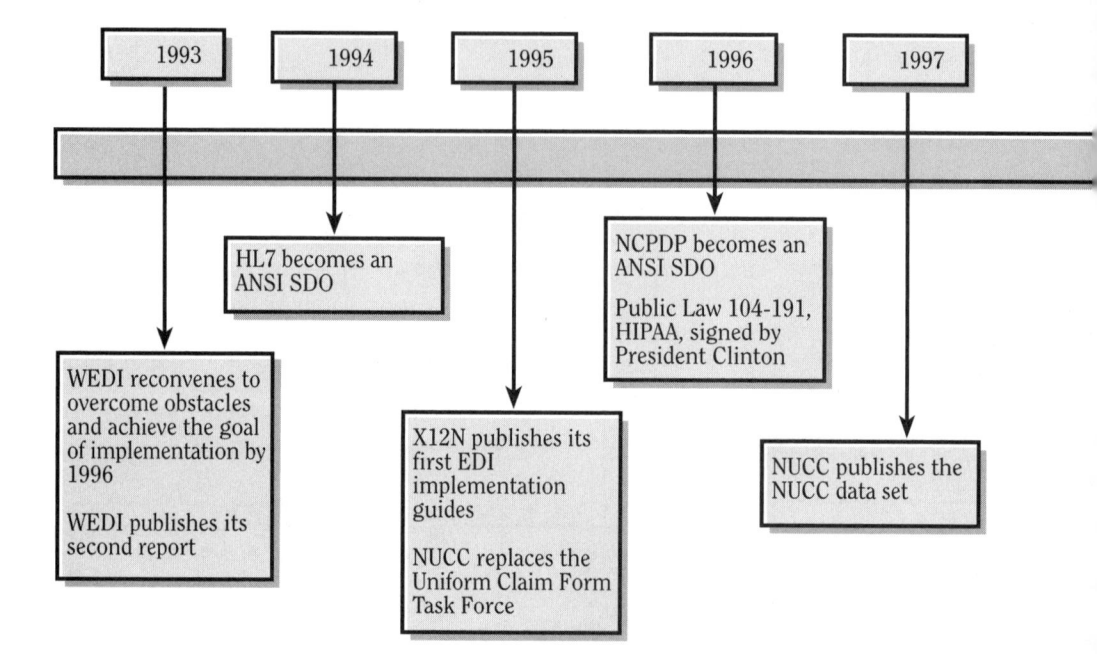

1993

WEDI reconvenes to overcome obstacles and achieve the goal of implementation by 1996

WEDI publishes its second report

1994

HL7 becomes an ANSI SDO

1995

X12N publishes its first EDI implementation guides

NUCC replaces the Uniform Claim Form Task Force

1996

NCPDP becomes an ANSI SDO

Public Law 104-191, HIPAA, signed by President Clinton

1997

NUCC publishes the NUCC data set

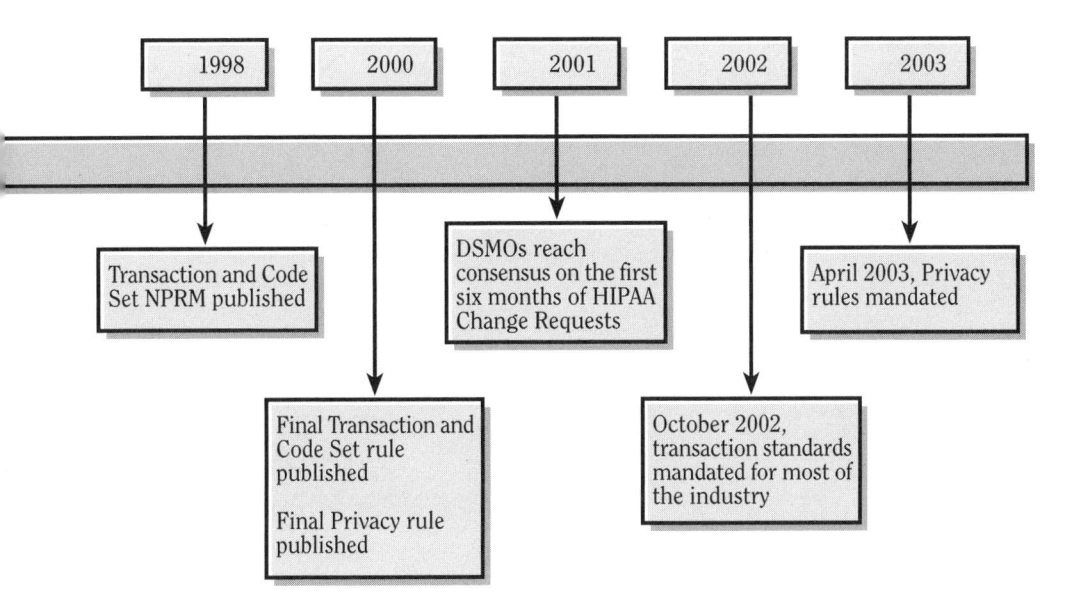

Timeline

1998	2000	2001	2002	2003

- **1998:** Transaction and Code Set NPRM published
- **2000:** Final Transaction and Code Set rule published; Final Privacy rule published
- **2001:** DSMOs reach consensus on the first six months of HIPAA Change Requests
- **2002:** October 2002, transaction standards mandated for most of the industry
- **2003:** April 2003, Privacy rules mandated

HIPAA Supplemental Information Contents*

Part I
(A HIPAA Glossary & Acronymary)

gives general definitions and explanations of HIPAA-related terms and acronyms.

Part II
(Consolidated HIPAA Administrative Simplification Final Rule Definitions)

shows all definitions included in the final HIPAA A/S rules as of 01/20/2001.

Part III
(Purpose & Maintenance)

is self-explanatory.

*Glossary republished by permission of the Workgroup for Electronic Data Interchange. Lead author: Zon Owen.

Part I

A HIPAA Glossary & Acronymary

Please note that whenever a definition occurs in both Part I and Part II, the Part II entry will be the more legally compelling one.

AAHomecare: See *American Association for Homecare*.

Accredited Standards Committee (ASC): An organization that has been accredited by *ANSI* for the development of *American National Standards*.

ACG: Ambulatory Care Group.

ACH: See *Automated Clearinghouse*.

ADA: See *American Dental Association*.

ADG: Ambulatory Diagnostic Group.

Administrative Code Sets: *Code sets* that characterize a general business situation, rather than a medical condition or service. Under HIPAA, these are sometimes referred to as *non-clinical* or *non-medical code sets*. Compare to *medical code sets*.

Administrative Services Only (ASO): An arrangement whereby a self-insured entity contracts with a *Third Party Administrator (TPA)* to administer a *health plan*.

Administrative Simplification (A/S): Title II, Subtitle F, of HIPAA, which gives HHS the authority to mandate the use of *standards* for the electronic exchange of health care data; to specify what *medical* and *administrative code sets* should be used within those *standards*; to require the use of national identification systems for health care patients, providers, payers (or plans), and employers (or sponsors); and to specify the types of measures required to protect the security and privacy of personally identifiable health care information. This is also the name of Title II, Subtitle F, Part C of HIPAA.

AFEHCT: See *Association for Electronic Health Care Transactions*.

AHA: See *American Hospital Association*.

AHIMA: See *American Health Information Management Association*.

AMA: See *American Medical Association*.

Ambulatory Payment Class (APC): A payment type for outpatient PPS claims.

Amendment: See *Amendments and Corrections*.

Amendments and Corrections: In the final privacy rule, an amendment to a record would indicate that the data is in dispute while retaining the original information, whereas a correction to a record would alter or replace the original record.

American Association for Homecare (AAHomecare): An industry association for the home care industry, including home IV therapy, home medical services and manufacturers, and home health providers. *AAHomecare* was created through the merger of the Health Industry Distributors Association's Home Care Division (HIDA Home Care), the Home Health Services and Staffing Association (HHSSA), and the National Association for Medical Equipment Services (NAMES).

American Dental Association (ADA): A professional organization for dentists. The *ADA* maintains a hardcopy dental claim form and the associated claim submission specifications, and also maintains the *Current Dental Terminology (CDT) medical code set*. The *ADA* and the *Dental Content Committee (DeCC)*, which it hosts, have formal consultative roles under HIPAA.

American Health Information Management Association (AHIMA): An association of health information management professionals. *AHIMA* sponsors some HIPAA educational seminars.

American Hospital Association (AHA): A health care industry association that represents the concerns of institutional providers. The *AHA* hosts the *NUBC*, which has a formal consultative role under HIPAA.

American Medical Association (AMA): A professional organization for physicians. The *AMA* is the secretariat of the *NUCC*, which has a formal consultative role under HIPAA. The *AMA* also maintains the *Current Procedural Terminology (CPT) medical code set*.

American Medical Informatics Association (AMIA): A professional organization that promotes the development and use of medical informatics for patient care, teaching, research, and health care administration.

American National Standards (ANS): Standards developed and approved by organizations accredited by *ANSI*.

American National Standards Institute (ANSI): An organization that accredits various standards-setting committees and monitors their compliance with the open rule-making process that they must follow to qualify for ANSI accreditation. HIPAA prescribes that the *standards* mandated under it be developed by ANSI-accredited bodies whenever practical.

American Society for Testing and Materials (ASTM): A standards group that has published general guidelines for the development of standards, including those for health care identifiers. ASTM Committee E31 on Healthcare Informatics develops standards on information used within healthcare.

AMIA: See *American Medical Informatics Association*.

ANS: See *American National Standards*.

ANSI: See *American National Standards Institute*. Also see Part II, 45 CFR 160.103.

APC: See *Ambulatory Payment Class*.

A/S, A.S., or AS: See *Administrative Simplification*.

ASC: See *Accredited Standards Committee*.

ASO: See *Administrative Services Only*.

ASPIRE: *AFEHCT's* Administrative Simplification Print Image Research Effort work group.

Association for Electronic Health Care Transactions (AFEHCT): An organization that promotes the use of *EDI* in the health care industry.

ASTM: See *American Society for Testing and Materials*.

Automated Clearinghouse (ACH): See *Health Care Clearinghouse*.

BA: See *Business Associate*.

BBA: The Balanced Budget Act of 1997.

BBRA: The Balanced Budget Refinement Act of 1999.

BCBSA: See *Blue Cross and Blue Shield Association*.

Biometric Identifier: An identifier based on some physical characteristic, such as a fingerprint.

Blue Cross and Blue Shield Association (BCBSA): The association that represents the common interests of Blue Cross and Blue Shield *health plans*. The *BCBSA* serves as the administrator for the *Health Care Code Maintenance Committee* and also helps maintain the HCPCS Level II codes.

BP: See *Business Partner*.

Business Associate (BA): A person or organization that performs a function or activity on behalf of a *covered entity*, but is not part of the *covered entity's workforce*. A *business associate* can also be a *covered entity* in its own right. Also see Part II, 45 CFR 160.103.

Business Model: A model of a business organization or process.

Business Partner (BP): See *Business Associate*.

Business Relationships:

- The term *agent* is often used to describe a person or organization that assumes some of the responsibilities of another one. This term has been avoided in the final rules so that a more HIPAA-specific meaning could be used for *business associate*. The term *business partner (BP)* was originally used for *business associate*.
- A *Third Party Administrator (TPA)* is a *business associate* that performs claims administration and related business functions for a self-insured entity.
- Under HIPAA, a *health care clearinghouse* is a *business associate* that translates data to or from a standard format on behalf of a *covered entity*.
- The HIPAA Security NPRM used the term *Chain of Trust Agreement* to describe the type of contract that would be needed to extend the responsibility to protect health care data across a series of subcontractual relationships.

- While a *business associate* is an entity that performs certain business functions for you, a *trading partner* is an external entity, such as a customer, with which you do business. This relationship can be formalized via a *trading partner agreement*. It is quite possible to be a *trading partner* of an entity for some purposes, and a *business associate* of that entity for other purposes.

Cabulance: A taxi cab that also functions as an ambulance.

CBO: Congressional Budget Office or Cost Budget Office.

CDC: See *Centers for Disease Control and Prevention*.

CDT: See *Current Dental Terminology*.

CE: See *Covered Entity*.

CEFACT: See *United Nations Centre for Facilitation of Procedures and Practices for Administration, Commerce, and Transport (UN/CEFACT)*.

CEN: European Center for Standardization, or Comite Europeen de Normalisation.

Centers for Disease Control and Prevention (CDC): An organization that maintains several *code sets* included in the HIPAA *standards*, including the *ICD-9-CM* codes.

Center for Healthcare Information Management (CHIM): A health information technology industry association.

CFR or C.F.R.: Code of Federal Regulations.

Chain of Trust (COT): A term used in the HIPAA Security NPRM for a pattern of agreements that extend protection of health care data by requiring that each *covered entity* that shares health care data with another entity require that that entity provide protections comparable to those provided by the *covered entity*, and that that entity, in turn, require that any other entities with which it shares the data satisfy the same requirements.

CHAMPUS: Civilian Health and Medical Program of the Uniformed Services.

CHIM: See *Center for Healthcare Information Management*.

CHIME: See *College of Healthcare Information Management Executives*.

CHIP: Child Health Insurance Program.

Claim Adjustment Reason Codes: A national *administrative code set* that identifies the reasons for any differences or adjustments between the original provider charge for a claim or service and the payer's payment for it. This *code set* is used in the *X12 835* Claim Payment & Remittance Advice and the *X12 837* Claim transactions and is maintained by the *Health Care Code Maintenance Committee*.

Claim Attachment: Any of a variety of hardcopy forms or electronic records needed to process a claim in addition to the claim itself.

Claim Medicare Remark Codes: See *Medicare Remittance Advice Remark Codes*.

Claim Status Codes: A national *administrative code set* that identifies the status of health care claims. This *code set* is used in the *X12 277* Claim Status Notification transaction, and is maintained by the *Health Care Code Maintenance Committee*.

Claim Status Category Codes: A national *administrative code set* that indicates the general category of the status of health care claims. This *code set* is used in the *X12 277* Claim Status Notification transaction, and is maintained by the *Health Care Code Maintenance Committee*.

Clearinghouse: See *Health Care Clearinghouse*.

CLIA: Clinical Laboratory Improvement Amendments.

Clinical Code Sets: See *Medical Code Sets*.

CM: See *ICD*.

COB: See *Coordination of Benefits*.

Code Set: Under HIPAA, this is any set of codes used to encode *data elements*, such as tables of terms, medical concepts, medical diagnostic codes, or medical procedure codes. This includes both the codes and their descriptions. Also see Part II, 45 CFR 162.103.

Code Set Maintaining Organization: Under HIPAA, this is an organization that creates and maintains the *code sets* adopted by the *Secretary* for use in the transactions for which *standards* are adopted. Also see Part II, 45 CFR 162.103.

College of Healthcare Information Management Executives (CHIME): A professional organization for health care Chief Information Officers (CIOs).

Comment: Public commentary on the merits or appropriateness of proposed or potential regulations provided in response to an *NPRM*, an *NOI*, or other federal regulatory notice.

Common Control: See Part II, 45 CFR 164.504.

Common Ownership: See Part II, 45 CFR 164.504.

Compliance Date: Under HIPAA, this is the date by which a *covered entity* must comply with a *standard*, an *implementation specification*, or a *modification*. This is usually 24 months after the *effective date* of the associated final rule for most entities, but 36 months after the *effective date* for *small health plans*. For future changes in the *standards*, the *compliance date* would be at least 180 days after the *effective date*, but it can be longer for *small health plans* and for complex changes. Also see Part II, 45 CFR 160.103.

Computer-based Patient Record Institute (CPRI)–Healthcare Open Systems and Trials (HOST): An industry organization that promotes the use of healthcare information systems, including electronic healthcare records.

Contrary: See Part II, 45 CFR 160.202.

Coordination of Benefits (COB): A process for determining the respective responsibilities of two or more *health plans* that have some financial responsibility for a medical claim. Also called *cross-over*.

CORF: Comprehensive Outpatient Rehabilitation Facility.

Correction: See *Amendments and Corrections*.

Correctional Institution: See Part II, 45 CFR 162.103.

COT: See *Chain of Trust*.

Covered Entity (CE): Under HIPAA, this is a *health plan*, a *health care clearinghouse*, or a *health care provider* who transmits any health information in electronic form in connection with a HIPAA transaction. Also see Part II, 45 CFR 160.103.

Covered Function: Functions that make an entity a *health plan*, a *health care provider*, or a *health care clearinghouse*. Also see Part II, 45 CFR 164.501.

CPRI-HOST: See the *Computer-based Patient Record Institute–Healthcare Open Systems and Trials*.

CPT: See *Current Procedural Terminology*.

Cross-over: See *Coordination of Benefits*.

Cross-walk: See *Data Mapping*.

Current Dental Terminology (CDT): A *medical code set*, maintained and copyrighted by the *ADA*, that has been selected for use in the HIPAA transactions.

Current Procedural Terminology (CPT): A *medical code set*, maintained and copyrighted by the *AMA*, that has been selected for use under HIPAA for non-institutional and non-dental professional transactions.

Data Aggregation: See Part II, 45 CFR 164.501.

Data Condition: A description of the circumstances in which certain data is required. Also see Part II, 45 CFR 162.103.

Data Content: Under HIPAA, this is all the *data elements* and *code sets* inherent to a transaction but not related to the format of the transaction. Also see Part II, 45 CFR 162.103.

Data Content Committee (DCC) See *Designated Data Content Committee*.

Data Council: A coordinating body within *HHS* that has high-level responsibility for overseeing the implementation of the *A/S* provisions of HIPAA.

Data Dictionary (DD): A document or system that characterizes the *data content* of a system.

Data Element: Under HIPAA, this is the smallest named unit of information in a transaction. Also see Part II, 45 CFR 162.103.

Data Interchange Standards Association (DISA): A body that provides administrative services to *X12* and several other standards-related groups.

Data Mapping: The process of matching *data elements* or individual code values of one set to their closest equivalents in another set. This is sometimes called a *cross-walk*.

Data Model: A conceptual model of the information needed to support a business function or process.

Data-Related Concepts:

- *Clinical* or *Medical Code Sets* identify medical conditions and the procedures, services, equipment, and supplies used to deal with them. *Non-clinical (non-medical)* or *administrative code sets* identify or characterize entities and events in a manner that facilitates an administrative process.

- HIPAA defines a *data element* as the smallest unit of named information. In X12 language, that would be a *simple data element*. But X12 also has *composite data elements*, which aren't really *data elements* but are groups of closely related *data elements* that can repeat as a group. X12 also has *segments*, which are also groups of related *data elements* that tend to occur together, such as street address, city, and state. These *segments* can sometimes repeat, or one or more segments may be part of a *loop* that can repeat. For example, you might have a claim loop that occurs once for each claim, and a claim service loop that occurs once for each service included in a claim. An X12 *transaction* is a collection of such loops, segments, etc. that supports a specific business process, whereas an X12 *transmission* is a communication session during which one or more X12 transactions is transmitted. *Data elements* and groups may also be combined into records that make up conventional files or into the tables or segments used by database management systems, or DBMSs.

- A *designated code set* is a *code set* that has been specified within the body of a rule. These are usually *medical code sets*. Many other *code sets* are incorporated into the rules by reference to a separate document, such as an *implementation guide*, that identifies one or more such *code sets*. These are usually *administrative code sets*.

- *Electronic data* is data that is recorded or transmitted electronically, and *non-electronic data* is everything else. Special cases include data transmitted by fax and audio systems, which is, in principle, transmitted electronically but lacks the underlying structure usually needed to support automated interpretation of its contents.

- *Encoded data* is data represented by some identification or classification scheme, such as a provider identifier or a procedure code. *Non-encoded data* is more free-form, such as a name, a street address, or a description. Theoretically, of course, all data, including grunts and smiles, is encoded.

- For HIPAA purposes, *internal* data, or *internal code sets*, are *data elements* that are fully specified within the HIPAA *implementation guides*. For X12 transactions, changes to the associated code values and descriptions must be approved via the normal standards development process and can only be used in the revised version of the standards affected. X12 transactions also use many coding and identification schemes that are maintained by *external* organizations. For these *external code sets*, the associated values and descriptions can change at any time and still be usable in any version of the X12 transactions that uses the associated *code set*.

- *Individually identifiable data* is data that can be readily associated with a specific individual. Examples include a name, a personal identifier, or a full street address. If life were simple, everything else would be *non-identifiable* data. But even if you remove the obviously identifiable data from a record, other *data elements* present can also be used to *re-identify* it. For example, a birth date and a

ZIP code might be sufficient to re-identify half the records in a file. The re-identifiability of data can be limited by omitting, aggregating, or altering such data to the extent that the risk of it being *re-identified* is acceptable.

- A specific form of data representation, such as an X12 transaction, will generally include some *structural data* needed to identify and interpret the transaction itself, as well as the *business data content* that the transaction is designed to transmit. Under HIPAA, when an alternate form of data collection such as a browser is used, such *structural* or *format-related data elements* can be ignored as long as the appropriate *business data content* is used.
- *Structured data* is data that has a meaning that can be inferred to at least some extent based on its absolute or relative location in a separately defined data structure. This structure could be the blocks on a form, the fields in a record, the relative positions of *data elements* in an X12 segment, etc. *Unstructured data*, such as a memo or an image, lacks such clues.

Data Set: See Part II, 45 CFR 162.103.

DCC: See *Designated Data Content Committee*.

D-Codes: A subset of the HCPCS Level II *medical code set* with a high-order value of "D" that has been used to identify certain dental procedures. The final HIPAA transactions and code sets rule states that these *D-codes* will be dropped from the *HCPCS*, and that *CDT codes* will be used to identify all dental procedures.

DD: See *Data Dictionary*.

DDE: See *Direct Data Entry*.

DeCC: See *Dental Content Committee*.

Dental Content Committee (DeCC): An organization, hosted by the *American Dental Association*, that maintains the data content specifications for dental billing. The *Dental Content Committee* has a formal consultative role under HIPAA for all transactions affecting dental health care services.

Descriptor: The text defining a code in a *code set*. Also see Part II, 45 CFR 162.103.

Designated Code Set: A *medical code set* or an *administrative code set* that *HHS* has designated for use in one or more of the HIPAA *standards*.

Designated Data Content Committee or Designated DCC: An organization that *HHS* has designated for oversight of the business data content of one or more of the HIPAA-mandated transaction *standards*.

Designated Record Set: See Part II, 45 CFR 164.501.

Designated Standard: A *standard* which *HHS* has designated for use under the authority provided by HIPAA.

Designated Standard Maintenance Organization (DSMO): See Part II, 45 CFR 162.103.

DHHS: See *HHS*.

DICOM: See *Digital Imaging and Communications in Medicine*.

Digital Imaging and Communications in Medicine (DICOM): A *standard* for communicating images, such as x-rays, in a digitized form. This *standard* could become part of the HIPAA claim attachments *standards*.

Direct Data Entry (DDE): Under HIPAA, this is the direct entry of data that is immediately transmitted into a health plan's computer. Also see Part II, 45 CFR 162.103.

Direct Treatment Relationship: See Part II, 45 CFR 164.501.

DISA: See *Data Interchange Standards Association*.

Disclosure: Release or divulgence of information by an entity to persons or organizations outside of that entity. Also see Part II, 45 CFR 164.501.

Disclosure History: Under HIPAA, this is a list of any entities that have received personally identifiable health care information for uses unrelated to treatment and payment.

DME: Durable Medical Equipment.

DMEPOS: Durable Medical Equipment, Prosthetics, Orthotics, and Supplies.

DMERC: See *Medicare Durable Medical Equipment Regional Carrier*.

Draft Standard for Trial Use (DSTU): An archaic term for any *X12 standard* that has been approved since the most recent release of X12 *American National Standards*. The current equivalent term is *"X12 standard."*

DRG: Diagnosis Related Group.

DSMO: See *Designated Standard Maintenance Organization*.

DSTU: See *Draft Standard for Trial Use*.

EC: See *Electronic Commerce*.

EDI: See *Electronic Data Interchange*.

EDIFACT: See *United Nations Rules for Electronic Data Interchange for Administration, Commerce, and Transport (UN/EDIFACT)*.

EDI Translator: A software tool for accepting an EDI transmission and converting the data into another format or for converting a non-EDI data file into an EDI format for transmission.

Effective Date: Under HIPAA, this is the date that a final rule is effective, which is usually 60 days after it is published in the Federal Register.

EFT: Electronic Funds Transfer.

EHNAC: See *Electronic Healthcare Network Accreditation Commission*.

EIN: Employer Identification Number.

Electronic Commerce (EC): The exchange of business information by electronic means.

Electronic Data Interchange (EDI): This usually means X12 and similar variable-length formats for the electronic exchange of structured data. It is sometimes used more broadly to mean any electronic exchange of formatted data.

Electronic Healthcare Network Accreditation Commission (EHNAC): An organization that tests transactions for consistency with the HIPAA requirements and that accredits *health care clearinghouses*.

Electronic Media: See Part II, 45 CFR 162.103.

Electronic Media Claims (EMC): This term usually refers to a flat file format used to transmit or transport claims, such as the 192-byte UB-92 Institutional EMC format and the 320-byte Professional EMC NSF.

Electronic Remittance Advice (ERA): Any of several electronic formats for explaining the payments of health care claims.

EMC: See *Electronic Media Claims*.

EMR: Electronic Medical Record.

EOB: Explanation of Benefits.

EOMB: Explanation of Medicare Benefits, Explanation of Medicaid Benefits, or Explanation of Member Benefits.

EPSDT: Early & Periodic Screening, Diagnosis, and Treatment.

ERA: See *Electronic Remittance Advice*.

ERISA: The Employee Retirement Income Security Act of 1974.

ESRD: End-Stage Renal Disease.

FAQ(s): Frequently Asked Question(s).

FDA: Food and Drug Administration.

FERPA: Family Educational Rights and Privacy Act.

FFS: Fee-for-Service.

FI: See *Medicare Part A Fiscal Intermediary*.

Flat File: This term usually refers to a file that consists of a series of fixed-length records that include some sort of record type code.

Format: Under HIPAA, those *data elements* that provide or control the enveloping or hierarchical structure or assist in identifying data content of a transaction. Also see Part II, 45 CFR 162.103. Also see *Data-Related Concepts*.

FR or F.R.: Federal Register.

GAO: General Accounting Office.

GLBA: The Gramm-Leach-Bliley Act.

Group Health Plan: Under HIPAA, an employee welfare benefit plan that provides for medical care and that either has 50 or more participants or is administered by another business entity. Also see Part II, 45 CFR 160.103.

HCFA: See the *Health Care Financing Administration*. Also see Part II, 45 CFR 160.103.

HCFA-1450: *HCFA*'s name for the institutional uniform claim form, or UB-92.

HCFA-1500: *HCFA*'s name for the professional uniform claim form. Also known as the UCF-1500.

HCFA Common Procedural Coding System (HCPCS): A *medical code set* that identifies health care procedures, equipment, and supplies for claim submission purposes. It has been selected for use in the HIPAA transactions. *HCPCS* Level I contains numeric *CPT* codes, which are maintained by the *AMA*. *HCPCS* Level II contains alphanumeric codes used to identify various items and services that are not included in the *CPT medical code set*. These are maintained by *HCFA*, the *BCBSA*, and the *HIAA*. *HCPCS* Level III contains alphanumeric codes that are assigned by Medicaid state agencies to identify additional items and services not included in levels I or II. These are usually called "local codes" and must have "W," "X," "Y," or "Z" in the first position. *HCPCS* Procedure Modifier Codes can be used with all three levels, with the WA–ZY range used for locally assigned procedure modifiers.

HCPCS: See *HCFA Common Procedural Coding System*. Also see Part II, 45 CFR 162.103.

Health and Human Services (HHS): The Federal government department that has overall responsibility for implementing HIPAA.

Health Care: See Part II, 45 CFR 160.103.

Health Care Clearinghouse: Under HIPAA, this is an entity that processes or facilitates the processing of information received from another entity in a nonstandard format or containing nonstandard *data content* into standard *data elements* or a standard transaction, or it is an entity that receives a standard transaction from another entity and processes or facilitates the processing of that information into nonstandard format or nonstandard *data content* for a receiving entity. Also see Part II, 45 CFR 160.103.

Health Care Code Maintenance Committee: An organization administered by the *BCBSA* that is responsible for maintaining certain coding schemes used in the X12 transactions and elsewhere. These include the *Claim Adjustment Reason Codes*, the *Claim Status Category Codes*, and the *Claim Status Codes*.

Health Care Component: See Part II, 45 CFR 164.504.

Healthcare Financial Management Association (HFMA): An organization for the improvement of the financial management of healthcare-related organizations. The *HFMA* sponsors some HIPAA educational seminars.

Health Care Financing Administration (HCFA): The *HHS* agency responsible for Medicare and parts of Medicaid. *HCFA* has historically maintained the UB-92 institutional EMC format specifications, the professional EMC *NSF* specifications, and specifications for various certifications and authorizations used by the Medicare and Medicaid programs. *HCFA* also maintains the *HCPCS medical code set* and the *Medicare Remittance Advice Remark Codes administrative code set*.

Healthcare Information Management Systems Society (HIMSS): A professional organization for healthcare information and management systems professionals.

Health Care Operations: See Part II, 45 CFR 164.501.

Health Care Provider: See Part II, 45 CFR 160.103.

Health Care Provider Taxonomy Committee: An organization administered by the *NUCC* that is responsible for maintaining the Provider Taxonomy coding scheme used in the X12 transactions. The detailed code maintenance is done in coordination with *X12N/TG2/WG15*.

Health Industry Business Communications Council (HIBCC): A council of health care industry associations that has developed a number of technical standards used within the health care industry.

Health Informatics Standards Board (HISB): An ANSI-accredited standards group that has developed an inventory of candidate standards for consideration as possible HIPAA standards.

Health Information: See Part II, 45 CFR 160.103.

Health Insurance Association of America (HIAA): An industry association that represents the interests of commercial health care insurers. The *HIAA* participates in the maintenance of some *code sets*, including the *HCPCS* Level II codes.

Health Insurance Issuer: See Part II, 45 CFR 160.103.

Health Insurance Portability and Accountability Act of 1996 (HIPAA): A Federal law that allows persons to qualify immediately for comparable health insurance coverage when they change their employment relationships. Title II, Subtitle F, of HIPAA gives *HHS* the authority to mandate the use of standards for the electronic exchange of health care data; to specify what *medical* and *administrative code sets* should be used within those standards; to require the use of national identification systems for health care patients, providers, payers (or plans), and employers (or sponsors); and to specify the types of measures required to protect the security and privacy of personally identifiable health care information. Also known as the Kennedy-Kassebaum Bill, the Kassebaum-Kennedy Bill, K2, or Public Law 104-191.

Health Level Seven (HL7): An ANSI-accredited group that defines standards for the cross-platform exchange of information within a health care organization. *HL7* is responsible for specifying the Level Seven OSI standards for the health industry. The *X12 275* transaction will probably incorporate the HL7 CRU message to transmit claim attachments as part of a future HIPAA claim attachments standard. The HL7 Attachment SIG is responsible for the HL7 portion of this *standard*.

Health Maintenance Organization (HMO): See Part II, 45 CFR 160.103.

Health Oversight Agency: See Part II, 45 CFR 164.501.

Health Plan: See Part II, 45 CFR 160.103.

Health Plan ID: See *National Payer ID*.

HEDIC: The Healthcare EDI Coalition.

HEDIS: Health Employer Data and Information Set.

HFMA: See *Healthcare Financial Management Association*.

HHA: Home Health Agency.

HHIC: The Hawaii Health Information Corporation.

HHS: See *Health and Human Services*. Also see Part II, 45 CFR 160.103.

HIAA: See *Health Insurance Association of America*.

HIBCC: See *Health Industry Business Communications Council*.

HIMSS: See *Healthcare Information Management Systems Society*.

HIPAA: See *Health Insurance Portability and Accountability Act of 1996*.

HIPAA Data Dictionary or HIPAA DD: A *data dictionary* that defines and cross-references the contents of all X12 transactions included in the HIPAA mandate. It is maintained by *X12N/TG3*.

HISB: See *Health Informatics Standards Board*.

HL7: See *Health Level Seven*.

HMO: See *Health Maintenance Organization*.

HPAG: The HIPAA Policy Advisory Group, a BCBSA subgroup.

HPSA: Health Professional Shortage Area.

Hybrid Entity: A *covered entity* whose covered functions are not its primary functions. Also see Part II, 45 CFR 164.504.

IAIABC: See *International Association of Industrial Accident Boards and Commissions*.

ICD & ICD-n-CM & ICD-n-PCS: International Classification of Diseases, with "n" = "9" for Revision 9 or "10" for Revision 10, with "CM" = "Clinical Modification," and with "PCS" = "Procedure Coding System."

ICF: Intermediate Care Facility.

IDN: Integrated Delivery Network.

IIHI: See *Individually Identifiable Health Information*.

IG: See *Implementation Guide*.

IHC: Internet Healthcare Coalition.

Implementation Guide (IG): A document explaining the proper use of a *standard* for a specific business purpose. The X12N HIPAA IGs are the primary reference documents used by those implementing the associated transactions and are incorporated into the HIPAA regulations by reference.

Implementation Specification: Under HIPAA, this contains the specific instructions for implementing a *standard*. Also see Part II, 45 CFR 160.103. See also *Implementation Guide*.

Indirect Treatment Relationship: See Part II, 45 CFR 164.501.

Individual: See Part II, 45 CFR 164.501.

Individually Identifiable Health Information (IIHI): See Part II, 45 CFR 164.501.

Information Model: A conceptual model of the information needed to support a business function or process.

Inmate: See Part II, 45 CFR 164.501.

International Association of Industrial Accident Boards and Commissions (IAIABC): One of their standards is under consideration for use for the First Report of Injury *standard* under HIPAA.

International Classification of Diseases (ICD): A *medical code set* maintained by the *World Health Organization (WHO)*. The primary purpose of this *code set* was to classify causes of death. A US extension, maintained by the *NCHS* within the *CDC*, identifies morbidity factors, or diagnoses. The *ICD-9-CM* codes have been selected for use in the HIPAA transactions.

International Organization for Standardization (ISO): An organization that coordinates the development and adoption of numerous international standards. "ISO" is not an acronym; it's the Greek word for "equal."

International Standards Organization: See *International Organization for Standardization (ISO)*.

IOM: The Institute of Medicine.

IPA: Independent Providers Association.

IRB: Institutional Review Board.

ISO: See *International Organization for Standardization*.

JCAHO: See the *Joint Commission on Accreditation of Healthcare Organizations*.

J-Codes: A subset of the HCPCS Level II *code set* with a high-order value of "J" that has been used to identify certain drugs and other items. The final HIPAA transactions and code sets rule states that these *J-codes* will be dropped from the *HCPCS*, and that *NDC codes* will be used to identify the associated pharmaceuticals and supplies.

JHITA: See *Joint Healthcare Information Technology Alliance*.

Joint Commission on Accreditation of Healthcare Organizations (JCAHO): An organization that accredits healthcare organizations. In the future, the *JCAHO* may play a role in certifying these organizations' compliance with the HIPAA A/S requirements.

Joint Healthcare Information Technology Alliance (JHITA): A healthcare industry association that represents *AHIMA*, *AMIA*, *CHIM*, *CHIME*, and *HIMSS* on legislative and regulatory issues affecting the use of health information technology.

Law Enforcement Official: See Part II, 45 CFR 164.501.

Local Code(s): A generic term for code values defined for a state or other political subdivision or for a specific payer. This term is most commonly used to describe HCPCS Level III Codes, but it also applies to state-assigned Institutional Revenue Codes, Condition Codes, Occurrence Codes, Value Codes, and so forth.

Logical Observation Identifiers, Names and Codes (LOINC): A set of universal names and ID codes that identify laboratory and clinical observations. These codes, which are maintained by the *Regenstrief Institute*, are expected to be used in the HIPAA claim attachments *standard*.

LOINC: See *Logical Observation Identifiers, Names and Codes*.

Loop: A repeating structure or process.

LTC: Long-Term Care.

Maintain or Maintenance: See Part II, 45 CFR 162.103.

Marketing: See Part II, 45 CFR 164.501.

Massachusetts Health Data Consortium (MHDC): An organization that seeks to improve healthcare in New England through improved policy development, better technology planning and implementation, and more informed financial decision making.

Maximum Defined Data Set: Under HIPAA, this is all of the required *data elements* for a particular *standard* based on a specific *implementation specification*. An entity creating a transaction is free to include whatever data any receiver might want or need. The recipient is free to ignore any portion of the data that is not needed to conduct his or her part of the associated business transaction, unless the inessential data is needed for coordination of benefits. Also see Part II, 45 CFR 162.103.

MCO: Managed Care Organization.

M+CO: Medicare Plus Choice Organization.

Medicaid Fiscal Agent (FA): The organization responsible for administering claims for a state Medicaid program.

Medicaid State Agency: The state agency responsible for overseeing the state's Medicaid program.

Medical Code Sets: Codes that characterize a medical condition or treatment. These *code sets* are usually maintained by professional societies and public health organizations. Compare to *administrative code sets*.

Medical Records Institute (MRI): An organization that promotes the development and acceptance of electronic health care record systems.

Medicare Contractor: A Medicare Part A Fiscal Intermediary, a Medicare Part B Carrier, or a Medicare Durable Medical Equipment Regional Carrier (DMERC).

Medicare Durable Medical Equipment Regional Carrier (DMERC): A Medicare contractor responsible for administering Durable Medical Equipment (DME) benefits for a region.

Medicare Part A Fiscal Intermediary (FI): A Medicare contractor that administers the Medicare Part A (institutional) benefits for a given region.

Medicare Part B Carrier: A Medicare contractor that administers the Medicare Part B (Professional) benefits for a given region.

Medicare Remittance Advice Remark Codes: A national *administrative code set* for providing either claim-level or service-level Medicare-related messages that cannot be expressed with a *Claim Adjustment Reason Code*. This *code set* is used in the *X12 835* Claim Payment & Remittance Advice transaction and is maintained by the *HCFA*.

Memorandum of Understanding (MOU): A document providing a general description of the responsibilities that are to be assumed by two or more parties in their pursuit of some goal(s). More specific information may be provided in an associated *SOW*.

MGMA: Medical Group Management Association.

MHDC: See the *Massachusetts Health Data Consortium*.

MHDI: See the *Minnesota Health Data Institute*.

Minimum Scope of Disclosure: The principle that, to the degree practical, individually identifiable health information should only be disclosed to the extent needed to support the purpose of the disclosure.

Minnesota Health Data Institute (MHDI): A public-private partnership for improving the quality and efficiency of heath care in Minnesota. *MHDI* includes the Minnesota Center for Healthcare Electronic Commerce (MCHEC), which supports the adoption of standards for electronic commerce and also supports the Minnesota EDI Healthcare Users Group (MEHUG).

Modify or Modification: Under HIPAA, this is a change adopted by the *Secretary*, through regulation, to a *standard* or an *implementation specification*. Also see Part II, 45 CFR 160.103.

More Stringent: See Part II, 45 CFR 160.202.

MOU: See *Memorandum of Understanding*.

MR: Medical Review.

MRI: See *Medical Records Institute*.

MSP: Medicare Secondary Payer.

NAHDO: See *National Association of Health Data Organizations*.

NAIC: See *National Association of Insurance Commissioners*.

NANDA: North American Nursing Diagnoses Association.

NASMD: See *National Association of State Medicaid Directors*.

National Association of Health Data Organizations (NAHDO): A group that promotes the development and improvement of state and national health information systems.

National Association of Insurance Commissioners (NAIC): An association of the insurance commissioners of the states and territories.

National Association of State Medicaid Directors (NASMD): An association of state Medicaid directors. *NASMD* is affiliated with the American Public Health Human Services Association (APHSA).

National Center for Health Statistics (NCHS): A federal organization within the *CDC* that collects, analyzes, and distributes health care statistics. The *NCHS* maintains the *ICD-n-CM* codes.

National Committee for Quality Assurance (NCQA): An organization that accredits managed care plans, or *Health Maintenance Organizations* (HMOs). In the future, the *NCQA* may play a role in certifying these organizations' compliance with the HIPAA A/S requirements. The *NCQA* also maintains the Health Employer Data and Information Set (*HEDIS*).

National Committee on Vital and Health Statistics (NCVHS): A Federal advisory body within *HHS* that advises the *Secretary* regarding potential changes to the HIPAA standards.

National Council for Prescription Drug Programs (NCPDP): An ANSI-accredited group that maintains a number of standard formats for use by the retail pharmacy industry, some of which are included in the HIPAA mandates. Also see *NCPDP Standard*.

National Drug Code (NDC): A *medical code set* that identifies prescription drugs and some over the counter products and that has been selected for use in the HIPAA transactions.

National Employer ID: A system for uniquely identifying all sponsors of health care benefits.

National Health Information Infrastructure (NHII): This is a healthcare-specific lane on the Information Superhighway, as described in the National Information Infrastructure (NII) initiative. Conceptually, this includes the HIPAA A/S initiatives.

National Patient ID: A system for uniquely identifying all recipients of health care services. This is sometimes referred to as the National Individual Identifier (NII) or as the Healthcare ID.

National Payer ID: A system for uniquely identifying all organizations that pay for health care services. Also known as Health Plan ID or Plan ID.

National Provider ID (NPI): A system for uniquely identifying all providers of health care services, supplies, and equipment.

National Provider File (NPF): The database envisioned for use in maintaining a national provider registry.

National Provider Registry: The organization envisioned for assigning National Provider IDs.

National Provider System (NPS): The administrative system envisioned for supporting a national provider registry.

National Standard Format (NSF): Generically, this applies to any nationally standardized data format, but it is often used in a more limited way to designate the Professional EMC *NSF*, a 320-byte flat file record format used to submit professional claims.

National Uniform Billing Committee (NUBC): An organization, chaired and hosted by the *American Hospital Association*, that maintains the UB-92 hardcopy institutional billing form and the *data element* specifications for both the hardcopy form and the 192-byte UB-92 flat file EMC format. The *NUBC* has a formal consultative role under HIPAA for all transactions affecting institutional health care services.

National Uniform Claim Committee (NUCC): An organization, chaired and hosted by the *American Medical Association*, that maintains the *HCFA-1500* claim form and a set of *data element* specifications for professional claims submission via the *HCFA-1500* claim form, the Professional EMC *NSF*, and the *X12 837*. The *NUCC* also maintains the *Provider Taxonomy Codes* and has a formal consultative role under HIPAA for all transactions affecting non-dental, non-institutional professional health care services.

NCHICA: See the *North Carolina Healthcare Information and Communications Alliance*.

NCHS: See the *National Center for Health Statistics*.

NCPDP: See the *National Council for Prescription Drug Programs*.

NCPDP Batch Standard: An *NCPDP standard* designed for use by low-volume dispensers of pharmaceuticals, such as nursing homes. Use of Version 1.0 of this *standard* has been mandated under HIPAA.

NCPDP Telecommunication Standard: An *NCPDP standard* designed for use by high-volume dispensers of pharmaceuticals, such as retail pharmacies. Use of Version 5.1 of this *standard* has been mandated under HIPAA.

NCQA: See the *National Committee for Quality Assurance*.

NCVHS: See the *National Committee on Vital and Health Statistics*.

NDC: See *National Drug Code*.

NHII: See *National Health Information Infrastructure*.

NOC: Not Otherwise Classified or Nursing Outcomes Classification.

NOI: See *Notice of Intent*.

Non-Clinical or Non-Medical Code Sets: See *Administrative Code Sets*.

North Carolina Healthcare Information and Communications Alliance (NCHICA): An organization that promotes the advancement and integration of information technology into the health care industry.

Notice of Intent (NOI): A document that describes a subject area for which the Federal Government is considering developing regulations. It may describe the presumably relevant considerations and invite *comments* from interested parties. These *comments* can then be used in developing an *NPRM* or a final regulation.

Notice of Proposed Rulemaking (NPRM): A document that describes and explains regulations that the Federal Government proposes to adopt at some future date, and invites interested parties to submit comments related to them. These *comments* can then be used in developing a final regulation.

NPF: See *National Provider File*.

NPI: See *National Provider ID*.

NPRM: See *Notice of Proposed Rulemaking*.

NPS: See *National Provider System*.

NSF: See *National Standard Format*.

NUBC: See *National Uniform Billing Committee*.

NUBC EDI TAG: The NUBC EDI Technical Advisory Group, which coordinates issues affecting both the *NUBC* and the *X12 standard*s.

NUCC: See *National Uniform Claim Committee*.

OCR: See *Office for Civil Rights*.

Office for Civil Rights: The HHS entity responsible for enforcing the HIPAA privacy rules.

Office of Management & Budget (OMB): A Federal Government agency that has a major role in reviewing proposed Federal regulations.

OIG: Office of the Inspector General.

OMB: See *Office of Management & Budget*.

Open System Interconnection (OSI): A multi-layer *ISO* data communications standard. Level Seven of this standard is industry-specific, and *HL7* is responsible for specifying the level seven OSI standards for the health industry.

Organized Health Care Arrangement: See Part II, 45 CFR 164.501.

OSI: See *Open System Interconnection*.

PAG: See *Policy Advisory Group*.

Payer: In health care, an entity that assumes the risk of paying for medical treatments. This can be an uninsured patient, a self-insured employer, a *health plan*, or an *HMO*.

PAYERID: HCFA's term for its pre-HIPAA *National Payer ID* initiative.

Payment: See Part II, 45 CFR 164.501.

PCS: See *ICD*.

PHB: Pharmacy Benefits Manager.

PHI: See *Protected Health Information*.

PHS: Public Health Service.

PL or P. L.: Public Law, as in PL 104-191 (HIPAA).

Plan Administration Functions: See Part II, 45 CFR 164.504.

Plan ID: See *National Payer ID*.

Plan Sponsor: An entity that sponsors a *health plan*. This can be an employer, a union, or some other entity. Also see Part II, 45 CFR 164.501.

Policy Advisory Group (PAG): A generic name for many work groups at WEDI and elsewhere.

POS: Place of Service or Point of Service.

PPO: Preferred Provider Organization.

PPS: Prospective Payment System.

PRA: The Paperwork Reduction Act.

PRG: Procedure-Related Group.

Pricer or Repricer: A person, an organization, or a software package that reviews procedures, diagnoses, fee schedules, and other data and determines the eligible amount for a given health care service or supply. Additional criteria can then be applied to determine the actual allowance, or payment, amount.

PRO: Professional Review Organization or Peer Review Organization.

Protected Health Information (PHI): See Part II, 45 CFR 164.501.

Provider Taxonomy Codes: An *administrative code set* for identifying the provider type and area of specialization for all health care providers. A given provider can have several *Provider Taxonomy Codes*. This *code set* is used in the *X12 278* Referral Certification and Authorization and the *X12 837* Claim transactions, and it is maintained by the *NUCC*.

Psychotherapy Notes: See Part II, 45 CFR 164.501.

Public Health Authority: See Part II, 45 CFR 164.501.

RA: Remittance Advice.

Regenstrief Institute: A research foundation for improving health care by optimizing the capture, analysis, content, and delivery of health care information. *Regenstrief* maintains the *LOINC* coding system that is being considered for use as part of the HIPAA claim attachments *standard*.

Relates to the Privacy of Individually Identifiable Health Information: See Part II, 45 CFR 160.202.

Required by Law: See Part II, 45 CFR 164.501.

Research: See Part II, 45 CFR 164.501.

RFA: The Regulatory Flexibility Act.

RVS: Relative Value Scale.

SC: Subcommittee.

SCHIP: The State Children's Health Insurance Program.

SDO: Standards Development Organization.

Secretary: Under HIPAA, this refers to the *Secretary* of *HHS* or his or her designated representatives. Also see Part II, 45 CFR 160.103.

Segment: Under HIPAA, this is a group of related *data elements* in a transaction. Also see Part II, 45 CFR 162.103.

Self-Insured: An individual or organization that assumes the financial risk of paying for health care.

Small Health Plan: Under HIPAA, this is a *health plan* with annual receipts of $5 million or less. Also see Part II, 45 CFR 160.103.

SNF: Skilled Nursing Facility.

SNOMED: Systematized Nomenclature of Medicine.

SNIP: See *Strategic National Implementation Process*.

Sponsor: See *Plan Sponsor*.

SOW: See *Statement of Work*.

SSN: Social Security Number.

SSO: See *Standard-Setting Organization*.

Standard: See Part II, 45 CFR 160.103.

Standard-Setting Organization (SSO): See Part II, 45 CFR 160.103.

Standard Transaction: Under HIPAA, this is a transaction that complies with the applicable HIPAA *standard*. Also see Part II, 45 CFR 162.103.

Standard Transaction Format Compliance System (STFCS): An EHNAC-sponsored WPC-hosted HIPAA compliance certification service.

State: See Part II, 45 CFR 160.103.

State Law: A constitution, statute, regulation, rule, common law, or any other State action having the force and effect of law. Also see Part II, 45 CFR 160.202.

State Uniform Billing Committee (SUBC): A state-specific affiliate of the *NUBC*.

Statement of Work (SOW): A document describing the specific tasks and methodologies that will be followed to satisfy the requirements of an associated contract or *MOU*.

STFCS: See the *Standard Transaction Format Compliance System*.

Strategic National Implementation Process (SNIP): A WEDI program for helping the health care industry identify and resolve HIPAA implementation issues.

Structured Data: See *Data-Related Concepts*.

SUBC: See *State Uniform Billing Committee*.

Summary Health Information: See Part II, 45 CFR 164.504.

SWG: Subworkgroup.

Syntax: The rules and conventions that one needs to know or follow in order to validly record information, or interpret previously recorded information, for a specific purpose. Thus, a syntax is a grammar. Such rules and conventions may be either explicit or implicit. In X12 transactions, the data-element separators, the sub-element separators, the segment terminators, the segment identifiers, the loops, the loop identifiers (when present), the repetition factors, etc., are all aspects of the X12 syntax. When explicit, such syntactical elements tend to be the structural, or format-related, *data elements* that are not required when a *direct data entry* architecture is used. Ultimately, though, there is not a perfectly clear division between the syntactical elements and the business data content.

TAG: Technical Advisory Group.

TG: Task Group.

Third Party Administrator (TPA): An entity that processes health care claims and performs related business functions for a *health plan*.

TPA: See *Third Party Administrator* or *Trading Partner Agreement*.

Trading Partner Agreement (TPA): See Part II, 45 CFR 160.103.

Transaction: Under HIPAA, this is the exchange of information between two parties to carry out financial or administrative activities related to health care. Also see Part II, 45 CFR 160.103.

Transaction Change Request System: A system established under HIPAA for accepting and tracking change requests for any of the HIPAA mandated transactions standards via a single Web site: *www.hipaa-dsmo.org*.

Translator: See *EDI Translator*.

Treatment: See Part II, 45 CFR 164.501.

UB: Uniform Bill, as in *UB-82* or *UB-92*.

UB-82: A uniform institutional claim form developed by the *NUBC* that was in general use from 1983 to 1993.

UB-92: A uniform institutional claim form developed by the *NUBC* that has been in general use since 1993.

UCF: Uniform Claim Form, as in UCF-1500.

UCTF: See the *Uniform Claim Task Force*.

UHIN: See the *Utah Health Information Network*.

UN/CEFACT: See the *United Nations Centre for Facilitation of Procedures and Practices for Administration, Commerce, and Transport*.

UN/EDIFACT: See the *United Nations Rules for Electronic Data Interchange for Administration, Commerce, and Transport*.

Uniform Claim Task Force (UCTF): An organization that developed the initial *HCFA-1500* Professional Claim Form. The maintenance responsibilities were later assumed by the *NUCC*.

United Nations Centre for Facilitation of Procedures and Practices for Administration, Commerce, and Transport (UN/CEFACT): An international organization dedicated to the elimination or simplification of procedural barriers to international commerce.

United Nations Rules for Electronic Data Interchange for Administration, Commerce, and Transport (UN/EDIFACT): An international EDI format. Interactive X12 transactions use the *EDIFACT* message syntax.

UNSM: United Nations Standard Messages.

Unstructured Data: See *Data-Related Concepts*.

UPIN: Unique Physician Identification Number.

UR: Utilization Review.

USC or U.S.C: United States Code.

Use: See Part II, 45 CFR 164.501.

Utah Health Information Network (UHIN): A public-private coalition for reducing health care administrative costs through the standardization and electronic exchange of health care data.

Value-Added Network (VAN): A vendor of EDI data communications and translation services.

VAN: See *Value-Added Network*.

Virtual Private Network (VPN): A technical strategy for creating secure connections, or tunnels, over the Internet.

VPN: See *Virtual Private Network*.

Washington Publishing Company (WPC): The company that publishes the X12N HIPAA *Implementation Guides* and the X12N HIPAA Data Dictionary, developed the X12 Data Dictionary, and hosts the EHNAC STFCS testing program.

WEDI: See the *Workgroup for Electronic Data Interchange*.

WG: Work Group.

WHO: See the *World Health Organization*.

Workforce: Under HIPAA, this means employees, volunteers, trainees, and other persons under the direct control of a *covered entity*, whether or not they are paid by the *covered entity*. Also see Part II, 45 CFR 160.103.

Workgroup for Electronic Data Interchange (WEDI): A health care industry group that lobbied for HIPAA A/S, and that has a formal consultative role under the HIPAA legislation. *WEDI* also sponsors *SNIP*.

World Health Organization (WHO): An organization that maintains the *International Classification of Diseases* (ICD) *medical code set*.

WPC: See the *Washington Publishing Company*.

X12: An ANSI-accredited group that defines EDI standards for many American industries, including health care insurance. Most of the electronic transaction standards mandated or proposed under HIPAA are *X12 standard*s.

X12 148: The X12 First Report of Injury, Illness, or Incident transaction. This *standard* could eventually be included in the HIPAA mandate.

X12 270: The X12 Health Care Eligibility & Benefit Inquiry transaction. Version 4010 of this transaction has been included in the HIPAA mandates.

X12 271: The X12 Health Care Eligibility & Benefit Response transaction. Version 4010 of this transaction has been included in the HIPAA mandates.

X12 274: The X12 Provider Information transaction.

X12 275: The X12 Patient Information transaction. This transaction is expected to be part of the HIPAA claim attachments *standard*.

X12 276: The X12 Health Care Claims Status Inquiry transaction. Version 4010 of this transaction has been included in the HIPAA mandates.

X12 277: The X12 Health Care Claim Status Response transaction. Version 4010 of this transaction has been included in the HIPAA mandates. This transaction is also expected to be part of the HIPAA claim attachments *standard*.

X12 278: The X12 Referral Certification and Authorization transaction. Version 4010 of this transaction has been included in the HIPAA mandates.

X12 811: The X12 Consolidated Service Invoice & Statement transaction.

X12 820: The X12 Payment Order & Remittance Advice transaction. Version 4010 of this transaction has been included in the HIPAA mandates.

X12 831: The X12 Application Control Totals transaction.

X12 834: The X12 Benefit Enrollment & Maintenance transaction. Version 4010 of this transaction has been included in the HIPAA mandates.

X12 835: The X12 Health Care Claim Payment & Remittance Advice transaction. Version 4010 of this transaction has been included in the HIPAA mandates.

X12 837: The X12 Health Care Claim or Encounter transaction. This transaction can be used for institutional, professional, dental, or drug claims. Version 4010 of this transaction has been included in the HIPAA mandates.

X12 997: The X12 Functional Acknowledgement transaction.

X12F: A subcommittee of *X12* that defines EDI standards for the financial industry. This group maintains the *X12 811* [generic] Invoice and the *X12 820* [generic] Payment & Remittance Advice transactions, although *X12N* maintains the associated HIPAA *Implementation Guides*.

X12 IHCEBI & IHCEBR: The X12 Interactive Healthcare Eligibility & Benefits Inquiry (IHCEBI) and Response (IHCEBR) transactions. These are being combined and converted to *UN/EDIFACT* Version 5 syntax.

X12 IHCLME: The X12 Interactive Healthcare Claim transaction.

X12J: A subcommittee of *X12* that reviews X12 work products for compliance with the X12 design rules.

X12N: A subcommittee of *X12* that defines EDI standards for the insurance industry, including health care insurance.

X12N/SPTG4: The HIPAA Liaison Special Task Group of the Insurance Subcommittee (N) of *X12*. This group's responsibilities have been assumed by *X12N/TG3/WG3*.

X12N/TG1: The Property & Casualty Task Group (TG1) of the Insurance Subcommittee (N) of *X12*.

X12N/TG2: The Health Care Task Group (TG2) of the Insurance Subcommittee (N) of *X12*.

X12N/TG2/WG1: The Health Care Eligibility Work Group (WG1) of the Health Care Task Group (TG2) of the Insurance Subcommittee (N) of *X12*. This group maintains the *X12 270* Health Care Eligibility & Benefit Inquiry and the *X12 271* Health Care Eligibility & Benefit Response transactions, and it is also responsible for maintaining the IHCEBI and IHCEBR transactions.

X12N/TG2/WG2: The Health Care Claims Work Group (WG2) of the Health Care Task Group (TG2) of the Insurance Subcommittee (N) of *X12*. This group maintains the *X12 837* Health Care Claim or Encounter transaction.

X12N/TG2/WG3: The Health Care Claim Payments Work Group (WG3) of the Health Care Task Group (TG2) of the Insurance Subcommittee (N) of *X12*. This group maintains the *X12 835* Health Care Claim Payment & Remittance Advice transaction.

X12N/TG2/WG4: The Health Care Enrollments Work Group (WG4) of the Health Care Task Group (TG2) of the Insurance Subcommittee (N) of *X12*. This group maintains the *X12 834* Benefit Enrollment & Maintenance transaction.

X12N/TG2/WG5: The Health Care Claims Status Work Group (WG5) of the Health Care Task Group (TG2) of the Insurance Subcommittee (N) of *X12*. This group maintains the *X12 276* Health Care Claims Status Inquiry and the *X12 277* Health Care Claim Status Response transactions.

X12N/TG2/WG9: The Health Care Patient Information Work Group (WG9) of the Health Care Task Group (TG2) of the Insurance Subcommittee (N) of *X12*. This group maintains the *X12 275* Patient Information transaction.

X12N/TG2/WG10: The Health Care Services Review Work Group (WG10) of the Health Care Task Group (TG2) of the Insurance Subcommittee (N) of *X12*. This group maintains the *X12 278* Referral Certification and Authorization transaction.

X12N/TG2/WG12: The Interactive Health Care Claims Work Group (WG12) of the Health Care Task Group (TG2) of the Insurance Subcommittee (N) of *X12*. This group maintains the IHCLME Interactive Claims transaction.

X12N/TG2/WG15: The Health Care Provider Information Work Group (WG15) of the Health Care Task Group (TG2) of the Insurance Subcommittee (N) of *X12*. This group maintains the *X12 274* Provider Information transaction.

X12N/TG2/WG19: The Health Care Implementation Coordination Work Group (WG19) of the Health Care Task Group (TG2) of the Insurance Subcommittee (N) of *X12*. This is now *X12N/TG3/WG3*.

X12N/TG3: The Business Transaction Coordination and Modeling Task Group (TG3) of the Insurance Subcommittee (N) of *X12*. TG3 maintains the X12N Business and Data Models and the HIPAA Data Dictionary. This was formerly *X12N/TG2/WG11*.

X12N/TG3/WG1: The Property & Casualty Work Group (WG1) of the Business Transaction Coordination and Modeling Task Group (TG3) of the Insurance Subcommittee (N) of *X12*.

X12N/TG3/WG2: The Healthcare Business & Information Modeling Work Group (WG2) of the Business Transaction Coordination and Modeling Task Group (TG3) of the Insurance Subcommittee (N) of *X12*.

X12N/TG3/WG3: The HIPAA Implementation Coordination Work Group (WG3) of the Business Transaction Coordination and Modeling Task Group (TG3) of the Insurance Subcommittee (N) of *X12*. This was formerly *X12N/TG2/WG19* and *X12N/SPTG4*.

X12N/TG3/WG4: The Object-Oriented Modeling and XML Liaison Work Group (WG4) of the Business Transaction Coordination and Modeling Task Group (TG3) of the Insurance Subcommittee (N) of *X12*.

X12N/TG4: The Implementation Guide Task Group (TG4) of the Insurance Subcommittee (N) of *X12*. This group supports the development and maintenance of X12 Implementation Guides, including the HIPAA X12 IGs.

X12N/TG8: The Architecture Task Group (TG8) of the Insurance Subcommittee (N) of *X12*.

X12/PRB: The X12 Procedures Review Board.

X12 Standard: The term currently used for any *X12 standard* that has been approved since the most recent release of X12 *American National Standards*. Since a full set of X12 *American National Standards* is only released about once every five years, it is the *X12 standard*s that are most likely to be in active use. These standards were previously called *Draft Standards for Trial Use*.

XML: Extensible Markup Language.

Part II

Consolidated HIPAA Administrative Simplification Final Rule Definitions

45 CFR 160.103 Definitions [from the 12/28/2000 Final Privacy Rule]

Except as otherwise provided, the following definitions apply to this subchapter:

Act means the Social Security Act.

ANSI stands for the American National Standards Institute.

Business associate:

(1) Except as provided in paragraph (2) of this definition, *business associate* means, with respect to a covered entity, a person who:

  (i) On behalf of such covered entity or of an organized health care arrangement (as defined in § 164.501 of this subchapter) in which the covered entity participates, but other than in the capacity of a member of the workforce of such covered entity or arrangement, performs, or assists in the performance of:

   (A) A function or activity involving the use or disclosure of individually identifiable health information, including claims processing or administration, data analysis, processing or administration, utilization review, quality assurance, billing, benefit management, practice management, and repricing; or

   (B) Any other function or activity regulated by this subchapter; or

  (ii) Provides, other than in the capacity of a member of the workforce of such covered entity, legal, actuarial, accounting, consulting, data aggregation (as defined in § 164.501 of this subchapter), management, administrative, accreditation, or financial services to or for such covered entity, or to or for an organized health care arrangement in which the covered entity participates, where the provision of the service involves the disclosure of individually identifiable health information from such covered entity or arrangement, or from another business associate of such covered entity or arrangement, to the person.

(2) A covered entity participating in an organized health care arrangement that performs a function or activity as described by paragraph (1)(i) of this definition for or on behalf of such organized health care arrangement, or that provides a service as described in paragraph (1)(ii) of this definition to or for such organized health care arrangement, does not, simply through the performance of such function or activity or the provision of such service, become a business associate of other covered entities participating in such organized health care arrangement.

(3) A covered entity may be a business associate of another covered entity.

Compliance date means the date by which a covered entity must comply with a standard, *implementation specification*, requirement, or *modification* adopted under this subchapter.

Covered *entity* means:

(1) A health plan.

(2) A health care clearinghouse.

(3) A health care provider who transmits any health information in electronic form in connection with a transaction covered by this subchapter.

Group health plan (also see definition of *health plan* in this section) means an employee welfare benefit plan (as defined in section 3(1) of the Employee Retirement Income and Security Act of 1974 (ERISA), 29 U.S.C. 1002(1)), including insured and self-insured plans, to the extent that the plan provides medical care (as defined in section 2791(a)(2) of the Public Health Service Act (PHS Act), 42 U.S.C. 300gg-91(a)(2)), including items and services paid for as medical care, to employees or their dependents directly or through insurance, reimbursement, or otherwise, that:

(1) Has 50 or more participants (as defined in section 3(7) of ERISA, 29 U.S.C. 1002(7)); or

(2) Is administered by an entity other than the employer that established and maintains the plan.

HCFA stands for Health Care Financing Administration within the Department of Health and Human Services.

HHS stands for the Department of Health and Human Services.

Health care means care, services, or supplies related to the health of an individual. *Health care* includes, but is not limited to, the following:

(1) Preventive, diagnostic, therapeutic, rehabilitative, maintenance, or palliative care, and counseling, service, assessment, or procedure with respect to the physical or mental condition, or functional status, of an individual or that affects the structure or function of the body; and

(2) Sale or dispensing of a drug, device, equipment, or other item in accordance with a prescription.

Health care clearinghouse means a public or private entity, including a billing service, repricing company, community health management information system or community health information system, and "value-added" networks and switches that does either of the following functions:

(1) Processes or facilitates the processing of health information received from another entity in a nonstandard format or containing nonstandard data content into standard *data elements* or a standard transaction.

(2) Receives a standard transaction from another entity and processes or facilitates the processing of health information into nonstandard format or nonstandard data content for the receiving entity.

Health care provider means a provider of services (as defined in section 1861(u) of the Act, 42 U.S.C. 1395x(u)), a provider of medical or health services (as defined in section 1861(s) of the Act, 42 U.S.C. 1395x(s)), and any other person or organization who furnishes, bills, or is paid for health care in the normal course of business.

Health information means any information, whether oral or recorded in any form or medium, that:

(1) Is created or received by a health care provider, health plan, public health authority, employer, life insurer, school or university, or health care clearinghouse; and

(2) Relates to the past, present, or future physical or mental health or condition of an individual; the provision of health care to an individual; or the past, present, or future payment for the provision of health care to an individual.

Health insurance issuer (as defined in section 2791(b)(2) of the PHS Act, 42 U.S.C. 300gg-91(b)(2) and used in the definition of *health plan* in this section) means an insurance company, insurance service, or insurance organization (including an HMO) that is licensed to engage in the business of insurance in a State and is subject to State law that regulates insurance. Such term does not include a group health plan.

Health maintenance organization (HMO) (as defined in section 2791(b)(3) of the PHS Act, 42 U.S.C. 300gg-91(b)(3) and used in the definition of *health plan* in this section) means a federally qualified HMO, an organization recognized as an HMO under State law, or a similar organization regulated for solvency under State law in the same manner and to the same extent as such an HMO.

Health plan means an individual or group plan that provides, or pays the cost of, medical care (as defined in section 2791(a)(2) of the PHS Act, 42 U.S.C. 300gg-91(a)(2)).

(1) *Health plan* includes the following, singly or in combination:
   (i) A group health plan, as defined in this section.
   (ii) A health insurance issuer, as defined in this section.
   (iii) An HMO, as defined in this section.
   (iv) Part A or Part B of the Medicare program under title XVIII of the Act.
   (v) The Medicaid program under title XIX of the Act, 42 U.S.C. 1396, et seq.
   (vi) An issuer of a Medicare supplemental policy (as defined in section 1882(g)(1) of the Act, 42 U.S.C. 1395ss(g)(1)).

(vii) An issuer of a long-term care policy, excluding a nursing home fixed-indemnity policy.

(viii) An employee welfare benefit plan or any other arrangement that is established or maintained for the purpose of offering or providing health benefits to the employees of two or more employers.

(ix) The health care program for active military personnel under title 10 of the United States Code.

(x) The veterans health care program under 38 U.S.C. Chapter 17.

(xi) The Civilian Health and Medical Program of the Uniformed Services (CHAMPUS) (as defined in 10 U.S.C. 1072(4)).

(xii) The Indian Health Service program under the Indian Health Care Improvement Act, 25 U.S.C. 1601, et seq.

(xiii) The Federal Employees Health Benefits Program under 5 U.S.C. 8902, et seq.

(xiv) An approved State child health plan under title XXI of the Act, providing benefits for child health assistance that meet the requirements of section 2103 of the Act, 42 U.S.C. 1397, et seq.

(xv) The Medicare+Choice program under Part C of title XVIII of the Act, 42 U.S.C. 1395w-21 through 1395w-28.

(xvi) A high risk pool that is a mechanism established under State law to provide health insurance coverage or comparable coverage to eligible individuals.

(xvii) Any other individual or group plan, or combination of individual or group plans, that provides or pays for the cost of medical care (as defined in section 2791(a)(2) of the PHS Act, 42 U.S.C. 300gg-91(a)(2)).

(2) *Health plan* excludes:

(i) Any policy, plan, or program to the extent that it provides, or pays for the cost of, excepted benefits that are listed in section 2791(c)(1) of the PHS Act, 42 U.S.C. 300gg-91(c)(1); and

(ii) A government-funded program (other than one listed in paragraph (1)(i)-(xvi) of this definition):

  (A) Whose principal purpose is other than providing, or paying the cost of, health care; or

  (B) Whose principal activity is:

   (1) The direct provision of health care to persons; or

   (2) The making of grants to fund the direct provision of health care to persons.

Implementation specification means specific requirements or instructions for implementing a standard.

Modify or modification refers to a change adopted by the Secretary, through regulation, to a standard or an implementation specification.

Secretary means the Secretary of Health and Human Services or any other officer or employee of HHS to whom the authority involved has been delegated.

Small health plan means a health plan with annual receipts of $5 million or less.

Standard means a rule, condition, or requirement:

(1) Describing the following information for products, systems, services, or practices:
   (i) Classification of components.
   (ii) Specification of materials, performance, or operations; or
   (iii) Delineation of procedures; or
(2) With respect to the privacy of individually identifiable health information.

Standard setting organization (SSO) means an organization accredited by the American National Standards Institute that develops and maintains standards for information transactions or data elements, or any other standard that is necessary for, or will facilitate the implementation of, this part.

State refers to one of the following:

(1) For a health plan established or regulated by Federal law, *State* has the meaning set forth in the applicable section of the United States Code for such health plan.
(2) For all other purposes, *State* means any of the several States, the District of Columbia, the Commonwealth of Puerto Rico, the Virgin Islands, and Guam.

Trading partner agreement means an agreement related to the exchange of information in electronic transactions, whether the agreement is distinct or part of a larger agreement, between each party to the agreement. (For example, a trading partner agreement may specify, among other things, the duties and responsibilities of each party to the agreement in conducting a standard transaction.)

Transaction means the transmission of information between two parties to carry out financial or administrative activities related to health care. It includes the following types of information transmissions:

(1) Health care claims or equivalent encounter information.
(2) Health care payment and remittance advice.
(3) Coordination of benefits.
(4) Health care claim status.
(5) Enrollment and disenrollment in a health plan.
(6) Eligibility for a health plan.
(7) Health plan premium payments.
(8) Referral certification and authorization.
(9) First report of injury.
(10) Health claims attachments.
(11) Other transactions that the Secretary may prescribe by regulation.

Workforce means employees, volunteers, trainees, and other persons whose conduct, in the performance of work for a covered entity, is under the direct control of such entity, whether or not they are paid by the covered entity.

45 CFR 160.202 Definitions
[from the 12/28/2000 Final Privacy Rule]

For purposes of this subpart, the following terms have the following meanings:

Contrary, when used to compare a provision of State law to a standard, requirement, or implementation specification adopted under this subchapter, means:

(1) A covered entity would find it impossible to comply with both the State and federal requirements; or

(2) The provision of State law stands as an obstacle to the accomplishment and execution of the full purposes and objectives of part C of title XI of the Act or section 264 of Pub. L. 104-191, as applicable.

More stringent means, in the context of a comparison of a provision of State law and a standard, requirement, or implementation specification adopted under subpart E of part 164 of this subchapter, a State law that meets one or more of the following criteria:

(1) With respect to a use or disclosure, the law prohibits or restricts a use or disclosure in circumstances under which such use or disclosure otherwise would be permitted under this subchapter, except if the disclosure is:

　(i)　Required by the Secretary in connection with determining whether a covered entity is in compliance with this subchapter; or

　(ii)　To the individual who is the subject of the individually identifiable health information.

(2) With respect to the rights of an individual who is the subject of the individually identifiable health information of access to or amendment of individually identifiable health information, permits greater rights of access or amendment, as applicable; provided that, nothing in this subchapter may be construed to preempt any State law to the extent that it authorizes or prohibits disclosure of protected health information about a minor to a parent, guardian, or person acting *in loco parentis* of such minor.

(3) With respect to information to be provided to an individual who is the subject of the individually identifiable health information about a use, a disclosure, rights, and remedies, provides the greater amount of information.

(4) With respect to the form or substance of an authorization or consent for use or disclosure of individually identifiable health information, provides requirements that narrow the scope or duration, increase the privacy protections afforded (such as by expanding the criteria for), or reduce the coercive effect of the circumstances surrounding the authorization or consent, as applicable.

(5) With respect to recordkeeping or requirements relating to accounting of disclosures, provides for the retention or reporting of more detailed information or for a longer duration.

(6) With respect to any other matter, provides greater privacy protection for the individual who is the subject of the individually identifiable health information.

Relates to the privacy of individually identifiable health information means, with respect to a State law, that the State law has the specific purpose of protecting the privacy of health information or affects the privacy of health information in a direct, clear, and substantial way.

State law means a constitution, statute, regulation, rule, common law, or other State action having the force and effect of law.

45 CFR 162.103 Definitions [from the 08/17/2000 Final Transactions & Code Sets Rule]

For purposes of this part, the following definitions apply:

Code set means any set of codes used to encode data elements, such as tables of terms, medical concepts, medical diagnostic codes, or medical procedure codes. A *code set* includes the codes and the descriptors of the codes.

Code set maintaining organization means an organization that creates and maintains the code sets adopted by the Secretary for use in the transactions for which standards are adopted in this part.

Data condition means the rule that describes the circumstances under which a covered entity must use a particular data element or segment.

Data content means all the data elements and code sets inherent to a transaction, and not related to the format of the transaction. Data elements that are related to the format are not data content.

Data element means the smallest named unit of information in a transaction.

Data set means a semantically meaningful unit of information exchanged between two parties to a transaction.

Descriptor means the text defining a code.

Designated standard maintenance organization (DSMO) means an organization designated by the Secretary under Sec. 162.910(a).

Direct data entry means the direct entry of data (for example, using dumb terminals or Web browsers) that is immediately transmitted into a health plan's computer.

Electronic media means the mode of electronic transmission. It includes the Internet (wide-open), Extranet (using Internet technology to link a business with information only accessible to collaborating parties), leased lines, dial-up lines, private networks, and those transmissions that are physically moved from one location to another using magnetic tape, disk, or compact disk media.

Format refers to those data elements that provide or control the enveloping or hierarchical structure, or assist in identifying data content of, a transaction.

HCPCS stands for the Health [Care Financing Administration] Common Procedure Coding System.

Maintain or maintenance refers to activities necessary to support the use of a standard adopted by the Secretary, including technical corrections to an implementation specification, and enhancements or expansion of a code set. This term excludes the activities related to the adoption of a new standard or implementation specification, or modification to an adopted standard or implementation specification.

Maximum defined data set means all of the required data elements for a particular standard based on a specific implementation specification.

Segment means a group of related data elements in a transaction.

Standard transaction means a transaction that complies with the applicable standard adopted under this part.

45 CFR 164.501 Definitions [from the 12/28/2000 Final Privacy Rule]

As used in this subpart, the following terms have the following meanings:

Correctional institution means any penal or correctional facility, jail, reformatory, detention center, work farm, halfway house, or residential community program center operated by, or under contract to, the United States, a State, a territory, a political subdivision of a State or territory, or an Indian tribe, for the confinement or rehabilitation of persons charged with or convicted of a criminal offense or other persons held in lawful custody. *Other persons held in lawful custody* includes juvenile offenders adjudicated delinquent, aliens detained awaiting deportation, persons committed to mental institutions through the criminal justice system, witnesses, or others awaiting charges or trial.

Covered functions means those functions of a covered entity the performance of which makes the entity a health plan, health care provider, or health care clearinghouse.

Data aggregation means, with respect to protected health information created or received by a business associate in its capacity as the business associate of a covered entity, the combining of such protected health information by the business associate with the protected health information received by the business associate in its capacity as a business associate of another covered entity, to permit data analyses that relate to the health care operations of the respective covered entities.

Designated record set means:

(1) A group of records maintained by or for a covered entity that is:
   (i) The medical records and billing records about individuals maintained by or for a covered health care provider;
   (ii) The enrollment, payment, claims adjudication, and case or medical management record systems maintained by or for a health plan; or
   (iii) Used, in whole or in part, by or for the covered entity to make decisions about individuals.

(2) For purposes of this paragraph, the term *record* means any item, collection, or grouping of information that includes protected health information and is maintained, collected, used, or disseminated by or for a covered entity.

Direct treatment relationship means a treatment relationship between an individual and a health care provider that is not an indirect treatment relationship.

Disclosure means the release, transfer, provision of access to, or divulging in any other manner of information outside the entity holding the information.

Health care operations means any of the following activities of the covered entity to the extent that the activities are related to covered functions, and any of the following activities of an organized health care arrangement in which the covered entity participates:

(1) Conducting quality assessment and improvement activities, including outcomes evaluation and development of clinical guidelines, provided that the obtaining of generalizable knowledge is not the primary purpose of any studies resulting from such activities; population-based activities relating to improving health or reducing health care costs, protocol development, case management and care coordination, contacting of health care providers and patients with information about treatment alternatives; and related functions that do not include treatment;

(2) Reviewing the competence or qualifications of health care professionals, evaluating practitioner and provider performance, health plan performance, conducting training programs in which students, trainees, or practitioners in areas of health care learn under supervision to practice or improve their skills as health care providers, training of non-health care professionals, accreditation, certification, licensing, or credentialing activities;

(3) Underwriting, premium rating, and other activities relating to the creation, renewal or replacement of a contract of health insurance or health benefits, and ceding, securing, or placing a contract for reinsurance of risk relating to claims for health care (including stop-loss insurance and excess of loss insurance), provided that the requirements of § 164.514(g) are met, if applicable;

(4) Conducting or arranging for medical review, legal services, and auditing functions, including fraud and abuse detection and compliance programs;

(5) Business planning and development, such as conducting cost-management and planning-related analyses related to managing and operating the entity, including formulary development and administration, development or improvement of methods of payment or coverage policies; and

(6) Business management and general administrative activities of the entity, including, but not limited to:

    (i) Management activities relating to implementation of and compliance with the requirements of this subchapter;

    (ii) Customer service, including the provision of data analyses for policy holders, plan sponsors, or other customers, provided that protected health information is not disclosed to such policy holder, plan sponsor, or customer.

    (iii) Resolution of internal grievances;

    (iv) Due diligence in connection with the sale or transfer of assets to a potential successor in interest, if the potential successor in interest is a covered entity or, following completion of the sale or transfer, will become a covered entity; and

(v) Consistent with the applicable requirements of § 164.514, creating de-identified health information, fundraising for the benefit of the covered entity, and marketing for which an individual authorization is not required as described in § 164.514(e)(2).

Health oversight agency means an agency or authority of the United States, a State, a territory, a political subdivision of a State or territory, or an Indian tribe, or a person or entity acting under a grant of authority from or contract with such public agency, including the employees or agents of such public agency or its contractors or persons or entities to whom it has granted authority, that is authorized by law to oversee the health care system (whether public or private) or government programs in which health information is necessary to determine eligibility or compliance, or to enforce civil rights laws for which health information is relevant.

Indirect treatment relationship means a relationship between an individual and a health care provider in which:

(1) The health care provider delivers health care to the individual based on the orders of another health care provider; and

(2) The health care provider typically provides services or products, or reports the diagnosis or results associated with the health care, directly to another health care provider, who provides the services or products or reports to the individual.

Individual means the person who is the subject of protected health information.

Individually identifiable health information is information that is a subset of health information, including demographic information collected from an individual, and:

(1) Is created or received by a health care provider, health plan, employer, or health care clearinghouse; and

(2) Relates to the past, present, or future physical or mental health or condition of an individual; the provision of health care to an individual; or the past, present, or future payment for the provision of health care to an individual; and

  (i) That identifies the individual; or

  (ii) With respect to which there is a reasonable basis to believe the information can be used to identify the individual.

Inmate means a person incarcerated in or otherwise confined to a correctional institution.

Law enforcement official means an officer or employee of any agency or authority of the United States, a State, a territory, a political subdivision of a State or territory, or an Indian tribe, who is empowered by law to:

(1) Investigate or conduct an official inquiry into a potential violation of law; or

(2) Prosecute or otherwise conduct a criminal, civil, or administrative proceeding arising from an alleged violation of law.

Marketing means to make a communication about a product or service a purpose of which is to encourage recipients of the communication to purchase or use the product or service.

(1) *Marketing* does not include communications that meet the requirements of paragraph (2) of this definition and that are made by a covered entity:
   (i) For the purpose of describing the entities participating in a health care provider network or health plan network, or for the purpose of describing if and the extent to which a product or service (or payment for such product or service) is provided by a covered entity or included in a plan of benefits; or
   (ii) That are tailored to the circumstances of a particular individual and the communications are:
      (A) Made by a health care provider to an individual as part of the treatment of the individual, and for the purpose of furthering the treatment of that individual; or
      (B) Made by a health care provider or health plan to an individual in the course of managing the treatment of that individual, or for the purpose of directing or recommending to that individual alternative treatments, therapies, health care providers, or settings of care.
(2) A communication described in paragraph (1) of this definition is not included in marketing if:
   (i) The communication is made orally; or
   (ii) The communication is in writing and the covered entity does not receive direct or indirect remuneration from a third party for making the communication.

Organized health care arrangement means:

(1) A clinically integrated care setting in which individuals typically receive health care from more than one health care provider;
(2) An organized system of health care in which more than one covered entity participates, and in which the participating covered entities:
   (i) Hold themselves out to the public as participating in a joint arrangement; and
   (ii) Participate in joint activities that include at least one of the following:
      (A) Utilization review, in which health care decisions by participating covered entities are reviewed by other participating covered entities or by a third party on their behalf;
      (B) Quality assessment and improvement activities, in which treatment provided by participating covered entities is assessed by other participating covered entities or by a third party on their behalf; or
      (C) Payment activities, if the financial risk for delivering health care is shared, in part or in whole, by participating covered entities through the joint arrangement and if protected health information created or received by a covered entity is reviewed by other participating covered entities or by a third party on their behalf for the purpose of administering the sharing of financial risk.
(3) A group health plan and a health insurance issuer or HMO with respect to such group health plan, but only with respect to protected health information created or received by such health insurance issuer or HMO that relates to individuals who are or who have been participants or beneficiaries in such group health plan;
(4) A group health plan and one or more other group *health plans* each of which are maintained by the same plan sponsor; or

(5) The group health plans described in paragraph (4) of this definition and health insurance issuers or HMOs with respect to such group health plans, but only with respect to protected health information created or received by such health insurance issuers or HMOs that relates to individuals who are or have been participants or beneficiaries in any of such group health plans.

Payment means:

(1) The activities undertaken by:
- (i) A health plan to obtain premiums or to determine or fulfill its responsibility for coverage and provision of benefits under the health plan; or
- (ii) A covered health care provider or health plan to obtain or provide reimbursement for the provision of health care; and

(2) The activities in paragraph (1) of this definition relate to the individual to whom health care is provided and include, but are not limited to:
- (i) Determinations of eligibility or coverage (including coordination of benefits or the determination of cost sharing amounts), and adjudication or subrogation of health benefit claims;
- (ii) Risk adjusting amounts due based on enrollee health status and demographic characteristics;
- (iii) Billing, claims management, collection activities, obtaining payment under a contract for reinsurance (including stop-loss insurance and excess of loss insurance), and related health care data processing;
- (iv) Review of health care services with respect to medical necessity, coverage under a health plan, appropriateness of care, or justification of charges;
- (v) Utilization review activities, including precertification and preauthorization of services, concurrent and retrospective review of services; and
- (vi) Disclosure to consumer reporting agencies of any of the following protected health information relating to collection of premiums or reimbursement:
  - (A) Name and address;
  - (B) Date of birth;
  - (C) Social security number;
  - (D) Payment history;
  - (E) Account number; and
  - (F) Name and address of the health care provider and/or health plan.

Plan sponsor is defined as defined at section 3(16)(B) of ERISA, 29 U.S.C. 1002(16)(B). [*Note:* Section 3(16)(B) of ERISA defines *plan sponsor* as "(i) the employer in the case of an employee benefit plan established or maintained by a single employer, (ii) the employee organization in the case of a plan established or maintained by an employee organization, or (iii) in the case of a plan established or maintained by two or more employers or jointly by one or more employers and one or more employee organizations, the association, committee, joint board of trustees, or other similar group of representatives of the parties who establish or maintain the plan.".]

Protected health information means individually identifiable health information:

(1) Except as provided in paragraph (2) of this definition, that is:
   (i) Transmitted by electronic media;
   (ii) Maintained in any medium described in the definition of *electronic media* at § 162.103 of this subchapter; or
   (iii) Transmitted or maintained in any other form or medium.
(2) *Protected health information* excludes individually identifiable health information in:
   (i) Education records covered by the Family Educational Right and Privacy Act, as amended, 20 U.S.C. 1232g; and
   (ii) Records described at 20 U.S.C. 1232g(a)(4)(B)(iv).

Psychotherapy notes means notes recorded (in any medium) by a health care provider who is a mental health professional documenting or analyzing the contents of conversation during a private counseling session or a group, joint, or family counseling session and that are separated from the rest of the individual's medical record. *Psychotherapy notes* excludes medication prescription and monitoring, counseling session start and stop times, the modalities and frequencies of treatment furnished, results of clinical tests, and any summary of the following items: diagnosis, functional status, the treatment plan, symptoms, prognosis, and progress to date.

Public health authority means an agency or authority of the United States, a State, a territory, a political subdivision of a State or territory, or an Indian tribe, or a person or entity acting under a grant of authority from or contract with such public agency, including the employees or agents of such public agency or its contractors or persons or entities to whom it has granted authority, that is responsible for public health matters as part of its official mandate.

Required by law means a mandate contained in law that compels a covered entity to make a use or disclosure of protected health information and that is enforceable in a court of law. *Required by law* includes, but is not limited to, court orders and court-ordered warrants; subpoenas or summons issued by a court, grand jury, a governmental or tribal inspector general, or an administrative body authorized to require the production of information; a civil or an authorized investigative demand; Medicare conditions of participation with respect to health care providers participating in the program; and statutes or regulations that require the production of information, including statutes or regulations that require such information if payment is sought under a government program providing public benefits.

Research means a systematic investigation, including research development, testing, and evaluation, designed to develop or contribute to generalizable knowledge.

Treatment means the provision, coordination, or management of health care and related services by one or more health care providers, including the coordination or management of health care by a health care provider with a third party; consultation between health care providers relating to a patient; or the referral of a patient for health care from one health care provider to another.

Use means, with respect to individually identifiable health information, the sharing, employment, application, utilization, examination, or analysis of such information within an entity that maintains such information.

45 CFR 164.504 Uses and Disclosures: Organizational Requirements
[from the 12/28/2000 Final Privacy Rule]

(a) *Definitions.* As used in this section:

Common control exists if an entity has the power, directly or indirectly, significantly to influence or direct the actions or policies of another entity.

Common ownership exists if an entity or entities possess an ownership or equity interest of 5 percent or more in another entity.

Health care component has the following meaning:

(1) Components of a covered entity that perform covered functions are part of the health care component.

(2) Another component of the covered entity is part of the entity's health care component to the extent that:

   (i) It performs, with respect to a component that performs covered functions, activities that would make such other component a business associate of the component that performs covered functions if the two components were separate legal entities; and

   (ii) The activities involve the use or disclosure of protected health information that such other component creates or receives from or on behalf of the component that performs covered functions.

Hybrid entity means a single legal entity that is a covered entity and whose covered functions are not its primary functions.

Plan administration functions means administration functions performed by the plan sponsor of a group health plan on behalf of the group health plan and excludes functions performed by the plan sponsor in connection with any other benefit or benefit plan of the plan sponsor.

Summary health information means information that may be individually identifiable health information and:

(1) That summarizes the claims history, claims expenses, or type of claims experienced by individuals for whom a plan sponsor has provided health benefits under a group health plan; and

(2) From which the information described at § 164.514(b)(2)(i) has been deleted, except that the geographic information described in § 164.514(b)(2)(i)(B) need only be aggregated to the level of a five digit ZIP code.

Part III

Purpose & Maintenance

Purpose

Part I provides a general glossary of terms and acronyms likely to be encountered by anyone dealing with the Administrative Simplification portions of HIPAA, or with any of the organizations, standards, and processes involved in developing, maintaining, and using HIPAA-related standards.

It evolved from a glossary developed in the Summer of 1998 to support the development of the *MOU* covering the *DSMO* process within *X12N/TG3/WG3*. That *MOU* explains how the *ADA*, *HHS*, *HL7*, the *NCPDP*, the *NUBC*, the *NUCC*, and *X12N* will coordinate their efforts to develop and maintain the HIPAA-related standards and implementation guides. In such a setting it is possible to talk for several days without using a word of English, and this document was an attempt to compensate for that.

Part II provides a single source for all definitions included in the body of the final HIPAA Administrative Simplification rules, and should reflect the cumulative effects of all related rules and correction notices. Including the complete text of those definitions in this part keeps the Part I entries comparatively short and informal. Related definitions in Part I reference the associated Part II definitions.

Part III explains the purposes of Parts I & II, and provides you with a way to complain whenever you feel that your favorite organization or subject has been abused or neglected in those parts.

Maintenance

The contents are necessarily limited by the maintainers' knowledge of and experience with the subjects and organizations included, and by the need to keep it finite. We have avoided including technical security-related terms beyond those needed to understand the rules themselves because there are so many of them, and because they are already fairly well documented by various industry and professional groups. When identifying organizations, we have tried to note when they have special responsibilities under HIPAA, such as the maintenance of a *transaction standard* or *code set*, or via the sponsorship of special educational programs.

Please send any suggestions or questions to zon4@earthlink.net.

Index

A

Accelerator. *See* BizTalk Accelerator for HIPAA
ADA (American Dental Association), claim form and procedure standardization, 16
A. D. Little, study on use of EDI in grocery industry, 5
administration, BizTalk Server, 59
Administrative Simplification
    HIPAA and, 32
    Web site, 2
agencies (public), as funding source for health care, 78–79
AHA (American Hospital Association), billing form standardization, 9
AMA (American Medical Association)
    requests to delay HIPAA by, 29
    role in standardization of health insurance claim form, 15
American Dental Association (ADA), claim form and procedure standardization, 16
American Hospital Association (AHA), billing form standardization, 9
American Medical Association (AMA)
    requests to delay HIPAA by, 29
    role in standardization of health insurance claim form, 15
American National Standards Institute (ANSI)
    Standards Development Organizations (SDOs), 10
    X12 standard for Electronic Data Interchange, 6
American Public Human Services Association (APHSA), requests to delay HIPAA by, 29
ANSI (American National Standards Institute)
    Standards Development Organizations (SDOs), 10
    X12 standard for Electronic Data Interchange, 6
APHSA (American Public Human Services Association), requests to delay HIPAA by, 29

B

Bass, Earl J. ("Buddy"), 5, 7
Bass, Steve, 5, 6
BCBSA (Blue Cross Blue Shield Association), requests to delay HIPAA by, 29
Benefit Enrollment and Maintenance-834, X12N HIPAA Implementation Guide Schemas, 61–62
Benefit Information (EB) segments, 63
benefits, Eligibility, Coverage or Benefit Information-271, 63–64
best practices concept, 21
billing forms, standardization of, 9–10
BizTalk Accelerator for HIPAA
    components of, 60–61
    as core technology in HIPAA Solution, 36
    envisioning potential benefits from, 74
    Healthaxis case study, 45
    as solution for HIPAA compliance, 55
    using in tandem with BizTalk Server 2000, 56
BizTalk Document Tracking, 59
BizTalk Editor, 56–57
BizTalk Mapper, 57–58
BizTalk Messaging Manager, 59
BizTalk Orchestration Designer, 58
BizTalk Server 2000
    components, BizTalk Document Tracking, 59
    components, BizTalk Editor, 56–57
    components, BizTalk Mapper, 57–58
    components, BizTalk Messaging Manager, 59
    components, BizTalk Orchestration Designer, 58
    components, BizTalk Server Administration, 59
    as core technology in HIPAA Solution, 36
    using in tandem with BizTalk Accelerator for HIPAA, 56
BizTalk Server Administration, 59
Blue Cross Blue Shield Association (BCBSA), requests to delay HIPAA by, 29
Braithwaite, William R., 1
BUSAP (Business Applications), as basis of X12 standard, 6
Bush, President George H. W., 12, 13
Business Applications (BUSAP), as basis of X12 standard, 6
business functions, HIPAA compliance and, 62

C

capitation model of health care, 75
Carley, Joseph, 5, 7
claims
    Electronic Remittance Advice (ERA), 67–68
    Health Care Claim Transaction (837), 64
    requesting current status of, 66–67
    standardization of forms, 15–16
clients, HIPAA Solution, 37
clinical trials, 78
Clinton, President William J., 13–14

Index

CMS/HCFA Common Procedure Coding System (HCPCS), 15
Code on Dental Procedures and Nomenclature, 16
compliance, HIPAA
   business functions and, 62
   mandatory and best practice considerations, 21–23
   OnlyConnect Methodology and, 43
   solution for, 55
consulting services, offered by Microsoft and WPC, 37
consumers, health
   benefits of HIPAA for, 77
   consumer-enabled technology, 81
core technologies, HIPAA Solution, 36
Current Components, Inc., 26–27

D

Data Interchange Standards Association (DISA), as X12 secretariat, 7
data standardization, NCVHS's role in, 8–9
Dental Electronic Content Committee (DeCC), claim form and procedure standardization, 16
Department of Health and Human Services (DHHS), on costs of implementing HIPAA, 31
dependents
   defined, 64
   as participant in enrollment process, 62
deployment phase. *See also* technical deployment
   Healthaxis case study, 53
   HIPAA Solution, 41
Designated Standards Maintenance Organization (DSMO), 17–19
   address to concerns about HIPAA, 31
   guiding principles of, 18
   organizations designated by HIPAA as DSMOs, 17
   recommendation process to NCVHS, 18–19
design goals, Healthaxis case study, 49
destination payer, 64
development phase
   Healthaxis case study, 51–53
   HIPAA Solution, 40–41
device manufacturers, benefits of HIPAA for, 78
DHHS (Department of Health and Human Services), on costs of implementing HIPAA, 31
DISA (Data Interchange Standards Association), as X12 secretariat, 7
document tracking, 59
DSMO. *See* Designated Standards Maintenance Organization (DSMO)

E

EB segments, 63
E-codes (injury codes), role of NCVHS in development of, 8
Ed Guilbert Professional Award, 7
EDI (Electronic Data Interchange)
   business value of, 25–27
   Colonel Ed Guilbert's role in founding, 4–5
   overview of, 1
   in petroleum industry, 28
   publication of standards of, 6–7
   using in grocery industry, 5
   X12 standard for, 6
EDI (Electronic Data Interchange), in health care industry, 7–19
   American Dental Association and Dental Electronics Content Committee, 16
   American Hospital Association and National Uniform Billing Committee, 9–10
   American Medical Association and National Uniform Claim Committee, 15–16
   business value of, 27
   Designated Standards Maintenance Organization (DSMO), 17–19
   Health Level Seven, 11–12
   National Committee on Vital and Health Statistics, 7–9
   National Council for Prescription Drug Programs, 10–11
   Workgroup for Electronic Data Interchange, 12–14
   X12N (insurance subcommittee), 14–15
editors, BizTalk Editor, 56–57
EFT (Electronic Funds Transfer), 62
Electronic Data Interchange. *See* EDI (Electronic Data Interchange)
Electronic Funds Transfer (EFT), 62
Electronic Media Claims (EMC), 10
Electronic Remittance Advice (ERA), 67–68
Eligibility, Coverage or Benefit Information-271, 63–64
Eligibility Request Document Specification, BizTalk Editor, 56–57
eligibility requests, 63, 64
EMC (Electronic Media Claims), 10
employers
   as domain of health care industry, 75
   private sector funding for health care, 78–79
enrollment process, participants in, 61–62
envisioning phase
   Healthaxis case study, 45–47
   HIPAA Solution, 39

Index 155

ERA (Electronic Remittance Advice), 67–68
Extensible Stylesheet Language (XSL), 57

F

Failure Mode Effects and Analysis (FMEA) tool, 47
Federal Register, publication of EDI standards in, 22
FirstPass, OnlyConnect, 71–72
FMEA (Failure Mode Effects and Analysis) tool, 47

G

Gap Analysis, 42
Gap Analysis Tool (GAT), 68–70
    connect frame of, 69–70
    implementation guide frame of, 68
    OnlyConnect Framework and, 42
grocery industry, using EDI in, 5
Guilbert, Colonel Ed, 4–5, 7

H

HCPCS (CMS/HCFA Common Procedure Coding System), 15
Health and Human Services (HHS), 12–13
Healthaxis, HIPAA Solution case study, 44
health care
    envisioning changes in, 73–75
    as secondary to profit motive, 75
    vision for new economy for, 79
health care administration, turbulence vs. streamlined approaches, 27
Health Care Claim Payment/Advice-835, 67–68
Health Care Claim: Professional, Institutional, and Dental, 64–65
Health Care Claim Status Request-276, 66–67
Health Care Claim Status Response-277, 67
Health Care Claim Transaction-837, 64
Health Care Eligibility Request-270, 63
Health Care Reform Task Force, 13–14
Health Care Services Review: Request for Review-278, 65–66
Health Insurance Portability and Accountability Act of 1996 (HIPAA). *See also* HIPAA Solution
    consequences of violations, 2–3
    countdown to implementation, 2
    electronic interchange for, 1
    "Final Rule on Standards for Electronic Health Care Transactions," 2
    HIPAA phobia, 29–30
    potential benefits from, 73
    relationship of transaction provisions within whole of HIPAA, 3–4
Health Insurance Portability and Accountability Act of 1996 (HIPAA), implementing, 21–34
    business value of EDI and, 25–29
    cost of, 31–33
    mandatory and best practice considerations, 20–24
    requests for delays, 29–31
    value of, 33–34
Health Insurance Reform: Standards for Electronic Transactions, 22
Health Level Seven (HL7), standards for interoperability, 11–12
health maintenance organizations (HMOs), capitation model and, 75
health plans, HIPAA compliance and, 21–23
HHS (Health and Human Services), 12–13
HIPAA Implementation Guide Schemas. *See* X12N HIPAA Implementation Guide Schemas
HIPAA parser, of BizTalk Accelerator, 60
HIPAA Solution, 35–53. *See also* Health Insurance Portability and Accountability Act of 1996 (HIPAA)
    components of, 55
    consulting and training services offered by Microsoft and WPC, 37
    core technologies, 36
    deployment phase, 41
    development phase, 40–41
    envisioning phase, 39
    OnlyConnect Framework, methodology of, 41–42
    OnlyConnect Framework, steps in, 42–43
    partnership model, 37
    planning phase, 39–40
    role of Microsoft and Washington Publishing Company in, 35
    specialized technologies, 36–37
HIPAA Solution, case study, 44–53
    deployment phase, 53
    development phase, 51–53
    envisioning phase, 45–47
    planning phase, 48–51
    project review, 53
    project timeline, 44
HL7 (Health Level Seven), standards for interoperability, 11–12
HMOs (health maintenance organizations), capitation model and, 75

I

ICD-9-CM (International Classification of Diseases, 9th Revision, Clinical Modification), 15

Implementation Architecture, OnlyConnect Methodology, 43
implementation team, Healthaxis case study, 49
Independent Software Vendors (ISVs), HIPAA partners, 37
information, integration of capture and management, 80
injury codes (E-codes), role of NCVHS in development of, 8
insured/members, as participant in enrollment process, 62
insurers, as participant in enrollment process, 61
International Classification of Diseases, 9th Revision, Clinical Modification (ICD-9-CM), 15
ISVs (Independent Software Vendors), HIPAA partners, 37

K

Kennedy-Kassebaum (K2) bill, 2

L

long-term care, 65

M

manufacturers
　device manufacturers, benefits of HIPAA for, 78
　as domain of health care industry, 74
Mapper. *See* BizTalk Mapper
Martin, Kendra, 28
MCS (Microsoft Consulting Services), 37
medical code sets, mandated by HIPAA, 15
Medical Group Management Association (MGMA), opposition to delays in administering HIPAA, 30
medical innovation, 78
medical service providers, Health Care Eligibility Request-270 and, 63
Messaging Manager, BizTalk, 59
MGMA (Medical Group Management Association), opposition to delays in administering HIPAA, 30
Microsoft BizTalk. *See* BizTalk Server 2000
Microsoft Consulting Services (MCS), 37
Microsoft, role in HIPAA Solution, 35
Microsoft SQL Server 2000
　as core technology, 36
　used by BizTalk Server 2000, 56
Microsoft Windows 2000 Server, as core technology, 36
Miller, Chris, 26

N

National Committee on Vital and Health Statistics (NCVHS), 7–9
　DSMO recommendations to, 18
　relationship of NUBC to, 10
　role in data standardization, 8–9
　role in HIPAA, 9
National Council for Prescription Drug Programs (NCPDP), 10–11
National Standard Format (NSF), 56
National Uniform Billing Committee (NUBC), 9–10
National Uniform Claim Committee (NUCC), 15–16
NCPDP (National Council for Prescription Drug Programs), 10–11
NCVHS. *See* National Committee on Vital and Health Statistics (NCVHS)
Notice of Proposed Rule Making (NPRM), 12
Notto, Ralph, 5, 7
NPRM (Notice of Proposed Rule Making), 12
NSF (National Standard Format), 56
NUBC (National Uniform Billing Committee), 9–10
NUCC (National Uniform Claim Committee), 15–16

O

OC. *See* OnlyConnect Framework (OC Framework)
OnlyConnect Framework (OC Framework)
　combining OnlyConnect Methodology (WPC) with Solution Framework (Microsoft), 38–39
　deployment phase, 41
　development phase, 40–41
　envisioning phase, 39
　methodology, 41–42
　phases overview, 38–39
　planning phase, 39–40
　steps in, 42–43
OnlyConnect Methodology
　FirstPass, 56, 71–72
　Gap Analysis Tool (GAT), 56, 68–70
　overview of, 41
　steps in, 42–43
Orchestration Designer, BizTalk, 58
Orchestration, OnlyConnect Methodology, 43

P

partnership model, HIPAA Solution, 37
patient events, 65–66

Index

patients, 64–65
payers
    benefits of HIPAA for, 33–34, 77
    destination payer, 64
    as domain of health care industry, 74
    as participant in enrollment process, 61
    secondary payers, 65
Payment Order/Remittance Advice-820, 62
pharmacies, standards for electronic transmission of retail pharmacy information, 10–11
physicians, benefits of HIPAA for, 76
planning phase
    Healthaxis case study, 48–51
    HIPAA Solution, 39–40
prescription drugs, standards for electronic transmission of retail pharmacy information, 10–11
privacy rules, in HIPAA, 3–4
private sector employers, as funding source for health care, 78–79
profit motive, health care and, 76
project structure document, Healthaxis case study, 47
project timeline, HIPAA Solution case study, 44
providers
    benefits of HIPAA for, 34, 75–76
    defined, 65
    as domain of health care industry, 74
    service providers, 66
public sector agencies, as funding source for health care, 78–79
purchase orders, X12, 6

R

R&D (research and development), benefits of HIPAA for, 78
red tape, decreasing, 21
Regulated Transactions (RTs), X12 Standard Implementation Guides, 24–25
Remittance Advice, 62
requesters, 66
request for eligibility transaction set, 77
Request for Review-278, 65
research and development (R&D), benefits of HIPAA for, 78
risk assessment, Healthaxis case study, 47
RTs (Regulated Transactions), X12 Standard Implementation Guides, 24–25

S

SDOs (Standards Development Organizations)
    address to concerns about HIPAA, 31
    ANSI, 10

secondary payers, 65
service providers, defined, 66
SGML (Standard Generalized Markup Language), 6
SIs (System Integrators), HIPAA partners, 37
smart devices, 80
Social Security Act, consequences of violations of HIPAA, 2–3
Solution. *See* HIPAA Solution
solution design document, Healthaxis case study, 50
specialized technologies, HIPAA Solution, 36–37
sponsors, as participant in enrollment process, 61
SQL Server 2000
    as core technology, 36
    used by BizTalk Server 2000, 56
Standard Generalized Markup Language (SGML), 6
Standards Development Organizations (SDOs)
    address to concerns about HIPAA, 31
    ANSI, 10
State Uniform Billing Committees (SUBCs), state counterparts of NUBC, 10
style sheets, used by BizTalk Mapper, 57
SUBCs (State Uniform Billing Committees), state counterparts of NUBC, 10
subscribers
    defined, 65
    as participant in enrollment process, 62
Sullivan, Dr. Louis, 12–13
System Integrators (SIs), HIPAA partners, 37

T

TAGs (Technical Advisory Groups), WEDI, 14
tax burden, for health care, 79
TDCC. *See* Transportation Data Coordinating Committee (TDCC)
Technical Advisory Groups (TAGs), WEDI, 14
technical deployment, BizTalk Server 2000 components, 56–61
    BizTalk Document Tracking, 59
    BizTalk Editor, 56–57
    BizTalk Mapper, 57–58
    BizTalk Messaging Manager, 59
    BizTalk Orchestration Designer, 58
    BizTalk Server Administration, 59–61
    OnlyConnect FirstPass, 71–72
    OnlyConnect Gap Analysis Tool, 68–70
technical deployment, X12N HIPAA Implementation Guide Schemas, 61–68
    Benefit Enrollment and Maintenance-834, 61–62
    Eligibility, Coverage or Benefit Information-271, 63–64

technical deployment, *continued*
    Health Care Claim Payment/Advice-835, 67–68
    Health Care Claim: Professional, Institutional, and Dental-837, 64–65
    Health Care Claim Status Request-276, 66–67
    Health Care Claim Status Response-277, 67
    Health Care Eligibility Request-270, 63
    Health Care Services Review: Request for Review-278, 65–66
    Payment Order/Remittance Advice-820, 62
technology
    accessible, 80
    adaptable, 81
    consumer-enabling, 81
    flexible, 80–81
technology validation, Healthaxis case study, 51–52
testing, Healthaxis case study
    pilot testing, 53
    preproduction testing, 52–53
Third Party Administrators (TPAs), as participants in enrollment process, 62
TPAs (Third Party Administrators), as participants in enrollment process, 62
training services, offered by Microsoft and WPC, 37
transactions
    defined, 24
    NCVHS's role in standardizing, 9
    provisions within whole of HIPAA, 3–4
    testing, 43
    X12N Identifiers, 24–25
transmission intermediaries, defined, 65
Transportation Data Coordinating Committee (TDCC)
    BUSAP initiative of, 6
    publication of EDI standards by, 5
    role in development of UPC, 5
turbulence vs. streamlined health care administration, 27

U

UB (Uniform Billing) manual, 9–10
UCC (Uniform Code Council), early history of, 5
UCS (Uniform Communication Standards), 5
UMO (Utilization Management Organization), 66
Uniform Billing (UB) manual, 9–10
Uniform Code Council (UCC), early history of, 5
Uniform Communication Standards (UCS), 5
Uniform Hospital Abstract Minimum Data Set, 8
Uniform Product Code Council (UPCC), 5
United Parcel Service (UPS), implementation of EDI by, 26

Universal Product Code (UPC), development of, 5
UPCC (Uniform Product Code Council), 5
UPC (Universal Product Code), development of, 5
UPS (United Parcel Service), implementation of EDI by, 26
U.S. Department of Health and Human Services, *Administration Simplification* Web site, 2
Utilization Management Organization (UMO), 66

V

VICS (Voluntary Interindustry Commerce Standard), X12 Purchase Order, 6
violations, consequences of, 2–3
vision for fundamental change, 73–82
    device manufacturers, 78
    new health care economy, 79–81
    new health care landscape, 74–75, 81–82
    payers, 77
    private and public funding, 78–79
    providers, 75–76
    technology empowering consumers, 73–74
vision statement, Healthaxis case study, 45
Voluntary Interindustry Commerce Standard (VICS), X12 Purchase Order, 6

W

Wal-Mart, implementation of EDI by, 26
Washington Publishing Company (WPC)
    consulting and training services offered by, 37
    publication of EDI standards by, 6–7
Web sites
    Administration Simplification Web site, 2
    DSMO, 19
    implementation of HIPAA, 25
    Uniform Code Council (UCC), 5
    Voluntary Interindustry Commerce Standard (VICS) for, 6
WEDI. *See* Workgroup for Electronic Data Interchange (WEDI)
Windows 2000 Server, as core technology, 36
Workgroup for Electronic Data Interchange (WEDI), 12–14
    applying EDI to health care, 12–13
    recommendations of, 13–14
    Technical Advisory Groups (TAGs) of, 14
WPC (Washington Publishing Company)
    consulting and training services offered by, 37
    publication of EDI standards by, 6–7

X

X12N HIPAA Implementation Guide Schemas, 61–68
    Benefit Enrollment and Maintenance-834, 61–62
    Eligibility, Coverage or Benefit Information-271, 63–64
    Health Care Claim Payment/Advice-835, 67–68
    Health Care Claim: Professional, Institutional, and Dental, 64–65
    Health Care Claim Status Request-276, 66–67
    Health Care Claim Status Response-277, 67
    Health Care Eligibility Request-270, 63
    Health Care Services Review: Request for Review-278, 65–66
    Payment Order/Remittance Advice-820, 62

X12N (insurance subcommittee), 14–15
    diverse membership of, 15
    specialized insurance task groups of, 14
    transaction set identifiers, 24–25

X12 standard
    EDI approach of, 27–29
    for EDI (Electronic Data Interchange), 6

XLANG schedules, 58

XSL (Extensible Stylesheet Language), 57

Get a **Free**
e-mail newsletter, updates,
special offers, links to related books,
and more when you
register on line!

Register your Microsoft Press® title on our Web site and you'll get a FREE subscription to our e-mail newsletter, *Microsoft Press Book Connections.* You'll find out about newly released and upcoming books and learning tools, online events, software downloads, special offers and coupons for Microsoft Press customers, and information about major Microsoft® product releases. You can also read useful additional information about all the titles we publish, such as detailed book descriptions, tables of contents and indexes, sample chapters, links to related books and book series, author biographies, and reviews by other customers.

Registration is easy. Just visit this Web page and fill in your information:

http://www.microsoft.com/mspress/register

Microsoft

Proof of Purchase

Use this page as proof of purchase if participating in a promotion or rebate offer on this title. Proof of purchase must be used in conjunction with other proof(s) of payment such as your dated sales receipt—see offer details.

HIPAA Compliance Solutions
0-7356-1496-2

CUSTOMER NAME

Microsoft Press, PO Box 97017, Redmond, WA 98073-9830